ENDURANCE

ENDURANCE
TOBY PRICE

with ANDREW VAN LEEUWEN

PENGUIN BOOKS

UK | USA | Canada | Ireland | Australia
India | New Zealand | South Africa | China

Penguin Books is part of the Penguin Random House group of companies
whose addresses can be found at global.penguinrandomhouse.com

First published by Penguin Books in 2022

Front cover photograph: Edoardo Bauer
Spine photograph: Kin Marcin/Red Bull Content Pool
Back cover photograph: Dean Mouhtaropoulos/Getty Images

Cover design by Alex Ross © Penguin Random House Australia Pty Ltd
Internal design and typesetting by Midland Typesetters, Australia

Printed and bound in Australia by Griffin Press, part of Ovato, an accredited
ISO AS/NZS 14001 Environmental Management Systems printer

 A catalogue record for this
book is available from the
National Library of Australia

ISBN 978 1 76104 387 1

penguin.com.au

For my sister, Min, and Kurt Caselli

Contents

FOREWORD

Alex Doringer,
KTM Factory Racing

Well done, mate!

I can still remember the Enduro World Champion finals, October 2010, in Noirétable, France. The weather was shitty and cold, but it was an amazing location and audience for off-road sport. The international KTM family is a big one, and we worked together and became good mates from the start.

My friend, Jeff Leisk, the MD at KTM Australia at the time, requested that we invite Toby to come compete at that final round, and the Wednesday before the race a young feller showed up in his board shorts, T-shirt and a big smile on his face. He was brave but shaking at the same time, because it was only five degrees Celsius that day.

'Hi, Alex. I'm Toby!'

From the first moment I met Toby, I knew it was going to be a good day – I felt the synergy immediately. I simply *knew* who Toby was and what this big feller was all about. His way of dealing with situations was simple: the only important thing for him was getting on his bike.

Toby's introduction to the Dakar Rally was years in the making. In a way it all started back in 2013, when my friend and KTM rally legend Marc Coma wasn't able to start Dakar because of a shoulder injury. I called American off-road racing legend Kurt Caselli and asked him, knowing the answer already, if he wanted to make his Dakar debut.

Kurt and I had already spent quite a bit of time together on racetracks and had become really good friends. He was a unique young gun: incredibly talented, an amazing teammate, a hard worker, very humble and gentle. And he always had this big smile on his face. He was loved by his family and friends, and he was the inspiration for many, including Toby.

The *real* start of Tobs's rally career had been earlier that year, 22 February 2013, in Santiago de Chile.

We had just won the Dakar again with Cyril Despres. Kurt was celebrating a successful debut that included two stage wins. Early in the morning – after a big celebration – Kurt; Stefan Huber, the KTM Rally Technical Director; and I enjoyed a quiet moment. The only thing the three of us did was watch videos of Toby.

He was everywhere! On the motorbike, on the pushbike, on his wakeboard, on any number of different tracks. This was the moment we signed Toby in for Dakar (without Toby knowing about our plan at this stage, of course!)

That year turned out to be a tough one. Kurt passed away,

but he left us with all of his plans and visions for the future. He wasn't with us at the track anymore, but we remembered him in everything we did. He was loved by us all.

Not having Kurt at Dakar with us the following year in South America, in 2014, was very difficult, and we dedicated Marc Coma's victory to Kurt. And I held onto a promise I'd made to Kurt about Toby.

It was a big day, and a big phone call! 'Mate, it's Alex. Are you ready to race a big bike at the Dakar 2015?!'

'Yes, mate,' Toby replied. 'I'm always ready!'

And Toby jumped on a plane, and he raced, and he raced fast . . . and he's kept going ever since! The love of racing is in his blood, and he's totally committed to that love.

Toby, mate, all the pain you've had to go through, all the injuries and the loss of your loved ones, all the pain . . . it never stopped you. We've been through so much on our racing journey together – the highs and the lows – and we live to race another day!

I'm grateful for all the time we've spent together, and I'm looking forward to all the times to come. One day we'll be old retired fellers, and we'll look back over the years, happy with everything we've accomplished. And we'll have a good laugh.

Toby, my dear friend – you are a true champion, a loyal friend and an inspiration to us all.

1
Roto

Roto. You've probably never heard of it and I don't blame you. It's not small, quite the opposite, but it's incredibly isolated and unpopulated. A vast expanse of land over 700 kilometres west of Sydney. It's a pretty insignificant place for most people, I suppose. But in the early 1980s it was the centre of the universe for my parents, John and Pauline Price.

Both of my parents came from rural areas and understood the bush. My dad John grew up in Harden-Murrumburrah in the South West Slopes area, where he lived until his career in banking took him to Moss Vale in the Southern Highlands. My mum Pauline grew up in Mittagong, 20-odd kilometres from Moss Vale, and trained to be a nurse. In 1975 their paths crossed, they hit it off and more than four decades later they're still together.

A few years into their life as a married couple, John and Pauline received a fascinating offer. A doctor at the hospital

Mum worked at was looking at buying a farm out at Roto, but he didn't want to put his money on the line unless there were people he could trust to go out there and run it. So the opportunity was presented to Mum and Dad, and Mum's brother Jeff and his wife, Diane. The place was pretty run down and the doctor wanted a five-year commitment from whoever took on the project. He didn't want somebody to go out there, freak out and pull the pin a few months later.

It was a huge call for my folks. They'd just built a brand new brick home in Mittagong, my brother, Matthew, was a baby and my sister, Amanda, was on the way. They'd been brought up in rural areas, but neither of them were born and bred farmers. But they decided to commit to the five years and give it a go. Obviously they didn't know it at the time – I wasn't even born – but that decision set me on my career path.

The move to Roto took a little longer than expected for my parents. There were a lot of loose ends to tie up in Mittagong, and when Amanda arrived a lot earlier than expected, that further complicated things. So my grandparents, Allan and Margaret, moved out to Roto first. Jeff and Diane followed a year later, and I finally arrived another year or so after that.

Life out in Roto wasn't for the faint-hearted, particularly in the early days. The property was 42,000 acres of cattle and sheep farm, sprawling across the western country. When my folks first got out there, there was no running water. Water itself was a scarce commodity, hot water even more so. Having a hot shower meant lighting a fire under a 44-gallon drum filled with water. There were snakes and spiders every-where. There was no electricity; food was stored in kerosene fridges. It wasn't until 1986, a year before I was born, that the property got electricity for the first time. The nearest neigh-bours were Jeff and Diane, who lived on a separate homestead on the same property, seven kilometres away. Adding to the challenge was that Amanda, having been born premature, required significant care, something that I'll expand on later. That move to Roto was an incredibly daunting task for my folks, but they loved it. They could quickly envisage the child-hood it could provide for us kids. The whole family learnt to appreciate what they had and make the best of it.

A few years into the stint at Roto I hit the scene, and from the word go I just couldn't sit still. The two-and-a-half-metre high fence around the homestead suddenly wasn't big enough. I was the complete opposite to Matthew; if my parents gave him a toy, he'd sit there and play quietly for hours. If they tried the same with me, I'd be out the door as soon as they turned their backs. I was a nightmare for my poor parents. When I was 18 months old I decided to climb this big tree in our front yard. Getting up there was easy, but I quickly realised I didn't know how to get down. Mum came out to hang the washing and could hear me calling, but couldn't work out where I was. She eventually looked up and there I was, eight metres in the air. If Dad had tried to climb the tree it would have snapped, so my uncle used the front end loader to lift him up high enough to grab me. I'd regularly scale that big fence around the homestead and go walkabout. Luckily, wherever I went, our Great Dane Harley went with me. Any time Mum realised I was gone, all she had to do was find the dog.

The big smoke to us was Hillston, population of around 1000 people. It wasn't exactly around the corner, either. Getting to school each day was an epic trek; first, Mum would drive us to the bus stop . . . which was 17 kilometres away. Then it was another 50-odd kilometres on the school bus. The bus didn't have air-conditioning and it was regularly 35, 40, even 45 degrees out there. And because it was dirt roads almost the entire way to school, the bus driver wouldn't let us open the windows. It was like a sauna on that old thing.

Being so remote, there were little luxuries that were always out of reach for us. Like ice cream. The kids that lived in town could go and get an ice cream or milkshake whenever they wanted one. For us, it was a special thing to go into Bill Morgan's cafe and have an ice cream. If I ever complained about wanting to get an ice cream Mum would say, 'It's a bit hard, Tobes. We live in the bush'. I heard that a lot as a kid. At least by the time I was born the electricity was connected and we had a freezer at home, so we could buy tubs of ice cream from the shops.

What we lacked in ice cream and milkshakes, we more than made up with space. We had buckets of it, and for us kids it was one big playground. One of my favourite things was our homemade water park. When I was around four years old, Dad would stick a life jacket on me, shove me inside a big irrigation pipe and then fire up the pump. It was a snug fit with the life jacket, so as the pipe filled with water out of the river the pressure would build behind me and eventually spit me into an irrigation channel. I loved it, but not many of my mates would sign up for that one. Another of our favourite games was riding billy goats. We called that the 'Roto initiation'. We'd drag an old billy goat, one with huge horns, back from the mallee growth and take turns riding it. Matthew took the record for longest ride; he held on for so long that the old goat decided the only way to get rid of him was to go through a mallee bush and wipe him out. It took two hours for us to find him. We knew he had to be down there in the mallee bush somewhere. Funnily enough, all those kids from Hillston I was sometimes jealous of couldn't wait to get out on the farm and ride motorbikes and swim in the dam. Sometimes they'd come for the weekend and stay for a week.

We spent most of our time outdoors, but we did have one living-room tradition. Like most Australian households in the early 1990s, we always watched the *Hey Hey It's Saturday* variety show on the weekend. There was a character called Plucka Duck that would give away prizes to guests. Big prizes, too. Things like cars and family holidays. When I was five years old I decided I wanted to enter, so I sent in an envelope with my name on it. To be honest I always thought our mail never left Hillston. A few weeks later we were watching the show and the host Daryl Somers announced the next contestant for Plucka Duck. 'Toby Price, we'll be in touch soon.' We were sitting there in complete shock. On the

Monday afternoon the phone rang at home. It was a producer for *Hey Hey*, asking to speak to Toby.

'He's at school,' said Mum.

'What? He's at school?'

'Yeah he's only five years old.'

The producer just assumed I was an adult. What was a five-year-old doing trying to win a car? For me it seemed like the most normal thing in the world. They eventually agreed I could go to Melbourne for the filming. If I couldn't physically spin the wheel around at least once, Dad would take my place. We did a practice spin and it didn't just make it all the way around, it landed on the new car! The cameras weren't rolling yet and I'd used up all my luck. In the recording I kept ending up with prizes that weren't suitable for a five-year-old. There was a king-size bed set, $2000 worth of kitchen appliances, $3000 worth of ladies' clothes . . . eventually I won a family holiday to the Gold Coast. Perfect. I think it was the longest ever Plucka Duck segment. When I got back to school at Hillston the next week I was basically a movie star.

***

Roto was the perfect place to breed a love of anything with a motor. I was into everything that had an engine strapped to it. My mum used to say that if a motor was going to blow up, it would take my face with it. I wasn't into toys, it was just bikes and cars. I wasn't the sort of kid that was happy to go into town and come home with a Matchbox car, either. It had to be the real deal. By the time I was three years old, the only place I wanted to go when we went to Hillston was the bike shop.

My obsession with motorbikes developed quickly, but that's not to say it was love at first sight. When I was two-and-a-half years old I jumped on my brother Matthew's old Suzuki JR50 to give it a go. I could barely walk. I couldn't ride a pushbike, let alone a motorbike. Anyway, I jumped on with Dad holding the back of the bike and off we went. After 20 metres or so, Dad let go and that's when I started to wobble. Seconds later I was on the ground. 'Do you want another go?' asked Dad. No way, I told him. The bike went back in the shed and I went back to the house. A few weeks later I turned to Dad and asked if we could get the bike back out. I wanted to give it another crack. We went through the same routine the second time around, Dad holding onto the bike, letting go, me having a bit of a wobble . . . and then I took off. That was it. I rode until the bike ran out of fuel.

As a working farm, with sheep, cattle and crops, bikes were part of life at Roto. We had heaps of them. We'd go out mustering and Matthew and I would cover 100 kilometres more than we needed to, just because we could. We all had bikes: Matthew, myself and our cousins Steve, Jenny and Becky. Because I was the youngest I always had the hand-me-down bikes that the others had outgrown.

We had a lot of fun riding on that property. We'd make short grass tracks and cut 500 laps at a time. We'd make jumps in the quarries. We had dirt tracks and motocross tracks. We were a bit young to use the earth-moving machinery on the farm, but Dad and my uncle would carve out tracks for us. What we really enjoyed were the trenches used to store the grain from the wheat crops. They were massive channels that would get lined with plastic, filled with grain and then covered with more plastic and dirt. Before all the plastic and grain went in, we'd have a lot of run riding through the trenches.

For the most part, though, Roto was dry, dusty land, perfect for riding flat out. I quickly became very comfortable hammering across a paddock at full throttle. That's how we got from one side to the other.

Bikes weren't the only form of motorised mischief we got up to. We used to race old cars around the place too. One time we found an old Ford Falcon – which would be worth a fortune these days – and we cut the roof off to turn it into a convertible. We drove around Roto like we were cruising through Hollywood. We had a go-kart that my dad made for us, and when it rained that was our favourite toy. We'd head straight to the clay pans and slide around for hours. The look on Mum's face when we'd get back to the house, covered head to toe in mud, was classic.

Most people get their first car when they're 17 or 18, but I was only six. It was an old, blue Datsun. Dad welded extensions onto the pedals so I could reach them and built a booster seat so that I could see over the dash. Mum quickly got sick of the 17-kilometre drive to the bus stop each morning, so from that point on I drove myself to catch the school bus. I'd get up, grab my bag, jump in the Datsun and head off down the road. I used to drive that thing all over the property. If Dad was out at one of the pumps or something like that, and he needed some tools that were back at the homestead, he'd radio through to Mum and say, 'Hey, tell Tobes to grab some stuff out of the shed for me and drive over to Pump 5.'

That all helped foster a deep love of going fast on four wheels that I have to do this day. But in those early days in Roto, we spent the majority of our time on two wheels. We'd spend entire days out on the bike. Mum had two strict rules. The first was that someone had to ride back to the homestead every two hours and do a couple of laps around the house, just to let her know everything was okay. The second was that if one of us did get hurt, someone had to ride straight back to the homestead to get help while the other one had to stay with whoever had come off their bike. Keep in mind that the closest hospital was 60 clicks down the road in Hillston.

My cousin Steve was the one who talked me into everything. He pushed me to my limit, and quite often beyond it. One of his favourite games was telling me I could do something he knew I wasn't capable of doing. Of course I'd believe him, give it a go and end up crashing. When I was still on a 50CC we'd go riding through the grain-storage trenches. These were seriously big pits and Steve, who was on a 125cc, would climb the walls and jump right out of the channel. The Crusty Demons were all the rage at the time and I thought it was so cool watching Steve fly through the air.

'I can't wait to do that,' I'd tell him. 'You can do it now. Just get in there, hit the wall and go for it,' he'd tell me. He'd convince me the little 50 had enough power, but he knew it'd never work. I'd try and climb out of the bank, get near the top and the 50 would run out of steam. I'd end up bouncing back down the wall on my head. He'd be pissing himself laughing as I tumbled through the dirt. At the time I'd be furious with him, but those bumps and bruises helped toughen me up.

Those kinds of exploits meant the JR50 didn't last long. It had spoked wheels, and the spokes would quickly snap when I started jumping off the dam wall and things like that. When Dad got sick of buying new wheels, he went and found a Honda QR50, which had steel wheels. The wheels were strong enough, but I started snapping frames in half. So we tried a Yamaha PeeWee 50, which was meant to be stronger again. Of course I still found a way to break the frame. Dad eventually got sick of buying bikes, so he redesigned the frame with additional bracing. That was good enough to see me out before I moved on to 60s, 80s and so on.

Given how much riding we did, we really didn't get badly hurt all that often. My first big injury was after a full day of mustering out on the bike when I was about seven years old. We were riding home and came across some kangaroos that were bouncing across the paddock. As kids, we would always try and chase down roos. There were thousands of them out on the property and catching and butchering them was our primary source of dog food. That's how it was on the farm. Anyway, I went after these roos and hit a concrete slab stuck in the ground. Bang, broken wrist. There was a brand new doctor in town, Dr Sanjay, and I was his first call-out. He said, 'I think I'm going to be seeing you quite a bit, Toby'. He wasn't wrong. He thought he'd come out to the bush for an easy life, only to be saddled with this crazy little daredevil.

Despite my cousin tricking me into crashing, I quickly fell in love with doing jumps. I'd turn nearly everything on the farm into something to jump off. Sometimes I'd find a steep bank and see how high I could go. Other times, I'd look for a rolling ramp in wide open space out in the middle of nowhere that I could hit at full throttle, to see how far I could fly.

I still love jumping motorbikes to this day. There's no better feeling than being 10, 15 metres in the air and floating 30 metres down the road. You're weightless. It's a feeling like nothing else. Jumping is a game of calculated guesses. There's this instinct you develop to assess how steep and long the ramp is, and how far you need to go. You can't learn how to do it without getting out there and doing it. You need to hone the ability to know how to hit the ramp just right without even thinking about it. You also need to work on body positioning; if you lean forward you'll push the front of the bike down, if you lean back you'll end up doing a backflip. Preloading techniques make a big difference too; if you want more height you can push into the up ramp to give you a bit more suspension compression. It's risky when you're learning all this by trial and error because you're putting your body on the line. If I had a dollar for every time I came up short on a jump, or overshot a jump, I'd be a million-aire. If you're going to get it wrong, overshooting is the better outcome. I'd rather go long than come up short. If you go from 60 km/h to a dead stop, it's going to hurt. If you can over-jump it's going to compress you pretty hard, but as long as there's nothing behind the down ramp, you might be okay. The worst situation is when you just tag the top of a down ramp and the bike compresses really quickly. That will flick you over the bars and slam you on the ground. It hurts.

But when you start nailing those jumps, wow. It's an unbeatable feeling. That's what keeps you coming back, even between the bumps, bruises and broken bones.

2
Juniors

One day Uncle Jeff arrived back on the farm with a bright idea. He'd driven past a bike club in Condobolin, about two hours from Roto, while there'd been a race meeting on. He told Dad, 'We should pack up all the kids and bikes and give it a go. Toby can come too, there must have been 50 of those little PeeWee bikes running around.' When the next club day rolled around that's exactly what we did. I was four years old. When we got there Dad started chatting with Geoff Smith, the club president. 'You know your young bloke has to race against seven-year-old kids, right?' he said. That was the youngest category, four to seven. 'He knows how to dodge sheep, so he'll be right,' said Dad.

I went out there and blew the lot of them to the weeds in my first race.

When we were finished, Geoff came up to Dad and said, 'I reckon you've got a bit of a speed demon on your hands there. You need to take him to a big meeting, see how he goes.' He gave Dad some information about a state meeting in Albury-Wodonga that was being held a few weeks later. There were riders from Victoria, South Australia, New South Wales, all over the place. We still didn't know what we were doing, but I lapped the field – despite the fact my over-braced PeeWee was a lot heavier than the standard bikes I was racing against.

Motorsport was already a family pastime. While living out at Roto, Dad and Uncle Jeff turned an old truck into an off-road racer in their shed and used it to compete in the Australian Off-Road Championship. They were pretty good, too, winning a national title in 1989. They didn't know it at the time, but this foray into two-wheel competition for us kids would cost them their truck. It was eventually sold off to pay for us to race bikes.

After those first couple of race meetings we were up and running. I raced that PeeWee 50 in long- and short-course and motocross events throughout New South Wales.

At the end of 1994, when I was seven years old, it was time for me to move to a Kawasaki KX60. It was a big shift; the little 50 is a fully automatic bike, but the 60 has a clutch, gears and more power. I already knew how to drive a manual car, so it wasn't a huge leap for me.

Moving to the bigger class meant more travelling. We were racing at state and national championship meetings. In that early part of my junior career, my focus was on long and short dirt-track racing. The races were generally held on either an oval or a flat track. They were short sprints, usually four to six laps. My goal was to eventually move into road racing – I wanted to be the next Mick Doohan – and the short and long track events were the best way to prepare.

In the early days of competing in 60s, I was on a second-hand bike. We'd only had the thing for a few weeks when the motor shit itself and we had an unexpected rebuild cost. As well as *Hey Hey It's Saturday*, another regular TV tradition in the Price household was to watch the *The Footy Show*. One night we were sitting there watching it and NRL player-turned-TV star Paul 'Fatty' Vautin rode a brand new KX60 onto the stage to start the show. He pretty much flipped the thing and ghosted it into the wall. I couldn't believe what I was seeing. 'What a waste of a bloody good bike'!' I said to Dad. 'That's exactly what I need for racing and he's just destroyed it.' Dad explained it was just part of the show and not to worry about it, but I wasn't having a bar of it. I went to my room and wrote a letter to Fatty. I told him I needed a new bike and, given he clearly had no idea how to ride, he should send his one to me. I told him I was going to be the next Mick Doohan and he could really help me out along the way. The very next week we sat down on the Thursday night to watch *The Footy Show* – and they read the letter out on TV! Fatty said, 'Yeah, no worries, we'll give him a bike. We'll give him two bikes if he wants them, no problem.' He was saying all this on live TV and there's me, just a kid, thinking, *Shit, I'm getting two new bikes*. It was like Christmas. I was over the moon! The next day Mum and Dad got in touch with the network and the backpedalling started. They were told, 'Yeah, we know what he said, but if we go through with it and it gets out, we'll be inundated with letters from kids asking for stuff.' Well, the Hillston community didn't like that one bit. Everyone had seen the show, so when there was suddenly no bike on offer, the letters to the network started. 'This is bullshit – you told the whole country you were going to give Toby a bike. If you don't come through, that's a low act.' They really copped some flack. There was a bit more back and forth, and eventually we struck a deal. Someone from the network told us, 'There's no way you're getting two bikes, but we'll send you one. You can't tell anyone where you got it from. If anybody asks, you just bought a new bike. We don't want to hear another word about it'.

Three weeks later a new KX60 showed up at the front door. I sometimes wonder if Fatty realises he played his part in the career of a world champion and two-time Dakar winner.

Once I was on that new bike things really got moving. For the first time I had something new, not something three or four years old. I started winning more races and more titles and we started to get a little more low-key support. At that point I started to realise I must be pretty good. More often than not I won. When I didn't win, I was usually on the podium.

For a long time, winning wasn't all that important. I just loved riding bikes. I wanted to be on two wheels, either on my BMX or my motorbike. I loved every second of it. To me, there was no better feeling than being wide open on the gas. It never mattered to me if it was in a paddock or on a motocross track. The success was basically a side effect of being out there on a bike having fun. At some point, though, winning did start to draw me back to competing. It wasn't the winning itself, it was me wanting to see how far I could go, whether I could actually turn riding bikes into a career. But even then, I was never the sort of kid who *had* to win. I don't ever remember chucking a tantrum when I didn't win for whatever reason. Dad always told me if I ever threw a bike on the ground, or even my helmet, goggles or gloves, we'd pack up, head home and stick a For Sale sign on everything. It was a stern warning against being a spoilt brat or a sore loser. No excuses, just get on with it. That played a big part in how I approach my racing to this day. I still don't make excuses. If something goes wrong and it was my fault, I'll blame myself.

That's not to say I wasn't competitive in the early days of my career. Even as a kid, if someone said, 'Let's race to the gate', it was on for young and old. If one of my mates said he could finish a sandwich faster than me, it would become a competition. To this day if the word 'race' comes up, it flicks a switch in my brain. But to me, it was always riding first, winning second. And it was always important to win in the right way.

Anyway, I had a great run on the KX60 during that 1996 season. I won New South Wales state titles in long track, dirt track and motocross. I also won my first national title at the Australian Long Track Championship in Maitland.

For the 1997 season I moved up a class, which meant a bigger bike, a Kawasaki KX80. The transition to the 60 a few years earlier had laid the foundation for my approach to learning new bikes. Once you're working with a clutch, throttle, rear brake and front brake, the tools at your disposal don't really change. It's just about how you use them. As you climb through the ranks you have more power, better suspension and you're going quicker.

I would carefully watch what other riders were doing on bigger bikes. When we were hanging around the pits, I'd listen closely to guys talking about things like clutch feel and throttle response, taking every little detail in and then seeing if I could feel something similar when I got back on my bike. When I was following other riders I'd watch their technique and their lines. I always responded best to learning by feel. If I had to learn how to ride a dirt bike from a textbook I would have been useless at it.

As well as the long and short track racing, I started doing more and more motocross. It's a very different discipline to dirt track racing. The tracks are built on land, where there's either man-made jumps or natural terrain. There's basically a path marked out in bunting and off you go. Given I always loved doing jumps, motocross was right up my alley. But it's a very physical discipline, something I learned the hard way at an event in Griffith on Mother's Day in 1997. I overshot a jump and had a huge crash. I knew my left wrist was broken straight away because I could see it was all out of shape. Dad called Mum and said, 'Look, we'll be here for a couple of days to get this sorted. Sorry for the shit Mother's Day present.' By the time we got to hospital I was complaining about my right wrist being sore as well. I was starting to think it might be broken too. The doctors poked and prodded at it and said, 'Nah, it should be okay, everything feels fine.' But when we got the scans done there it was. Two broken wrists. So we had to call Mum back and apologise again. Happy Mother's Day!

I had surgery to get everything put back into place, and they put my arms up in slings to keep my wrists above my heart to reduce swelling. I couldn't move my arms at all, so someone had to feed me. At some point, while my dad was out of the room having a cigarette break (he was a nervous smoker back then), a nurse brought my dinner in, threw it on the little table in front of me and just left. I was starving, but there was nothing I could do. It was like torture. I tried to shove my head far enough forward to grab it off the plate with my mouth, but I couldn't quite reach. She came back 20 minutes later and said, 'Oh, aren't you hungry?' and wanted to take the plate away. Luckily, Dad arrived back in the room in time and stopped her. Having two broken wrists isn't all that much fun when you're a schoolkid. There's nothing quite as embarrassing as your mum having to pop into school at lunch to see if you need help wiping your backside. You cop a fair bit of flack from your mates over that one, trust me.

That wasn't the only snag we hit that year. Three days after my dad's 40th birthday he had a heart attack. It was a tough time, for a while there we didn't know if he was going to make it. He was always a healthy, energetic guy so it was a real shock. It happened out on the property; he hit the deck while opening a gate. It slowed down my racing program, although we had some family friends in Hillston who took me to a few events. But racing without Dad just wasn't the same.

Even once he recovered, there was no way Dad could keep up with running the farm and doing all the travelling to moto events. Mum and Dad made the difficult decision to leave Roto and buy a property in Hillston. The property included the local squash centre, a big concrete building with two courts, and a small gym right next to the house. Twice a week we hosted competitions and the whole thing just kept us afloat. I got plenty of squash practice. I ended up playing representative squash for my high school, even though I wasn't exactly built like a typical squash player.

The move to Hillston was a bit of a culture shock. We went from 42,000 acres to an acre-and-a-half. We knew the people who took over the farm, so we still spent time out there. But not being there full-time was a big change. Luckily we had some state forest just across the road from us at the new place, so I could still spend plenty of time on my bike. I'd cut across the road, ride up a laneway and then I was straight into the forest. We built a bike track in Hillston as well, on a parcel of land near the local tip.

The council gave us the green light to ride there, just to help out the community.

After laying low in 1997 we were back at it in 1998. The highlight was a huge trek all the way over to Perth for the Australian Junior Motocross Championship at Coastal Park, where I won my first national motocross title in the under-11s class.

Throughout my junior career, our little 'race team', if you could call it that, was pretty humble. There were some fancy set-ups out there in terms of trucks and marquees, but ours wasn't one of them. When we started out it was me, my parents and my brother all crammed into a Nissan Patrol, which we used to tow an open three-bike trailer. We'd take tents and sleeping bags and either sleep on the side of the road or at caravan parks if we wanted to have a shower. We couldn't afford motels. It was like a camping trip. We had a $20 tarpaulin that we used as a makeshift awning to work on the bike and I hated the thing. With a passion. We looked like farmers not racers. Most kids would go and buy stickers for their bikes, but I'd sit at home printing out numbers to make die cuts for my number, 287. We'd buy a 12-metre roll of coloured contact, the stuff you usually cover schoolbooks with, and there I was with a pair of scissors cutting my own numbers out. We couldn't afford the fancy number stickers. They were $6 each and a whole roll of contact, enough for a year's worth of stickers, cost less than that.

My bike was completely stock. I didn't have any trick parts. I tried to keep a lid on it, because I could see the work

Mum and Dad were putting in for me to be there in the first place . . . but sometimes it would get to me. I'd look at these other kids with their fancy marquees and spare rims and tyres in case they wanted to use a different tread patterns. I'd turn to Dad and say, 'Jeez, Dad, look at this bloke. He's going to be fast.' His answer was always the same. 'Just wait until you get out there, mate. We'll see how it goes.' More often than not, I'd go out there and win. The fancy gear doesn't necessarily make you faster on track.

Once I was riding in the 80cc class, Mum stopped coming to the races. She was fine when I was racing 50s and 60s, but when I started going faster she didn't like it. She decided she'd rather stay home and give her nerves a rest. That's when we got an old Ford Econovan to haul the bikes around in. It only had two seats, but by then it was just me and Dad travelling anyway.

How long we were away for depended on where we were going and what we were doing. An Australian champion-ship meeting went for a week. When we went to Perth for nationals in 1998 we were basically away for three weeks. There were times when Mum had to come with us even if she didn't want to, just so she could help Dad out with the driving to get home. Once I got a little older I could help Dad out with the driving. Not legally. I wasn't old enough to have my licence. But given I'd been driving cars since I was six years old, Dad trusted me on the road. When it was night time and we were in the middle of nowhere I'd take over for two or three hours so Dad could get some sleep. We weren't exactly driving through the middle of Sydney. These were roads you'd struggle to find on a map.

Money was constantly an issue. Even when you're doing motorsport on the cheap like we were, it's an insanely expensive hobby. And as a junior you're not allowed to win prize money. When I won a race, I got a $5 trophy. Mum and Dad had probably spent something like $1500 for me to win that small bit of plastic. People thought my folks were crazy, but it was great family time for us, travelling all over the place. By the time I was 10 years old, we'd seen so much of the country.

We had some creative ways to keep money in the racing kitty. Early in my junior career the wild goats out at Roto were a handy source of extra income. They are vermin, like wild boars and roos, and go through heaps of crops. They're a pest capable of destroying so much acreage. So it was good for the farm to get rid of them. Back then, a decent-sized billy goat went for a decent price, around $25 to $28 a piece. For smaller goats you'd still get $15 to $18. On weekends we weren't racing we'd dedicate a day to mustering goats. We'd head out on our bikes and set up yards. Timing was critical, you had to muster them into the yard before they got into the mountains. Once they got into the mountains you had Buckley's chance of getting them back out. Once we'd caught the goats they were loaded into a big trailer. We had a guy that would come around every two weeks with a prime mover. We'd usually have 30 to 40 goats in the pen, and he'd pay cash for them on the spot. If there were ten billy goats in there, you could rack up a fair bit of money. That was our racing budget. It wasn't just about the money, either. It was a nice family day out and a hell of a lot of fun, chasing goats and tying them up.

The goat-wrangling business ended when we left Roto, so we needed a new way to make extra cash. The good thing about farming communities is there's always something you can do. The bad thing is that it's usually hot, hard work.

There was a big lettuce and onion farm about ten kilometres out of Hillston. For three years, during the summer school holidays, Mum and I would work out there chipping weeds. We'd head out about 5 am with little torches strapped to our heads so we could see as we cut weeds away from the lettuce and onion plants. How long we worked depended on the weather. It was usually hot, like 40 degrees, so we'd finish between mid-morning and lunch. On the few days it was below 40 we'd work on until 1 pm. The rows of lettuce were anywhere from 800 metres to 1.2, 1.3 kilometres long. It felt like they went forever. At the end of the rows there were irrigation channels full of water. On those 40-degree days, I'd dive into the channel and drench myself for ten seconds or so. It was a small bit of relief from the heat before starting all over again on the next row. The channels only ran between two rows, so when you got to the last row in a paddock you had to go up and back before you could dive into the water to cool off. I was getting paid $13 an hour, but as a kid that seemed reasonable. Mum made about $10 more per hour than I did. It was bloody tough work. Even when I was in my early teens and pretty fit, I'd leave that farm feeling pretty second hand. I can still feel those aches and pains. And there was my mum, doing the same work in the same heat. Looking back, it blows me away how hard she worked. Mum and Dad let me keep a bit of the cash as pocket money, but most of it was used to keep the racing going.

As time went on we got some sponsorship. It was never anything too serious, mostly tyres, fuels and lubricants, and it never matched the money that was being poured into the racing by my parents. But every little bit helped. The Hillston community was hugely supportive. The local newspaper would keep track of what I was doing, and the town's fuel station would often donate a tank of fuel for the car when we took off somewhere to go racing. When we travelled to Perth for the 1998 nationals, nearly every business in Hillston helped us out. A family friend was an artist and she drew a motorbike on this big board in town. People could stick money to the board and it really helped us out. The town did what it could. There weren't many people living there, so it wasn't an endless money pit, but if everyone chucked in two or three dollars it added up. That motorbike drawing paid for us to get to Perth. It wasn't just money, either. In my early teens the local AFL club, the Hillston Swans, would let me train with them, just to keep fit. I never played for them, but it was a fun way to maintain my fitness to ride the bike.

In the very early part of my career it was hard to get a bike sponsor. In the 60cc class there was only one option, the KX60, so Kawasaki didn't need to be handing out discounts on bikes. You had to have one. But once I moved up to the 80cc class I had options. It gave us a bit of bargaining power. Our closest Kawasaki dealer was J & P Motorcycles in Griffith, about 200 kilometres away. Dad hammered out a deal with them that meant we got bikes at cost price and they'd throw in some parts. By the time I was on 125s, they would loan us bikes for the season and give us a little bit of a race budget.

Not being flush with cash made things difficult, but the good thing about racing bikes is that it wasn't a deal breaker. If you're racing karts or cars, equipment is everything. Finding the limit of your gear is easy. On bikes, the equipment makes a difference, sure, but there's still a very human element to it. It's dangerous. You're very exposed. You can get hurt. You need to not only have the raw ability to ride the bike quick, but complete trust in that ability. If you lack either of those two things, it doesn't matter how much you spend. You'll be slow. Even when I didn't have the latest and greatest bits for my bike, I could still win races.

I won NSW motocross titles in 1998 and 2000 before what I thought was my big break came along in 2001. Peter Goddard, a grand prix racer in his own right, called up Dad and offered me a test on a Moriwaki 80cc road racing bike at Wakefield Park. Peter said, 'Look, Toby's winning a lot of races, he seems to have good corner speed, and he's got a lot of potential. I think this could be a good future for him.' It was exactly where I wanted my career to go. Two days before the test, Peter called back to grab some more details. He asked for my weight and height. It turned out I was eight or nine centimetres too tall and 12 kilograms too heavy for the bike. I wasn't about to drop more than ten kilos and shrink almost ten centimetres in two days.

My whole career plan was turned on its head. I had to accept that my lifelong goal of racing in MotoGP was never going to happen. I was a big kid and there was nothing I could do about it. Luckily, motocross was a viable career path on its own. So I put road racing out of my mind and focussed solely on the transition to 125cc dirt bikes.

I won a second consecutive NSW motocross title in 2001, followed by a third in 2002. I was then picked to represent Australia at the Oceania Motocross Championship across the ditch in Wellington, where I finished second in the 125cc junior class.

My last junior season was 2003, when I was 16. I won a fourth consecutive NSW motocross title and had more success across the Tasman, winning my class at the NZ Junior Motocross Championship in Palmerston North. Then I set my sights firmly on the Australian championship at Old Noarlunga in South Australia.

About 12 weeks prior to that event I crashed during training and broke both my wrists. I then got compartment syndrome in my left arm. Anybody who's ever ridden a dirt bike will know what arm pump is. Sometimes when you're on a bike, your arm muscle swells and cuts off the blood circulation to your hand. Your fingers go numb and you start losing control of the bike. The same thing had happened with the compartment syndrome. Due to the injury, the circulation was cut off to my left hand and it started to turn all shades of blue and purple. The doctor had to slice my arm open from the inside of my palm to the inside of my elbow to relieve the pressure. If he hadn't gone and done it, I probably would've been 15-odd hours away from having my whole arm amputated. It would have killed all the muscle and left me with a dead arm.

They sliced my arm up in hospital and I had to wait eight days for the pressure to come down to the point that they were comfortable with stitching me back up. It was a pretty gruesome process for a 15-year-old to deal with. Particularly when doctors are discussing how your arm might have to be cut off.

The whole thing cast a huge amount of doubt over whether I'd make it to the Australian championship. I couldn't believe it. This was my last nationals as a junior and I really wanted to be there. The doctor told me it would be a five- or six-month turnaround, in terms of healing and getting my body sorted to ride a bike again. When I told him I had to be fit in 12 weeks for nationals he was pretty blunt about it. 'You won't be racing by then,' he said.

I spent the first six weeks letting the bones heal before I went and got the cast cut off. The bones were perfectly fine, all healed and back in place. Eight weeks after the crash I was back on a bike. I felt okay, but my left arm was pretty weak. I still had four weeks up my sleeve and I felt that if I spent time on the bike every day, built up some match fitness, I might just make it.

Ten weeks after the injury it was time for the annual Hillston Show. Each year I'd put on a display with my bike, to give something back to a community that supported me so much. It was a showcase of what they were helping me do. We'd started out building a few jumps but each year it grew. It became a hot topic around town. What's Toby going to jump this year? First it was cars, then a bus, then a semitrailer . . .

Anyway, there I was, ten weeks after breaking both wrists, jumping a B-double truck on my bike. Lengthways. Two weeks later I was at Old Noarlunga as planned and I won national titles in both the 125cc class and the 250F class. Winning the 250F title was a little unexpected as I had next to no experience riding four-stroke bikes. I'd done a bit of four-stroke racing the previous season, but that was on a KLX model. It was a full-blown road bike with mirrors, indicators and everything. We tried to turn it into a race bike, but it was nothing like it.

The KX250F was a brand new model and was a proper four-stroke race bike. Kawasaki gave me the very first one to land in the country to ride at that Australian titles. It was all a bit rushed – we picked it up from a local Kawasaki dealer in SA the day before the meeting kicked off. Kawasaki had told us they were serious about winning the four-stroke title, and that the bike only had four hours of running on it. It was meant to be race-ready and brand new. But it turned out it was a press bike that had been loaned out to journalists and dealers all over the country. It had a shitload of hours on it and it was flogged out. The sprockets were worn, the chain was basically dragging on the ground and the tyres were bald. The shimming for the valving was starting to lock up, so I had to bump-start it down a hill to get to the starting gate. If I'd stalled the bike once I got to the gate, my race would have been over on the spot. I'll never forget the look on Dad's face when he first saw the bike. Four hours? More like 50. It wasn't an ideal situation, but I was still thankful Kawasaki gave me the bike. To then go and hand them junior titles in both of the main classes was really cool. Particularly as I was never even meant to be fit for that meeting in the first place.

In my mind there was never really any doubt over where my career was headed. I went through the motions of schooling at St Joseph's Parish School and then Hillston Central right up to Year 10. I was a fairly big kid for my age, so I was pretty popular when it came to school sports. If we were playing footy I was always one of the first to be picked, because I was a bulldozer with a crazy streak. I tried to play as much sport as I could, simply because I enjoyed it much more than sitting in a classroom. Footy, squash, volleyball, basketball, whatever. My size meant I didn't get bullied too much during my school years. I could hold my own. Every now and then someone would chirp up about how big I was, but I could always pull them back into line quickly enough if the trash talk went too far.

Academically, I was nothing special. My favourite classes were recess and lunch. I wasn't a troublemaker as such, but I could be a bit of a distraction for other kids. I could have listened more and I could have worked harder. I never really focussed 100 per cent on what was happening in the classroom. My aim was to basically pass each class with as little effort as possible. I'd still generally end up in the 65 to 70 per cent range, so my results weren't terrible, but I was never an A-plus student. I did enough to get by and spent the rest of the time thinking about my next race.

It was difficult to sell the idea to my teachers that I could turn racing motorbikes into a job. They didn't follow the sport like I did. I was watching these guys racing in the US and making a good living from it, but to my teachers it all seemed a bit far-fetched. Their job was to encourage kids to work hard at school and get a good nine-to-five job. They loved how passionate I was about bikes and respected what I was achieving. But all I'd hear when I laid out my career plan to them was, 'It's not going to happen. It's great that you love racing bikes and you've done really well . . . but the chances of it going anywhere are slim to none.' I didn't want to know. It probably made me work even harder at it, just to prove them wrong.

Even without working as hard as I could have, I passed my way through to the end of Year 10. Not necessarily with flying colours, but I did quite well. At the time the principal, Barbara Novelli, organised a meeting with me and my parents. 'We know we can get your grades up even further, Year 11 and 12 is a good option for you. I'd be great to have you back for the next two years to see if you can get into university.'

'Ms Novelli, I appreciate you saying that, but no thanks,' I said. 'I've already wasted too many good years here at this school. It's time for me to go and race some bikes.' My mum nearly died of embarrassment. Ms Novelli shook her head for a second and then cracked up laughing.

'Well, Toby, I wish you all the luck in the world.'

3
Seniors

My parents supported the decision for me not to continue with school. Not because they thought it was a given I'd hit the big time, but the risk of not making it in motorsport was huge.

Of course I was confident I could make it, but so is everybody when they start out on the journey to professional racing. The investment my parents had made just to get me through my junior career was so big. And sometimes it just takes one injury, one thing outside your own control, to bring it all down. But my parents supported me because they understood that I was a hands-on learner. Even if racing bikes didn't work out, another career was unlikely to come from a classroom. I never saw myself as someone who would move to the big city and work in an office, so what good was a degree? My first back-up plan was to join the police motorcycle force. Failing that, I could always fall back on my farming experience.

But I wasn't seriously considering any of that heading into the 2004 season. I was 16 years old and I had a factory Kawasaki deal to race in seniors. Throughout my junior career I'd grown close to Kawasaki because I was always winning on their bikes. It left me first in line for a promotion. Ross McWatters from the Kawasaki Racing Team had helped me get hold of the 250F for the junior nationals meeting in 2003 and, after I won the two titles, he made the call to give me a proper shot in seniors. It was hardly big money; my base wage was only about $15,000. Mind you, at 16 I felt like I was on my way to buying a Lamborghini. We used the $15,000 to get to the events and Kawasaki was then paying for the racing itself, so the profit came from prize money. But that meant I pretty much had to be racing at any senior event on any given weekend to try and pick up the few thousand bucks that were on offer.

The Kawasaki deal meant the family had to move again, which was a huge thing given we'd just got back on our feet after dad's heart attack. About a year after we'd moved to Hillston, he and Mum had rented what used to be a cafe in the main street and set up a sports store. Once that was up and running, Mum ran the store on her own and Dad took a job managing an orange juice factory. Now he had to quit that job so we could move closer to Kawasaki HQ in Sydney. I couldn't move on my own because I was still a kid, I didn't even have my driver's licence. I still needed Mum and Dad to drive me to training sessions and things like that. It was another example of my parents not getting to enjoy the fruits of their own labour because of me and my racing. Kawasaki wanted me in Sydney itself, but that wasn't our scene. City life seemed too chaotic for us. We reached a compromise with Kawasaki that we'd be within two hours of where the team was based. Ian Whiteman, a sponsor of mine, had a property in Singleton where we could test and train. It was going to take a while for Mum and Dad to sell their place in Hillston and find somewhere else to live, so initially I lived with Ian. The Kawasaki team would then make the two-hour trip out to Singleton for testing sessions.

Once Mum and Dad had tied up all the loose ends in Hillston, they moved to Singleton. They were part-way through buying a property for us all to live on when Dad had another heart attack. They had to pull out of the sale and we ended up moving to Country Acres Caravan Park instead. The three of us moved into one caravan that was on a permanent site. It had two bedrooms (one at either end), a kitchen in the middle and then a hard annex that was the living room. It was only meant to be a temporary thing while Dad recovered, but we lived in that park for the best part of a decade. Matthew, who had been living in Wagga Wagga for a few years, moved to Singleton a few months after my parents and bought a van in the same park. Amanda decided to stay where she'd been living in Griffith.

I'd been heavily focussed on motocross for some time, but Kawasaki wanted me to add the Aussie SX series to my program. I'd only ever ridden on a couple of supercross tracks and never raced on one, but why not? If that's what Kawasaki wanted, that's what I was going to do.

Supercross is a modern version of motocross. The tracks are short, relatively slow, entirely man-made and built inside showgrounds and stadiums. It's in effect an indoor sport and it's all about big, tall jumps. It's a highly technical discipline. If there's a long pile of dirt stretching 20 metres – what we call a tabletop – and you want to jump from one end to the other, it's easy. You'll do it 40 times in a row without even blinking an eye, because there's so much margin for error. There's all this dirt underneath you. The comfort of knowing you can get it wrong means you won't get it wrong. But if someone suddenly dug out the middle, and you had to jump from one mound of dirt to the other, well, that changes everything. The distance is the same, but you *have* to time it perfectly. There's no margin for error. That messes with your head. When you land, you're going straight into the up-ramp for the next jump . . . and you've got to time that one perfectly too. That's what supercross is all about – timing and not making mistakes.

I was given a small insight into the pain that was ahead of me when I broke my femur while training for my supercross debut out in Singleton. Luckily there was time to have a rod put in my leg and recover before the first round of the Aussie SX season.

That opening round was at the Sydney Super Dome. It was incredible. Here I was lining up against all these professional riders, guys that were getting paid real wages, guys I'd been looking up to for years. In my first heat I had Troy Dorron and Mitchell Hoad either side of me. It was a terrifying reality check. This wasn't going to be easy. But I couldn't have predicted just how hard it would get.

A supercross event is split in to heats, with a certain number of riders, usually four or five going straight through to the final. Those that are left then take part in the last chance qualifier (LCQ) – one final shot at the money race. The top two make it through. It's generally a desperate affair and I found that out the hard way when Bronte Holland jumped over me and landed on my back. It put me in hospital and sent me spiralling into a deep panic. When you're a rookie, every shot on a factory bike might be your last. The team was telling me to relax, that I had a year or two to prove myself, there was no rush. But my ears were deaf to what they were saying. I was desperate for a breakthrough race to repay the faith they'd shown in me. I was putting so much pressure on myself, and being injured wasn't part of the plan. I rushed my recovery and set a game of physical catch-up in motion that would plague me for years.

Between 2004 and 2007 I was never properly fit. Every time I got close, something else would happen. The dumbest, most random shit you could ever imagine. One day I was practising starts. The start is so important in both motocross and supercross; if you can get the holeshot and beat the field into the first corner, you can control the race. I knew I had to improve my starts, so I was in a paddock, all on my own, practising starts. On a flat bit of ground, nothing dangerous around me at all. We had a start gate set up to properly simulate a race start. I think I burnt through three or four clutches just launching the bike over and over. Towards the end of the day I'd shortened my reaction time and things were looking great. I decided to do a couple more before we packed up. I took off from the gate, got to the shut-off point and jumped on the brakes. Because I'd been ripping along the same path all day a big stone that started the day way underground had worked its way to the surface. As I dragged my rear brake across the rock, the bike bucked me over the handlebars and into a fence. I broke my shoulder and my collarbone.

That's how the first part of my senior career went. There were times when things were okay, I won plenty of lower-level events and a state supercross championship. But when it really mattered on the big, national stage, I just couldn't piece it together. The longer it all went on, the more it got to me. The pressure was mounting. The Kawasaki guys were so understanding, but surely their patience was going to run out and I was going to be dropped. I had factory bikes, I couldn't blame the hardware. It was just rotten, shit luck that was holding me back. And it was all snowballing out of control. I would rush back from injury because I could see my hopes and dreams slipping away. And that left my body vulnerable to more injuries. I made so many mistakes, the product of sheer desperation to get results. All I wanted to do was prove to Kawasaki, to the guys that sign the cheques, that they weren't wasting their money. That I could deliver. It was a never-ending cycle of rushing back and getting injured again. After three years, every time I picked up the phone the response was 'All right, what is it this week?'

By the end of 2006 I was burnt out, physically and mentally exhausted and my worst nightmare had finally come true: I lost all my sponsorship deals and I was dropped as a factory Kawasaki rider. I didn't blame Kawasaki for that decision. They gave me three years, it was a fair crack. They'd been supportive the whole way through. But my body was beaten to hell. The rod that had been put in my right leg back in 2004 had been bent in another crash in 2005. I was in constant pain; I woke up in agony and went to sleep in agony. I couldn't train, I couldn't run. The enjoyment of riding a bike had disappeared entirely.

I eventually realised that I couldn't keep going. To have any chance of salvaging my career, I needed a year off. I had to get my body right. Then, maybe my head would follow. I spent 2007 on the sidelines. Actually, I spent most of it on the operating table. I had the rod in my leg replaced and a few other ligaments and joints cleaned up. I had a nine-to-five job wiring motors and making plastic impellers for electric fans. I'd learnt my lesson about rushing things, I needed time to heal. But, as an athlete, you don't have all that much time. At the end of that 12 months nobody knew my name anymore. I'd gone from being a promising junior to being completely forgotten. I wished I could make everybody understand how physically damaged I was by the end of 2006, there was no way I could have kept going. I had to put my health first, but it was hard to see it as the right decision when my career had vanished into thin air. I felt like a failure. I was 19 years old and I'd stuffed up.

By the time the 2008 season rolled around I was physically fit and raring to make a comeback, but nobody wanted me. My factory deal was long gone and there was no hope of getting a new one with any manufacturer. Nobody would answer my calls. I seriously considered throwing in the towel. I was fit and I wanted to race, but I had to face up to the reality of the situation. I was well down the path of plotting my next career move.

The lifeline ended up coming from my old sponsor, J & P Motorcycles in Griffith. They told me that if I was serious about it, they could help. They had some favours they could call in to get me a couple of bikes and some support for the season. But they wanted me to do it properly. I had to move to Griffith so I could be close by and help promote the shop at events. So I packed up and moved back out west. This time I moved on my own, my parents stayed in Singleton. I took a day job driving earth-moving machinery, working 40 hours a week. The racing budget came from the support of local businesses that saw me trying to get back on my feet. We ended up with around $25,000 to stretch over the 15-odd races we wanted to do. That barely covered running the bike. The money I earned from my day job was used for fuel to get to the races and hotels. When there was no money left for hotels, we slept in swags. It was like being back in juniors. I missed the first round of the Australian Motocross Championship (Australian MX) because it was down in Tasmania, and I didn't have the budget to get on the boat. But once I got up and going, I had a decent season and finished ninth in the points. I was a regular Top 10 finisher in the Australian Supercross Championship at the end of the season as well. For a privateer it was a good effort. I felt like I'd turned a corner, that I'd put myself back on the map . . . but I was wrong. When I started looking ahead to 2009, I realised I was in the same position I'd been a year earlier. There were no factory offers, and I couldn't keep asking these local businesses for money to keep racing. It was an exhausting process and it wasn't fair on those that had supported me in the past. I was once again faced with the idea that my racing career was over.

4
Comeback

Just when I thought it was all over the phone finally rang. It was Kawasaki and they had a very unexpected proposal.

They were impressed that I'd stayed loyal to the brand and they'd noticed how well I'd gone as a privateer. They couldn't offer me any funding in terms of motocross and supercross, but they did provide factory support to an off-road enduro team called MSC. And they needed a rider for the 2009 season. There was no base salary, but the performance incentives were decent.

My first instinct was to turn it down. I wanted to race motocross and supercross, not enduros. I hardly knew anything about enduro racing, which is entirely different. I'd only ever competed in one enduro event, a round of the Australian Off-Road Championship (AORC) in Port Macquarie in late 2007. I used it as a low-key, off-the-radar way to test out my body before I returned to moto and supercross in 2008. I borrowed a Honda CRF 450 from a mate of mine; it was the only bike that wasn't a Kawasaki I'd raced since I was seven years old. The first day I spent the whole time throwing the bike into the bush and smashing myself to bits. On the second day I got on top of it. I finished third in the E2 class and fifth outright. It was a decent result for a first-timer, but I didn't really enjoy it all that much.

With that in mind, my first thought was that this Kawasaki enduro offer wasn't the deal for me. So I said thanks, but no thanks.

As soon as I hung up the phone I started to think about where my career was at. This was the only factory offer I had. It was the only thing that was going to keep me on a motorcycle. It suddenly hit me; If I didn't take this deal, I was an idiot. This was my way back in. Take the deal, smoke everybody in enduros, make some cash and then switch back to moto and supercross. If I could make $50,000 at these enduro events I'd have a good foundation to run my own show again the following year. This wouldn't be a permanent switch, it would just be a small bump in the road to where I wanted to be. I called them back and agreed to take the ride. In the stroke of a pen I went from being a full-time motocross rider to being a full-time enduro rider.

I had no idea at the time, but my career, and my whole life, had taken a new course. It was a pivotal moment in my journey to Dakar.

***

Enduro or off-road racing is completely different to moto-cross and supercross. The races are held out in the bush and the tracks, around the width of a bobcat bucket, winding through the trees, rocks and bushes. A loop can be anywhere from six minutes long to 12, 13 minutes long. The events are split into classes – E1 is 250s, E2 is 450s, and E3 is the big bore class, 500s, 550s and so on. There's a class winner and an outright winner. There are usually two tracks for each event. For a sprint round you'll do four timed runs on one track in the morning, and four on the other in the afternoon. You're not physically racing anybody else, you're racing the stop-watch. Then there's cross-country events, where you'll do a three-hour enduro using a combination of both loops. You start in groups, but it's still timed rather than first across the finish line. It's a dead engine start, so you have both hands on your helmet. When the starting gun goes off, you've got to kick- or button-start your bike and get going. If your bike won't fire, you can easily end up in the dust at the back of your group. In the Australian Off-Road Championship there are two rounds per weekend, one on Saturday and one on Sunday. Often one day is a sprint, the other cross-country.

Before the 2009 AORC season Stefan Merriman moved home from Europe, where he'd been competing against the world's best enduro riders. He returned as a four-time World Enduro Champion and had won the last world champion-ship round he'd competed in at the end of 2008. According to everyone on the Aussie enduro scene, we were all racing for second place in 2009. Nobody was going to beat Stefan.

I seemed to be the only person who wasn't all that fazed about Stefan's return. It didn't mean too much to me. I was completely new to the sport, I didn't understand it properly. And that meant I was less focussed on Stefan. I knew who he was, but him being back in Australia wasn't some mental barrier for me. I didn't have anything to lose, apart from a factory deal I wasn't even sure I wanted.

I moved back to the caravan park in Singleton and started preparing for the season ahead. Five days before the first round of the AORC at Port Macquarie, I had a huge scare at MSC's practice track. We went out to do some last-minute testing, my first run on my actual race bike. What I didn't know is that a young kid who'd never been on the track before was out doing some training as well, right at the other end. I got my gear on and took off in the direction that we always went when we used that track. I wasn't messing about, either. I got to a blind corner and bang, out of nowhere there was this kid right in front of me. He thought the track went the other way. We collided, head on, and both went flying. As I was lying on the ground my heart sank. Here we go again. Surely I'm hurt. Something random has ruined my season before it can even get going. I had a quick feel around and I couldn't believe it. I was all right. Incredible. The kid was all right too. It was a miracle, it could have been really nasty. My bike wasn't quite as lucky, though; everything on the front end was bent. I couldn't even push the thing back because the front wheel and brake disc were so out of shape. After giving the kid a piece of my mind, I took off my helmet and started the long walk back to the workshop. I wasn't looking forward to telling the boys that I'd wrecked my race bike on the very first lap of testing . . . just days before the race.

As I walked I began to feel really hot. Then I started to sweat. It was all very strange. I looked at my pants and there were pools of red forming on the fabric. What the fuck is going on here? When I got back to the shop I ducked into a room and pulled off my pants. I had a hole in my ballsack the size of a five-cent piece. The chat I was already dreading with the boys just got even more awkward. I walked out and said, 'Hey, someone has to take me to hospital. I've put a hole in my sack and I need to get it fixed.' There was a stunned silence . . . followed by roaring laughter across the workshop floor. They couldn't believe how calm I was, but deep down I was freaking out for two reasons. One, I'd split my nut sack. Enough said. Two, it felt way too much like the bad old days I thought I'd left behind.

I went to see the doctor and he took a look and left me with the nurse. I was 21 years old and not entirely against the idea of a pretty nurse playing with my bits and pieces. But this wasn't quite how I might have imagined the situation.

'You'll be fine, I'll get a needle and start sewing you up,' she told me.

'Bullshit. You aren't going near my sack with a needle. Ain't gonna happen.'

'What do you want me to do, then?'

'Literally anything else. There's got to be another way.'

'I can wrap it in bandages, I suppose, but it will need to be tight.'

'Okay. Not too tight.'

Having grown up on a farm, I knew exactly what happened when blood flow was cut off to the nether regions. But a bandage sounded a hell of a lot better than a needle and string.

It was good enough to patch me up for the first race weekend in Port Macquarie, even if I was walking around like I'd shit myself. That made the track walk on the Friday very uncomfortable. Enduro tracks are long, so I was hobbling about for three or four hours.

Sitting on the bike on the Saturday morning wasn't all that comfortable either, but it was bearable. The same couldn't be said about the Saturday evening. After finishing fifth for the day, I went looking for something to help my body recover for the next day. Usually you'd use an ice bath, but all they had at the hotel was a swimming pool. That'll do. I jumped in, bandage and all. It took me about five seconds to realise it was a saltwater pool. They would have heard my scream back in Singleton. I walked on water to get out of there. For the second time in a couple of days the crew were all laughing their heads off.

I finished third on the Sunday to cap off a decent first event. Stefan romped away to two wins, but I was happy enough with what I'd achieved.

I was a little surprised by how much I enjoyed the enduro racing. And when I'm having fun, the results tend to quickly follow. I finished second at my first Australian 4 Day Enduro (A4DE) in Orange and followed that up with a third and sixth at the second AORC round in Blayney. At Murray Bridge, South Australia, for rounds five and six of the AORC, I finished second to Stefan. Then, the floodgates opened. We went to Cherrabah Resort, Queensland, for rounds seven and eight and on the Saturday I won by 46 seconds followed by another win on Sunday. And another on the first day of the final event of the season in Young, back in NSW. That put me level with Stefan on points in the outright standings. On the Sunday it was winner-takes-all for the title. I beat him by nothing, just over a second. It was unbelievable. I was the Australian champion, at my very first attempt. I think it took Stefan by surprise. It felt like he'd come back to Australia thinking that winning an Australian title should be easy enough. Even by world championship standards, he was still at the top of his game. I don't think getting beaten by a rookie was part of the plan.

Even more importantly, I was having fun on a motorbike again. Enduro riding suited me. Bashing through the bush, that was my bread and butter. It's what I'd grown up doing. It honestly felt like I was heading out to ride with my mates, but we were actually competing for an Australian title. And being a bigger guy, it physically suited me better than moto and supercross. To this very day, I am convinced signing that Kawasaki deal for the 2009 season was the smartest decision I ever made.

I finished off the 2009 season by being selected to represent Australia at the International Six Days Enduro (ISDE) in Portugal. The ISDE is an annual multi-discipline event.

There are different tests on each day, and you work to a timecard and checkpoints like a rally. You compete both on your own and as part of the national team, which takes all of your results into account. Initially, I was only picked for the four-man under-23 team, but when we were on the plane on the way over we got word that Shane Watts, one of the senior riders, had been hurt in testing. I was given the spare spot on the six-man senior team. It was a huge physical test. I was used to getting through two-day AORC events. The four-day in Australia had been hard enough. To add another two days of racing was brutal. But once I got into the zone, my brain started blocking out the pain and I got into a rhythm. I ended up as the best-placed Aussie, seventh in class and 14th outright. As a team we finished fourth. It was an incredible end to an incredible year.

***

Apart from that one ride on a borrowed Honda, I'd been a Kawasaki man since I first threw a leg over a KX60 when I was seven years old. We'd had our ups and downs, but I was loyal to the brand. Kawasaki was over the moon about winning the AORC title in 2009 as it was their first big enduro win. At the end of the season we had a chat about the future. I wasn't necessarily planning on leaving, but Kawasaki had other ideas. 'We can better our offer from 2009 but . . . you're going to have people knocking the door down. We won't be able to compete with the offers you're going to get. It'll be sad to see you go, but we just don't have the money.' We agreed that if nothing else came up, we'd hammer out a deal. But they didn't seem too confident I'd be wearing green for the 2010 season.

I'd spent most of my career to that point trying to catch Jeff Leisk's eye.

Jeff is one of the best motocross/supercross riders Australia has ever produced. He was one of the first Aussies to crack the US and Europe, and had an amazing career as a Honda factory rider. After finishing his riding career, he rose through the corporate ranks to become general manager of the KTM Group in Australia.

Along the way, Jeff set up a junior factory development program. It was a flash set-up, the bikes were incredible. I raced against a lot of those guys when I was in juniors, on my near-stock bike covered in my cheap hand-cut stickers. The KTM guys had fancy rims, new tyres, pre-cut factory sticker packs, all the factory pipes, everything. And they had a clear pathway to the KTM senior factory team. In the early 2000s, the latter stages of my junior career, I was so jealous of those KTM guys. It was a world I desperately wanted to be in. I'd see Jeff at events all the time, he was very hands-on. You'd see him at everything from the big state and national events, right down to local club days. He was always roaming around the pits, keeping tabs on what was going on. He was known for having a keen eye for young talent, and I was constantly hoping I could catch it. For whatever reason I never did, at least not as a junior.

In November 2009 KTM finally came calling. Winning the national enduro title, on what was far from the most competitive bike in the field, had made Jeff sit up and take notice of me. He made the call to stick a deal on the table. The timing was great; KTM Group was selling heaps of enduro-style bikes, so it wanted to shift its focus away from motocross and onto off-road racing. Jeff offered me a deal to race in the AORC, the A4DE, they'd support me for the ISDE, and give me a crack at desert racing. They wanted me to spearhead their program and made it clear I'd have the best equipment at my disposal, a 450 EXC for the enduro events and a 450 SX-F for the desert races. In December, I signed on with the KTM Off-Road Racing Team. A KTM contract. It was a dream come true.

I made a perfect start to life as a KTM rider by winning the first two rounds of the 2010 AORC in Port Macquarie and the A4DE in Portland. I then kept my streak alive at the next AORC event in Moruya.

Next up was the Finke Desert Race – my first desert racing event.

Desert racing is another style of enduro event. The tracks are about as wide as a grater-blade and are in the middle of nowhere. They're usually fast, you're hitting speeds of up to 175 km/h. At the Finke Desert Race, the biggest event of its kind in Australia, you average around 125 km/h. It's wild. It's a whole different world again. I knew events like the Finke and Hattah existed, but I didn't know much about them.

I thought I'd given my body and brain a workout when I did my first ISDE, but that was nothing compared to my first Finke Desert Race experience in 2010. Two hundred and thirty kilometres each way from Alice Springs to Finke, flat-out through the desert. I couldn't get my head around it. How do you spend two hours on the bike going that quick? The speed is the challenge at Finke. When we went out to Alice Springs to do some pre-running for the first time I was blown away. I thought I knew a thing about riding flat-out, but it was a whole new level. The first time riding that track, I felt like my eyelids were folding back on themselves under my goggles . . . and my eyeballs were being sandblasted.

My secret weapon for my first Finke was actually my rival-slash-teammate Ben Grabham. Grabbo was already an experienced desert racer and had three Finke wins to his name. It would have been understandable if he'd wanted to keep what he knew about the race to himself, rather than sharing it with the newcomer. But that's not how Grabbo works. He didn't treat me like a threat. Not because he didn't think I was one, but because that's not his style. Grabbo was an open book from the word go, he took me under his wing and shared everything.

It may not have seemed that way back when I was at school, but listening and learning has always been one of my great strengths. I think it catches people out sometimes because I'll be standing there with a dumb look on my face when they are talking. They think I'm off with the fairies, zoned out, not paying attention at all. But that's just how

I seem when I'm deep in thought. As we prepared for Finke, I latched onto Grabbo and soaked up everything he said.

Once I had my head around the speed, I felt remarkably composed going into the event. It all came down to the resources at KTM. I flew out there three times in the lead-up to do pre-running, to help get both my head and body in the right place for what I was about to go through. Jeff knew preparation was key and he is never happy unless he feels he's put 100 per cent effort into something. He wasn't the sort of boss who was happy to just sit in the corner office at KTM HQ. He always wanted to be in the thick of it and he wanted to make sure he was giving his riders the best opportunity to succeed. Between that, and some fine-tuning from Grabbo, I felt ready for what Finke might throw at me.

At Finke you start two at a time, with a one-minute gap in between. Like an enduro event it's a timed race, so you can cross the line behind another rider but beat them on time if they started ahead of you. Grabbo topped prologue and took off in the first group. I qualified third, which meant I started on the second row, a minute later. I put my head down and focussed on my first goal, which was to catch Chad Billett, who had started with Grabbo. I caught him by about the 40-kilometre mark. Once I was past Chad, the dust cleared – a sign that Grabbo was a fair way down the road. I wasn't worried, second behind him would have been an epic result for my first Finke. Nobody had given Grabbo a hurry-up for years, he'd been winning this thing by eight, nine minutes. I was already exceeding my own expectations. Around the

120-kilometre mark I started to see a bit of dust. It kind of felt like I was catching someone, but I didn't really think it was Grabbo. Often you get some dust from cars on the service road that runs alongside the track, so I put it down to that. There are fuel stops at 80 kilometres and 160 kilometres – it takes three tanks of fuel to get from one end to the other – and as I approached the second stop the dust was getting thicker and thicker. *Shit*, I thought, *maybe it is Grabbo*. I didn't have to pass him. I just had to be within a minute of him. Then, whatever advantage I had, I'd get to start with that for the return leg the next day.

By the time we got to the fuel stop we were running side-by-side. And boy did that give the KTM guys a headache to deal with. Jeff, ever the hands-on boss, always helped out at that 160-kay fuel stop. And the last thing he expected to see was two of his bikes approaching the stop all crossed up, racing each other like mad. They had to work out how to refuel two bikes at once, without giving either of us an advantage. It was thrilling, I get a chill just thinking about it to this day. Jeff refuelled my bike, which meant spending a moment of time with our faces about 30 centimetres apart. He was amazed at how composed I was, given I was in the middle of my first ever Finke, and in this incredible battle for the lead. He could take the credit for that; all of the pre-running was paying off. As I came into that stop I felt completely calm, I felt like a diesel engine in a tractor, just chugging along.

Once I was fuelled I snapped the bike into gear and Grabbo and I took off, side-by-side again, racing through the desert at 150 km/h. All I wanted to do was mimic everything Grabbo did and stay glued to his tail (without swallowing too much dust in the process). About six kilometres from Finke his motor blew up. I was gutted for him. I slowed down immediately, I wanted him to grab on to my camel back so I could drag him to the finish. But he wouldn't have a bar of it, he started waving me on like a madman. He yelled at me to tear the plastics off the bike as I raced past him. Him retiring from the event was obviously great news for me; Grabbo and I were about 12 minutes up on the field when his bike broke down.

That gave me a pretty handy overnight lead for the run home. I didn't do anything crazy on the way back to Alice Springs the next day, my focus was just keeping it all together. When I arrived in Alice I was crowned King of the Desert for the first time. I was the first rookie to win the race since David Armstrong in 1987 – the year I was born! It was an amazing feeling, but man I would have loved to have seen how it had played out if Grabbo had kept going. I reckon I would've started the second leg with around a 45-second lead and it would've been a fascinating race back to Alice Springs. A lot of people focussed on how I'd beaten Grabbo at my first Finke, which wasn't entirely fair. One, it wasn't a fair fight given he was taken out by a mechanical failure. And two, I was only in the fight in the first place because of the help Grabbo had given me in the lead-up to the event. There wasn't a hint of bitterness over the result from Grabbo, either. In fact, he felt like I'd helped lift his game. He'd taken some dominant Finke wins, but nothing like the 12-minute advantage we'd had when his bike failed.

Winning on my Finke debut cemented my spot in the KTM line-up. It was a clear sign that my success in 2009 wasn't a fluke and gave Jeff and his crew confidence in their decision to get me on board. Jeff knows a thing or two about spotting young talent, but there's always a risk when you sign a new rider, particularly one with so little experience in that particular discipline. He later told me that when I won that first Finke, he felt like he'd won the lottery.

The next desert race was the Hattah the following month. The Hattah is a four-hour race around a 38-kilometre sandy loop in the northwest of Victoria. There's usually 300-odd bikes in the field, so you can imagine how beaten up the track gets throughout the race. The Hattah was another event that Grabbo had dominated in recent years before I joined KTM. I would have completely understood if he'd said 'Stuff this kid' and played his cards a little closer to his chest after what had happened at Finke. But that's just not how Grabbo does business. Once we started testing he was as open and helpful as ever, sharing set-ups, lines and every other tip and trick he could think of. We diced and duelled it out again and I beat him. It takes someone comfortable and confident in their own ability to nurture a young talent like that. By the time I got there, Grabbo had been there and done it all. He was nowhere near the end of his career, but he had nothing to prove. Everyone knew how good he was. That's why he was happy to help me out, rather than being threatened by me. He fast-tracked my desert racing career and laid the foundation for so much of my success. I'll be forever grateful for that.

If 2009 was a good season, 2010 was something else. I won both my class and outright in the AORC, won the A4DE, and won Finke and Hattah on my first attempts. The only thing missing was a second crack at the ISDE; there were some security concerns about travelling to Mexico at the time so the Aussie team didn't enter.

I may have been a two-time Australian champion and a KTM factory rider, but I was still living in the caravan park in Singleton. At least I wasn't sharing with Mum and Dad anymore; I bought my very own van in the same park for $18,000. It was a happy little home for me, until I unexpectedly moved in with my mate Ben Richards, better known as Reggie.

I first met Reggie in the early Singleton days as he did a fair bit of bike racing, but we weren't close mates or anything. In 2005 I took a trip with my then-girlfriend to the Gold Coast and randomly bumped into Reggie and his missus in Cavill Avenue. We recognised each other, had a quick chat and decided to catch up for dinner. We hit it off straight away. Back in Singleton we started hanging out and going riding. He quickly became a real mate and confidant. We used to love taking impromptu trips to the Gold Coast. We wouldn't tell anyone, not even our girlfriends. We'd hit the road after work on a Friday, turn off our phones and just pin it up the highway. One time we wanted to go to Movie World; we drove all night and pulled into the car park at 7 am. We got three hours' sleep in the car and then the adventure continued. He's the sort of mate I can see once a year, or every day, and nothing changes between us. He's also the sort of mate who'll help you move or paint, those kinds of shitty jobs. When I signed my first KTM deal he threw a party for me to celebrate at his house. I'm a bit of a lightweight when it comes to booze, so after three or four beers I was sideways. Reggie found me in his pantry mowing through a bag of raw potatoes like they were apples.

Anyway, Reggie owned a house in Singleton at the time and one Friday I needed his help to get out of a bind. I'd been chatting to a couple of girls online. They were both in Sydney and looked like they lived nice, comfortable lives. Out of the blue, one of the girls sent me a message saying she had the weekend off and that she wanted to come to Singleton and meet me in person. I loved my caravan, it was more than enough for me. I'd live in a caravan again tomorrow. But it wasn't going to cut it for this girl. After all, I was a KTM factory rider. Surely I was living the high life.

I called Reggie and asked if he was home.

'Yeah, why's that?'

'Mate, I just need to borrow a room for the weekend.'

'What do you mean?'

'There's no time to explain, I'll see you in a minute.'

It was like something out of a TV sitcom. I grabbed my van and threw a dirt bike in the back. I chucked in a heap of trophies, a handful of clothes and a few pots and pans, pretty much whatever I could get my hands on. She was leaving Sydney, so I had less than two hours to get sorted. I raced over to Reggie's and backed the van up to this front door. He still didn't know what was going on. 'I need to take over your house. I'm coming in whether you like it or not.'

Typical Reggie, he just went along with it. He said, 'Well, we need to make it look like you own the place and I'm renting a room from you. You better move into the master bedroom.'

He moved out of his own room. What a good bloke.

I set my bike up in the lounge room and spread a bit of my stuff around before the girl pulled up out the front. We told her it was my house and I was doing Reggie a solid by renting the spare room to him. After an hour or so, this girl asked if I could turn on the air-conditioner. I had no idea where the switch was. So there I was, awkwardly fumbling from wall to wall looking for it.

As this was all going on I got a message from the second girl I'd been talking to. She had Sunday off and wanted to drive out to Singleton to hang out. I pulled Reggie into the garage and asked him what I should do. 'Just go for it. See if you can get this girl out before the next one arrives.' He was pissing himself laughing as he said it. He was clearly trying to set me up for disaster. But, in the spirit of the madness that was unfolding in front of us, turning back didn't feel like an option. I messaged the second girl back and told her I was tied up until about 10 am, but she could come after that. I was hoping and praying the existing house guest would clear off first thing on the Sunday morning. Best case scenario, they'd drive past each other on the freeway.

On the Saturday evening me and my first date were discussing dinner options. We talked about going out or getting takeaway. Trying to be romantic I offered to make dinner, desperately hoping she'd choose to go out. I had no idea how to cook and this wasn't my kitchen. Of course, she chose the home-cooked meal. Fuck. Reggie is the sort of bloke who turns every switch off in his house when he's not using something to save power. He's obsessive about it. So there I was in the kitchen, throwing potatoes in a pot of water on the stove and, 20 minutes later, nothing was boiling. I made an excuse to go and see Reggie in the spare room to find out what was going on. 'Oh yeah, the switch on the back wall is turned off. That'll switch the stove and oven on.' As I walked out of the room he was rolling on the floor laughing. Once the appliances were on I could at least cook something, although it must have seemed odd that I had no idea where the plates, cutlery, utensils and anything else was in what was meant to be my own home.

The plan worked to perfection from there. Visitor #1 left just in the nick of time before Visitor #2 arrived. By then I'd had some practice and I knew where everything was.

Once the madness was over and the second girl had gone home, Reggie emerged from his bedroom. He looked like he'd been laughing for two days straight. 'That was the single most entertaining thing that's happened in my life,' he told me. I actually felt like an idiot; it wasn't great form. But it made for a good story. Reggie looked around and said, 'Mate, I'm not knocking you for living in a caravan . . . but pretty much everything you own is right here in my place now. Why don't you just move in?' He agreed to rent me the spare room for what I was paying in site and power fees at the caravan park, which was next to nothing. I sold the caravan and moved in with Reggie.

We lived together in Singleton until I bought my first house in Maitland at the end of 2012. He then moved into my house – for real, this time – shortly afterwards while his place was on the market. We're still great mates to this day. The thing about Reggie is that while he loves bikes, he doesn't look at me as a rider. We're just mates, he doesn't care about what I do for a living. It's always been like that. We normally don't talk about bikes at all. He's my way to switch off from that world. It's so important to have that outlet. Hanging out with Reggie, going to the pub or whatever, it always brings me back to earth. I could win ten Dakars and he wouldn't give a shit. For as long as I've known him, he's never hit me up for a free part for his own bike. He rides a KTM and I could easily get him either free parts or parts at cost. But every time I go to visit him and he's working on his bike, he's fitting brand new KTM parts that he's paid full retail for at the local shop.

'I could have got you that for nothing, mate,' I'd tell him.

'Why? I've got money, I just paid for it,' he'd say.

There are people who've blown in and blown out of my life who were constantly asking for free stuff. Free parts, free riding gear, free everything. There's an expectation that I can just get more gloves and boots whenever I want. It can be exhausting. The thing is, I'd happily do it for Reggie – but he doesn't expect a single thing from me. It sums him up as a bloke.

5
Min

We all had nicknames growing up. I was Bushman, Matthew was Boo and our sister Amanda was Mini, Min for short.

Min was born 14 weeks premature. It was right when my parents were in the middle of moving from Mittagong to Roto. Mum didn't feel right one day and went to hospital in Bowral. She was in early labour and was rushed to hospital in Sydney in an ambulance to see if it could be stopped. It couldn't, and along came Min. All 844 grams of her.

Back then, babies born that early didn't survive, simple as that. Dad was still travelling from Mittagong to Sydney, so the doctors kept her on some oxygen until he could get there, just to say hello before he said goodbye. When he arrived they turned off the oxygen, expecting her to pass away peacefully. Instead, she started screaming at the top of her lungs. Suddenly it was panic stations in the hospital room. Unfortunately, she'd been on 100 per cent oxygen to keep her alive in the first place, which left her blind and with cerebral palsy. But she was alive, which was a miracle. She was, at the time, the smallest baby to have ever survived in New South Wales.

My parents were told that she would never see, never walk, never eat solid food, never talk, never live anything like a normal life. It was a daunting prospect. Min had arrived so early; Matthew was still a baby. And they were half packed up and about to move to the middle of nowhere. But Min loved proving people wrong. She never walked and she could never see, but she could do pretty much everything else. She could smash through a steak and she could talk your leg off.

Min was six years old when I came on the scene, so having a disabled sister was always a completely normal thing for me. I didn't see her as disabled. It was not until I started walking, talking and riding bikes that I twigged on to the fact she was different to the rest of us.

I loved her from the word go, and she loved me. We just clicked. It was a special bond, unbreakable. She enjoyed being involved in whatever we were doing, and in a way I was her eyes, arms and legs. I'd grab her wheelchair and push her around outside, looking for mounds of dirt to use as jumps. I'd take her on the back of the four-wheeler motorbike and the faster I went, the bigger the skids, the more wheelies I pulled, the happier she was.

We used to take her water skiing; Dad would strap Min on top of Matthew in the tube and then drag them around the lake behind the boat. If Dad went too slow, Min would crack the shits. People thought we were nuts. They'd come up and tell us she shouldn't be out on the water. But she loved it. She had a life jacket on, and she'd laugh and scream the whole way around the lake. They just didn't understand Min. We used to joke that if she wasn't disabled she would be the craziest out of all of us, me included. She was a wild child.

They say when people lose one sense, another becomes more powerful. Min couldn't see, but her sense of smell was incredible. She was like one of those drug dogs at the airport. I would always try and sneak up on her, creeping in without making a noise. Without fail, before I'd got even remotely close, she'd yell, 'Toby!' I used to think the whole blindness thing was a load of shit and she could actually see just fine. But nope, she was as blind as a bat. We had her checked, trust me. She could just smell you coming from a mile off. And her memory . . . I've never met anyone with a memory like hers. We'd watch her meet someone new and pat their dog. Five years later, she'd meet up with the same person and ask how 'Fluffy', or whatever the dog was called, is going. She'd even remember things like what colour scarf they'd been wearing the last time they met.

Both Matthew and I were very protective of Min, although she didn't get bullied much. It was one of the nice things about country life. There was this one time that a kid said something unpleasant about her. Matthew proceeded to beat the shit out of him. You could argue it wasn't the most mature response, but it looked pretty satisfying.

Min spent a lot of her childhood at a school suited to her needs in Sydney. Roto just wasn't the place for somebody with her disabilities to be living year-round. I missed her a lot when she was gone. Maybe we should have all moved to Sydney, but the quality time we had on the farm was worth the times we were apart. And Min loved school. When she came home for school holidays she'd last a couple of weeks with us and then start missing her friends and wanting to go back.

When Min finished school, she initially moved back in with us in Hillston. It was great for us, we got to spend a lot of time with her, but we could all sense she wasn't quite herself. She didn't understand why she couldn't hang out with her friends. She'd spent her whole life in a wheelchair, but it was like this was the first time she felt trapped. Stuck. Not stuck with her family, but isolated from a social life, which is all any teenager really wants. She wanted to live her own life. Mum and Dad found a group home in Griffith, which was about 100 kilometres away. That's nothing by country standards, it was barely an hour's drive. In Aussie lingo you'd call that 'just down the road'.

Min moving to Griffith was a win–win. She was close enough that we could maintain a healthy level of contact with her, but she could live in this group home and basically have her own life. She loved it. Straight away, she made all these new friends. She couldn't see the people she was friends with, but she could sense they were like her. She knew she was different to us and she liked to be around people like her. It made her feel comfortable.

Sometimes she'd come home on weekends; a lot of the time we'd find ourselves calling into Griffith if we were driving past going to and from races, or just shopping for things we couldn't get in Hillston. But nearly every time we'd call and ask if Min was there, or try and call in to the home to have lunch with her, she wasn't there. Or she'd tell us not to bother coming as she was out with her friends. It was hilarious. If we tried to surprise her, nine times out of ten she'd be gone. They were always off doing something. Her and her friends would talk the carers into taking them to the bakery to grab pies and then they'd sit in the park. Or they'd go to the shopping centre for coffee. One time we called in and they told us Min was at the Murrumbidgee Farm Fair. We couldn't believe it. 'What's she doing there, buying tractors?' asked Mum. They told us she just wanted to go, so they organised a bus and off her and her friends went. It was some random, crazy idea that had popped into her head. She was busier than we were. She was having the time of her life and leading a normal young adult life.

The one thing Min always made time for was when I raced in Griffith. We'd let the home know there was a race coming up, and they'd pack up the residents and come out to watch the bikes. In one way she loved it, she thought she was a local legend when I was out there racing. But I know she was scared for me as well. She'd always tell me to come back in one piece. She couldn't see me, she didn't know what was happening in the race, but whoever she was with would talk her through it. We have some old family videos of those days and you can see her face light up if I was having a good race. For me it was so special.

I never, ever felt sorry for Min. To me, her situation wasn't something to be sad about. Yes, it was a lot of hard work for my parents – particularly alongside all of the dumb shit I got up to as a kid. But Min was special, I felt lucky to have a sister like her. And it made me appreciate the things I could do, the freedoms I had. It gave me a strong mentality and good outlook on life. A sense of never taking anything for granted and to grab hold of any opportunity that comes your way . . . because it can all be taken away from you tomorrow. The way she lived what was almost a normal life despite her exceptional circumstances was always a huge inspiration to me. She accomplished the things that she wanted to do. If she could do that, what was my excuse? It was a constant reminder that if you want something, you've got to go and get it. I had everything in front of me. Okay, we could have used a bit more money back when I was racing juniors, but in the scheme of things that didn't matter. I had a family who was doing everything they could for me so I could chase my dream of racing motorcycles. I had the physical ability to walk and see. If my sister was out working hard to live the life she wanted, there was nothing stopping me doing the same.

When we moved to Singleton we looked at similar homes in the areas. There were some good options, but Min didn't want a bar of it. We tried to tell her it was eight hours away, that we wouldn't be able to swing by weekly. 'All right, see you later. I'm happy here,' she told us. She was determined to do things her way and she didn't need us on her doorstep to do it. She was fiercely independent. My parents never pushed us into anything we didn't want to do. They didn't push me into racing bikes, they never tried to stop me racing bikes. And it was the same for Min. She was happy, she was comfortable, so they didn't make her move. We went back to how it was when she was younger and living in Sydney. Despite the distance, we spent as much time together as we could. Or, at least, as much as she could handle before she'd get sick of us and start missing her friends.

***

My 2011 season was solid, but far from spectacular. In the AORC I ran out of fuel while leading the first round in Bulahdelah, but bounced back to win the second round the following day. I grabbed another couple of round wins in cold conditions in Hedley before it was off for a second crack at Finke.

I was looking forward to another epic showdown with Grabbo. And, for just shy of 200 kilometres, that's what it was. Like the year before, we went at it for almost the entire run from Alice Springs to Finke, racing side-by-side through the desert. About 20 kilometres past the second fuel stop we came out of a right-left chicane. It was a slightly tighter section, but it's all relative at Finke. It was still very fast and flowing, we only dropped back to fourth gear. Between four and fifth gear, Grabbo hit a false neutral and it bucked him off the bike. It was a pretty solid crash and left him with a busted wrist. That gave me a comfortable lead, around one minute and 30 seconds, which was great. But once again, it was a shame that we didn't get to race it out to the bitter end.

But the bitter end was coming for me sooner than I expected. And boy, was it bitter. An engine failure not far out of Finke left me sitting on the sidelines and Grabbo, nursing his broken wrist, blazed back into the lead. He got to Finke with around four minutes up his sleeve over second place and very purposely kept his injury a secret overnight. He didn't want anyone catching wind of it and sensing he would be vulnerable on the run back to Alice. He only lost about half of his lead on the return leg, it was a real ironman effort.

I won both the A4DE and the Hattah Desert Race for a second time, but my AORC campaign was derailed by a crash during the sixth round in Callington in late August. It forced me out for a couple of rounds and cost me a shot at the title. It was annoying, but I knew I'd be back soon enough. Unlike the injuries earlier in my career, I felt like I had a little more time on my side. I was doing plenty of winning and I was making a comfortable living. Not millions of dollars, but I could pay the bills and I was doing something that I loved. Life was still pretty good.

On 26 September in 2011 my phone rang. It was Mum and Dad, and it didn't take long to work out something wasn't right. They told me Min was gone. I was devastated.

Each night the carers at the home would put Min to bed, tuck her in, and then just keep an ear out for if she needed anything. Min was never a problem sleeper, she generally didn't make a sound during the night. For whatever reason, one morning she just didn't wake up. It was hugely unexpected. Going to the Murrumbidgee Farm Fair had become a yearly tradition for her and that's what she did the day before she died. The carers told us she'd been in great spirits all day and hadn't complained of being sick or headaches or anything like that before she went to bed that night. But the next morning she wasn't there anymore. I basically hid myself away until I could get back on a bike. Even when I returned to competing, it took me a long time to come out of my shell. It hurt to think I would never see Min again. She wouldn't be there at Christmas. We couldn't call in and see if she was home. I was drained and I was down. I didn't feel like myself. I didn't know how I'd ever feel like myself without having Min in my life. And at the same time I had to watch the rest of my family go through the same thing. That broke my heart all over again, particularly watching Mum and Dad struggle with it. They did their best to stay strong for me and Matthew, but we could see how much they were hurting and they could see how much we were hurting.

Eventually I hauled my way out of the hole by focussing on all the good things that had come from having Min in my life. It gave me comfort to think about her finally being able to walk and see in whatever wonderful afterlife she was living. As the weeks and months passed, I was overcome with this sense that she was up there, somewhere, watching on – and I wanted to make her proud. I wanted to get out there and win races, whatever it took. I felt this burning desire inside me to put more work, more effort, into what I was doing than ever before. The pain wasn't gone; it never will be gone, I feel it to this day. But I turned that pain into a driving force to live life to the fullest.

6
Overseas

By the time 2012 rolled around I felt like I was back to normal. I was physically fit and felt I could focus without the sadness of losing Min drowning everything else out. The pain didn't turn off like a switch, but I was ready to harness it as motivation for the brand new season. I had clarity. This was my shot and I had to take it – because you never know what's going to happen tomorrow. That was Min's influence. Plus being busy, focussing on my racing, was exactly what I needed.

The year kicked off with a single-round championship event called the Melbourne Enduro-X. It was almost like an off-road version of supercross with a relatively contained loop featuring obstacles like old tyres, rock gardens and water pits. There were logs that you had to ride along like a balance beam in gymnastics. But every time you'd approach one, there were ten other blokes trying to get onto it before you. I beat my new teammate Chris Hollis, who had joined

KTM after winning the AORC title on a Yamaha in 2011, and won the Enduro-X title and the $5000 that came with it.

Before the 2012 Australian Off-Road Championship season I sat down with KTM to discuss our options. I felt like I needed a fresh challenge, so we started looking at moving out of the E2 class, which is dominated by 450cc four-stroke bikes. The 450s are just so smooth, so easy to ride. The torque is so manageable and the bikes are easy to throw around. That's what makes E2 the premier class in enduro competition. The other options were a 250cc bike in the E1 class, or a 500cc bike in the big-bore E3 class. Being a bigger guy, the real challenge would have been trying to win a title on a 250cc four-stroke. We did briefly discuss it and KTM may have given me a shot if I'd pushed hard enough for it, but deep down I knew I was going to struggle. I wanted a challenge, not an impossible task.

So we looked at running in the big bore class with KTM's 500cc bike. With an E3 bike you have more power and more torque than a 450cc, but you've also got additional inertia from the motor, more overall weight and things like that to deal with. The handling is entirely different. The engine braking is entirely different. Nobody had ever won the outright title on an E3 bike. Everyone had always said, 'Ah, you can't throw a big bike like that around for twelve rounds. You'll win a few rounds, but you'll never be consistent enough to win the Australian title'. Of course, we couldn't help ourselves. The more we discussed it, the more the idea of trying to tame the bigger bike was irresistible to both myself and KTM.

It proved to be a stroke of genius. I was unstoppable from the word go on that bike in the AORC. By mid-May we'd completed eight of the ten rounds, and I'd taken seven wins and a second place.

In June we travelled out to Alice Springs for the Finke Desert Race and, after the mechanical failure the year before, I was able to get the title back. But, once again, Grabbo and I didn't get the battle royale we really wanted. Just once we wanted to duke it out until the end, cross the line together and see who would come out on top. But it was never to be. In 2012 Grabbo wasn't even there; a crash during the Australasian Safari left him with a broken back. He was bloody lucky to get away without ending up in a wheelchair. Or worse. Without Grabbo in the field, the door was wide open for me to grab a second win. I topped the prologue and, back on the 450cc bike, I got out to Finke with five minutes up my sleeve. I'd stretched that advantage out to more than nine minutes by the time I reached Alice Springs.

I won the Hattah Desert Race in Victoria, and then took a second and a first in the final two rounds of the AORC at Kapunda in South Australia. Eight wins and a worst finishing position of second; it was a dominant AORC campaign, to say the least.

The Aussie season couldn't have gone better, and it was great bouncing back from such a difficult 2011. It feels like sometimes, from the outside, it all looks so simple. You're just riding a bike as fast as it will go. But behind the scenes, there's so much that has to come together for it to work for you. That's not even getting into the business side of being a professional sportsperson. I'd enjoyed a bit of success since making the enduro switch in 2009, but it felt like 2012 was the first season that everything came together. Boy, did it feel good.

By that point I was really starting to think about what would come next. I'd won pretty much everything worth winning in Australia, so I began properly considering what the rest of the world had to offer. Grabbo had gone to do the Dakar Rally in South America at the start of 2012, so for the first time that was on my radar . . . but I knew nothing about navigation rallies. The Enduro World Championship was a decent option, given I was doing so well in the AORC, but I had reservations about living in Europe and dealing with things like language barriers. So my big dream was to crack the USA and race in the Grand National Cross Country (GNCC) series. The US was the promised land. You could make a good living, race in incredible events like the Baja 1000, and live in a country where English was the first language. The more I thought about it, the more it became my goal.

Back then, my overseas experience was mostly limited to a handful of appearances on the Aussie team at the International Six Days Enduro. After my debut in Portugal in 2009, the next ISDE I went to was in 2011 in Finland, where I finished as the best-placed Aussie and fourth in the E2 class. I had, however, started to explore my options in the US with what was pretty much a self-funded trip to the States in late

2011. I wanted to take a look at things over there and start making some contacts, just in case. I paid for my own flights over and entered in the last two rounds of the GNCC in Indianapolis and Tennessee. They were dead-start, three-hour cross-country events, similar to some of the AORC rounds, which made it a good opportunity to see where I stacked up against the guys in the US. Before I made that first trip, I sat down with Jeff Leisk and explained that I wanted to start thinking about the next phase of my career. I asked him if my contract could include some help to take part in overseas events. It was a tricky conversation to have. On one hand, having an Aussie go overseas and do well would be a good thing for KTM Australia. On the other hand, Jeff was the guy paying my wages. I was asking him to let me, his rider, take off to the other side of the world with the very obvious intention of trying to impress KTM USA and sign a contract with them. But Jeff being Jeff, he never tried to stand in my way. He always loved seeing his riders do well on the world stage. It all comes back to the fact Jeff is a racer, happiest when he's got his feet in the dirt at an event. He understood what I wanted and did everything he could to support me.

Jeff organised for KTM USA to provide me with a bike. They told me that, as I was one of Australia's best riders, they'd take care of me. There were emails telling me not to bring any parts with me, the bike would be good to go. But when I got there and took a look at the bike I was disappointed. No disrespect to KTM USA or the guys that were running the program, but the bike was basically stock standard. It was a thud back to reality. I was the shining star in the Aussie KTM team that had all the go-fast bits, but to these guys, I was a foreigner who had paid for his own plane ticket to get there. I asked the crew if they were going to throw some proper suspension on it, and all I got back was blank stares. They told me the bike was ready to race. If I'd known, I would've taken the forks and shocks off my bike in Australia with me but, based on what I'd been told, I'd left all the good bits at home. So, only a few hours after arriving, I picked up the phone and called Reggie. It was a Friday afternoon back in Australia and I knew he'd just got back from a two-week swing on a mine site and had a week off.

'Feel like a trip to the US to bring me some parts?'

'Why? What's happened?'

'I just need you to pop out to the workshop and grab the forks, shocks and a few other bits off one of the practice bikes, chuck them in a bag and jump on a plane to Indianapolis.'

'When?'

'ASAP. Now. Today.'

'Yeah, sweet, no worries. See you soon.'

It was a three-minute phone call that led to a 24-hour flight. I didn't think my dad could get the time off work, hence why I called Reggie, but the old man caught wind of what was happening and wanted in. They quickly worked out a plan, ripped some bits off my bike, and turned up in a motor home a couple of days later. They were pissing themselves laughing when they arrived. Being used to Australian fuel prices, when they'd picked up the motor home they'd asked the rental agent how much gas it used. 'Guys, this thing absolutely guzzles it. You're going to have a ball,' he proudly told them.

That trip was an eye-opening experience. I thought the events in Australia were big, but I was blown away by what I saw in the States. It was crazy. As the KTM factory team in Australia we had a decent set-up, but even that was modest compared to what was going in the USA. There was a 20-acre paddock filled with huge motor homes and pantech trucks. It was insane. I remember seeing one of these massive trucks pull up and, when the tailgate came down, there were three 50cc KTMs inside. That was it. They weren't pit bikes for a factory team. That was the transporter for one kid racing in juniors. I was gobsmacked. It was a world away from the old trailer and tarpaulin I'd used at events when I was a junior. There were some more humble pit set-ups too, but the top end of town really blew my mind. I finished that first race tenth, a decent result but not spectacular. You could argue that it wasn't worth flying Reggie and Dad all the way out. Not that Reggie and Dad cared; they had a blast cruising around in their gas-guzzling RV. They ended up somewhere in Texas trying to fly home, only for a tornado to come through and rip the airport to shreds. It was a wild old trip. I finished fourth at the final GNCC round of the season, but the results weren't overly important. All I wanted to do was open some doors with KTM USA.

***

In 2012 I joined the Aussie team for the ISDE in Germany, and on the first day I took a digger and hit the ground. It left me with three cracked ribs on my left side. Broken ribs aren't the most serious injury in the world, but when it comes to riding bikes it's one of the most painful to deal with. Of course, the old sinking feeling came back. I'd worked so hard to get my career up and running, things were looking good both home and abroad, and now I was injured. Again. There's never any external pressure to keep going when you're injured – teams will usually argue against it, to be honest – but I just hate letting people down. I'd learned plenty about letting the body heal from my 2004–2006 ordeal, but I was – *am* – still guilty of pushing the boundaries.

The way the ISDE points system works is that, from the six riders on each team, the best five are counted. So if I'd pulled out on Day 1, we'd have been left with no margin for error for the rest of the competition. Even if my results weren't being counted, I was a handy back-up. I lapsed back to my old thinking. I wanted to become a great of the sport and it was easy to convince myself that it would never happen if I threw in the towel because of a few broken ribs. If the bikes were still going, I was going to keep going. So I pushed on through the next five days, busted up, broken and beaten to hell. It wasn't easy but I gritted my teeth and just kept on. It's funny how once your goggles are on you can block so much of the pain out. But every now and then you hit a bump the wrong way or something like that, and suddenly you know all about it.

There were times it felt like those three ribs were hanging out the back of my rib cage. Even trying to sleep at night to try and get ready for the next day of racing was nearly impossible. That's one of the biggest things when you're trying to nurse an injury through a multi-day event like that. You can't block the pain out when you're trying to sleep, and that means you don't get the rest you need. Rest is the key to success when it comes to endurance events. Even when you're at full fitness, exhaustion is a never-ending battle. Throw a few sleepless nights in there and it's debilitating. Even losing an hour of sleep, which doesn't sound like much, is a huge disadvantage over the course of a six-day event. Your competition end up with almost a full night's worth of rest over you and that's going to cost you, regardless of how well you can ride a bike. If you're losing three or four hours a night, like I was in Germany, you're in big trouble. You've also got to consider the legalities of your pain and sleep management. Professional sporting events always have a doping code which cuts down your options for medicating along the way. You're pretty much limited to paracetamol, and trust me, it does jack shit when you're dealing with broken ribs.

The other pitfall of trying to ride injured is the risk of doing even more damage. The more exhausted I became, the more I put myself in danger of having another crash and breaking something else. Or sending a rib through a lung or something nasty like that. It was, in hindsight, a risky move to keep going. But as I have proven, time and time again in my career, I'm compelled to roll the dice when it comes to riding through injuries. There's something inside me that tells me to keep going even when I shouldn't. It almost ruined my career in the early days of seniors. And if the way my body feels now is any indication, that attitude is going to come back to haunt me as some crippling arthritis in the years to come. Anyway, I got to the end of the 2012 ISDE and the Aussie team left Germany with a second place overall.

7
Pain

The Baja 1000 is the most famous desert race in the world. It's this completely mad dash that either runs point-to-point over the 1000 miles (or about 1610 kilometres) from Ensenada to La Paz in Mexico, or on a loop in and out of Ensenada. It's open to bikes, trucks, buggies and everything in between. They don't even close the roads to local traffic. There's nothing else like it.

Having got my foot in the US door in 2011 and 2012, I wanted to really test myself on the desert racing scene. The best way to do that was to do the small series of Baja races – the San Felipe 250, the Baja 500 and the Baja 1000.

During my trips to the International Six Day Enduros I'd got to know Kurt Caselli and we hit it off straight away. Kurt was one of the top off-road riders in the world and a giant of the US scene, dominating the AMA National Hare and Hound Championship. He was a guy I really looked up to professionally long before I actually met him – I was one of his fans before I was one of his friends. When you're starting out your career you look up to the guys at the top of the sport, and Kurt was the best of the best in North America. It just so happened that we had a personal connection as well. As I got to know him he became my hero both on and off the bike, and I treasured the time we spent together at those ISDEs. At the end of 2012 an American number popped up on my phone. I assumed it was someone from KTM.

'Hey, it's Kurt Caselli. I just wanted to chat about what you want to do over here, and how we can get you to the Baja 1000.'

My first thought was that it was somebody taking the piss out of me, a wind-up. But it was an international call, so it couldn't have been any of my Aussie mates. I must have sounded a little hesitant. I recognised his voice, but I was shocked that he was on the other end of the phone. He must have picked up on it because he said, 'Toby, it's definitely Kurt, I promise.'

Once I'd got over the initial shock we started to properly chat. 'I've seen your videos from Finke and I think you're a perfect fit for desert racing,' he told me. 'You're the right physical build, you can clearly ride, and I'd love to get you on our team over here. If you're keen, we can try and put a deal in place for you.'

It was amazing. There I was ahead of the 2013 season with my KTM deal in Australia and this side deal with my hero to do the three Baja races. My dream was starting to come true, I was stupidly excited. Over the moon.

I kicked off the season by finishing second and first in the first two rounds of the Australian Off-Road Championship to give myself a nice little points lead. Then I flew to Mexico to compete in the San Felipe 250, a 250-mile loop around the Baja California Peninsula. There were four riders, split into two pairs, on the KTM team. One pair was Kurt and Ivan Ramirez, the other was myself and Mike Brown. That was another absolute thrill, to be paired with Browny. As a kid I'd watched him racing on TV in big moto and supercross events, and here I was teaming up with him to race in the San Felipe 250. I felt like I was in a cyclone, everything was spinning around me, everything was happening at once. The work I'd put in was finally paying off. All the hard work in Australia. All those self-funded trips to the States trying to get noticed. It was finally happening.

On the first day I went out for a pre-run with Kurt. It was all foreign to me, I knew nothing about the sections we'd be competing on. I'd never even been to Mexico before. Kurt, on the other hand, had ridden these tracks before, so I just pulled in behind him and started following. Kurt was ripping along at a decent pace and I just watched what he was doing. When we were finished he said, 'You've never been on these tracks before, right? Every time I looked back you were sitting on my tail. And I was working pretty hard out there. Every time I pushed harder, I turned back and there you were. I think this race is going to suit you extremely well.'

It may have seemed like I was doing it easy, but the truth was I was hanging on to the bike pretty hard. Being my first time I was a bit on edge. We had this small GPS that had the track marked out on it, but to be able to see the line on it you'd have to stop the bike and take a close look at the little screen. There are so many roads, tracks, ravines, washes and everything else around Baja and the track's not that well-marked, so it's very, very easy to get very, very lost. I figured the best way to avoid that was to stick with Kurt. For my first time through those sections I probably shouldn't have been running at that pace, but it left Kurt extremely impressed. And that was important, because he had a lot of influence within KTM and its desert racing program. He'd basically laid the foundation for KTM's presence on the desert racing scene and whatever he told them to do, they would do. To have him on my side and pumped about what I was doing was very exciting.

How the race works is that the first rider in the pair keeps going until the halfway point, then you swap riders, change tyres, refuel the bike and off you go. It's the same bike for both riders, so you have to settle on a set-up that works for two individual riding styles. That means you inevitably make some compromises on handlebars and things like that. You'll never be as comfortable as you would be on a bike that's been set up specifically for you. It's a tough challenge, but myself and Browny worked well together. We were basically the B-team, the runners for Kurt and Ivan. If they had a problem, it would be our job to stop and help them fix their bike. But if we ended up in a position to win the race, we were allowed to go and win it.

Browny and Kurt were our starting riders and Kurt was first to get to the pitstop where Ivan and I were waiting. Browny arrived about 17 minutes later and we'd only started two minutes behind the lead bike, so the gap to Ivan was around 15 minutes. I got on the bike and just did what came naturally – went flat out. I'd ridden my section three or four times so I felt comfortable and I really hooked in. I remember passing Mark Samuels in a riverbed and after the race he came up and said, 'Dude, you scared the absolute hell out of me. You went by me like I was standing still. I didn't even hear you coming and before I could blink twice you were checked out, gone.' He was running fourth at that stage. When I got on the bike we were in sixth place and 15 minutes off the pace, and by the end of the race I was seven minutes down and in fourth place. It was a hell of an achievement to make up that ground. When we went through the individual section times, I was a lot quicker than the guys in front.

That first race cemented my spot in the US squad. I'd proven beyond doubt that I was the real deal, that I could ride that motorcycle. I flew back home and won the third and fourth rounds of the AORC in Wonthaggi. It felt like things were going even better than the year before.

I'd originally planned to travel back to Mexico for the Baja 500, but I made a last-minute call to head to the States a few weeks early to spend some time with the team and build on the goodwill from the San Felipe 250. I wanted to show them I was committed to the program and could be seen as one of the crew. Once I got there we prepared my practice bike and made plans to head down to Mexico to kick off the pre-running and testing. Kurt was racing in the AMA National Hare and Hound series and there was a round in Lucerne Valley, California, on 13 April. We decided to go there and support him, and then travel to Mexico the following day. I thought it would be good to go along, have a look and see what the National Hare and Hound series was all about. At some point, as we were getting everything ready, I had an idea. My bike was going to be there, why not enter the race? If I was going to move to the States full-time, this was a championship I'd probably compete in, so it felt like the perfect opportunity to make sure I enjoyed that style of event. The team were all for it. The bike was ready to go and they had a healthy bank of spare parts if it needed to be fixed before we started Baja training. So we loaded up the bike, I threw my gear bag in the truck and off we went.

I wish I'd never made that decision.

We travelled out to Lucerne Valley and set up camp in the motorhome the team provided for us. I was stoked, it was a big step up from sleeping in my swag in the Aussie bush somewhere. I felt like I'd hit the big time. I had no plans to try and chase a result, I was just happy to be there.

It was like a Grand National Cross Country event with a dead-engine start, so you had to start the bike when the flag fell. Then you had what's called the bomb run. That's basically the first couple kilometres of the track, and the only part you're allowed to pre-run. Once you get to the end of the bomb run you're into the unknown. You're facing three laps of a 40-kilometre loop and you have no idea where it goes. There are pink ribbons tied to posts, trees and stones, or rocks that have been painted, and you've got to follow the trail. I did some testing on the bomb run and felt like I'd worked out a decent line. I made a pretty good start and settled into sixth or seventh and then started to work my way to the front. By the time I was halfway through the first lap I'd worked my way onto the back of Kurt. I was never going to beat Kurt and I didn't even want to try. I was there to learn, and sitting behind him, watching what he was doing, was the best way to go about it. I was looking at when he was charging, when he was conserving energy, things like that. I felt completely comfortable; I wasn't on edge, there were no 'moments', I was just cruising.

All I can remember is a hard thud. Lights out. My next memory is waking up in a hospital bed in Palm Springs. It felt like I'd torn a few muscles in my neck, like I'd been in a car accident and I had a nasty case of whiplash. I was hot and I felt a bit sick. I was tender, sure, but it was hardly excruciating pain. I didn't think for a moment there was anything seriously wrong. I had a neck brace on and they sent me off to have some scans and X-rays. When they wheeled me back to the room, before the bed could even come to a complete stop, a team of doctors burst through the door. One of them was holding this halo contraption and he screamed at me to lie completely still. 'Can you feel your legs? Can you feel your arms?' I had no idea what was going on.

'You've broken your neck in three places.'

I could feel everything, I showed the doctors I could move my arms and legs. They were shocked. In that moment there was this wave that came over me, a realisation I was in a bad way. These doctors, medical professionals used to dealing with traumatic situations, were freaking out. I now know why. People who have the sort of injuries I had are usually quadriplegics . . . at best. A lot of them are dead. Being both alive and able to move my arms and legs was some sort of miracle.

As I began to process what was going on the doctors started to fit the halo to my head. There was no pain medication, nothing. They drilled these sharp steel bolts through my skin and into my skull. There was blood pouring down my face, it was like a horror film and I was about to become a murder victim. It was excruciating. It was the worst pain I'd ever felt in my life. I was begging them to put me to sleep, to give me a needle and just knock me out. I wanted the pain to stop, but they were freaking out so much that they either didn't hear me or they didn't want to waste any time getting the halo on. When they were done screwing into my skull, they started tightening the halo with something that looked like a torque wrench. It was like someone was letting off sticks of dynamite in my brain, an explosion of pain over and over again. Once the halo was in place they put this big sheepskin suit over my chest. There were four rods that came off the suit which connected to the halo, so there was no way my neck or head could move.

Then the headache set in, the worst you could imagine. My brain felt like it was being squeezed from four points.

I was losing my mind. Finally, once everything was set up, they gave me some pain relief. I still don't really know why they didn't give me anything before they started fitting the halo, but I often wonder if, as horrifying as it was, it's what saved me. Maybe if they'd knocked me out my body would have relaxed too much, something would have moved and I wouldn't be able to walk today. Maybe I wouldn't be here at all. But at the time it was torture, there's no other way to describe it.

To this day nobody knows why I crashed. I can remember the brutal thud, so I must have hit something hard like a rock. But it's impossible to piece together what happened. Later on I spoke with Skyler Howes, who now competes in the Dakar Rally. He was one of the first on the scene and stopped to help me. With off-road races and rallies there's a compassionate time rule; any time you lose stopping to assist someone who's been injured will be taken off your race time. Yes, it's a race and yes, the other riders are your competition, but we're usually out in the middle of nowhere at these events. You'd have to be a real arsehole to keep riding while somebody is lying on the deck. Somebody's life is worth a lot more than a race win or a trophy. There's an understanding between us as riders that if you see somebody injured, you stop and help them regardless of what it means for your own race. That's what Skyler did for me that day in Lucerne Valley. He didn't see the crash itself; once he got there, I was on the ground and completely dazed and confused. When he later heard how serious my injuries were he couldn't believe it.

He called me and said, 'You were knocked out and then you got back on the bike. It was the gnarliest thing I've ever seen. How are you not in a wheelchair?'

He says I made it about 100 metres down the road – with a broken neck! – but that I was all over the shop. Somebody else crashed in front of us, so I stopped to try and help him. But once I got off the bike I just laid down and started groaning in pain. He says my first worry was that I'd lost my GoPro. Then I started taking all my riding gear off. I was lying in the middle of the desert wearing nothing but my jocks. I don't remember any of it. I've pressed him about it a few times, asking if he's given it the 'round the campfire' treatment and embellished the story a bit. But he's dead serious about it.

If it really happened, then I must have a guardian angel. And I reckon I know who it is. When things like that happen, I think of Min sitting up there keeping me safe. As far as I'm concerned, she played a big part in this whole thing. But even with her intervention I got so damn lucky. I'll never buy a lotto ticket in my life, because I used up all my luck when I survived that crash.

I was alive, the pain from the halo finally subsided, but I wasn't out of the woods. In fact, there was a week of hell ahead of me. It was initially tough for me to comprehend the full seriousness of the injury. Apart from the halo I'd never been in serious pain, and I could still move my arms and legs. But I kept having the same conversation with the doctors over and over: 'You'll never ride a motorbike again. What were you doing it for in the first place? It's a stupid sport.'

If there's one thing I've learnt over the years it's that doctors do not like people who ride motorcycles. I'm not sure why, we keep them in a job.

The doctors looked through the scans and X-rays. Usually each vertebrae overlaps the next all the way down, but I'd bent my neck so far forward that it had basically inverted the bones in my neck. That had to be sorted before they could do anything, even surgery. So they put me in traction to slowly pull my head away from my body, to get my neck to stretch and then pop back the right way. They also worked out the best surgical option for when that was done, which involved fitting some rods in my neck. It was going to cost around US$500,000.

I wasn't worried about the money, I'd carefully chosen an insurance policy that had me covered for this very situation. At least so I thought. When I lodged the claim for the money the insurance company went silent. Then they rolled out a clause that said the only race I was covered for was a running race. They said they had no idea I was going to be racing a motorbike, which was complete bullshit. I'd gone through a broker to get the best insurance I could have for those trips overseas. I had outlined exactly what I was travelling to North America for – to race a motorbike. And I wanted to be covered if I got injured on the job. It wasn't cheap and the insurer happily took my money and told me I'd be covered. But there I was, lying in hospital with a broken neck being told 'If you look at Section Whatever and Clause 525.2 in Column C, it says we don't have to pay for your surgery.'

I was devastated. My life was dangling by a thread, almost literally, and they were pulling this shit on me.

'Sorry, sir, that's how the policy works. We wish you all the best.'

The harsh reality was that I didn't have what was the best part of a million Australian dollars to pay for the surgery. I was doing all right for myself, but I wasn't flush with cash. Two years earlier I'd been living in a caravan. I was still in the share house with Reggie. I asked the hospital what my options were and they told me that, without the surgery, the only thing I could do was stay in the halo for four months. I'd heal, but not properly. I'd be stuck in a wheelchair for the rest of my life. Forget ever riding a motorbike again. Even with the surgery, they told me not to even think about bikes. Whatever I did, my career was over. But at least with surgery I could live some sort of normal life.

Every little bit of it was bad news. Everything I'd worked for was gone. I was laying there with a broken neck and being kicked in the balls over and over. The insurance was screwing me over. I was uncomfortable. I was facing a choice between a wheelchair and financial ruin. The last thing I needed was these fucking doctors telling me over and over and over that I was never going to ride a bike again. It didn't help my process in dealing with what was going on, it didn't help my try and work out a way out of this mess. I found myself getting angry every time I was told I'd never ride a bike again. I'd tell these doctors to shut up and get out of my room.

It was hard to get information back to Mum and Dad in Australia. They'd initially only heard about the crash via something they spotted on Facebook, a post from someone saying, 'I hope Toby Price is okay'. Then someone else commented on it with 'It looks like he's broken his neck.' They were panicking. Dad tried to call me and then tried to call the team. After the longest hour of their lives, the team manager called Dad back to fill him in.

Meanwhile, I was about to be incapacitated by the traction process and I was spiralling into depression. I called home and said, 'Hey, I'm in big trouble here. I'm going to either be in a wheelchair for the rest of my life, or forever working to pay off a crippling debt because the insurance company has done a runner on me.'

Mum and Dad scrambled to get over to Palm Springs and arrived just as I was being put into traction. When they popped their heads over the top of the bed and into my line of sight there was initially this comforting feeling of seeing familiar faces – but those faces told me a story I didn't want to hear. I hadn't sat up, I hadn't showered, I had barely moved since the crash. When I saw Mum and Dad's reaction to me laying there with this halo screwed into my skull, it hit me harder than ever that I was in a bad way.

The traction meant I was stuck on this bed, flat on my back, with what looked like a Meccano set behind me. There was a V-plate that was screwed to the halo, which was connected to a pulley and a rope and they'd hang weights off it.

Once I was in traction the really dark thoughts set in. I still didn't know what was going to happen with the insurance, but did it really matter? If I wasn't going to be able to ride a motorbike anyway, what was the point? What was the point of even being alive? All I wanted to do was race motorcycles. Why bother dealing with all this shit with the insurance company? I started to think that maybe it would be better if someone just gave me a needle that put me to sleep. The sort of sleep you don't wake up from. They were deep, dark thoughts. I'd been teetering on the edge of depression and suddenly I found myself firmly in its grip. My thoughts were as black as they get. I wanted to turn the lights out permanently.

It wasn't all about riding bikes. There was an underlying feeling of guilt on top of the physical and mental anguish. I was putting my poor parents, who had been through so much, through more shit. As a family we were still dealing with losing Min, even though it was two years later. I knew how hard it was for my parents to look after Min when she was alive. And here I was lying in a bed, facing a life of needing a similar sort of care. Maybe, I thought, it would be better for them if I wasn't around. They could just get on with their lives and not have to worry about wheeling me around. I'd spent the last 26 years causing them stress and grief. All I could see now was that I'd be in a wheelchair and they'd have to go through all the pain and problems again. I thought about how selfish I'd been to get myself into this situation in the first place. And now I was going to be even more selfish and need my parents to take care of me for the rest of their lives, 24 hours a day, wiping my backside, showering me, feeding me, putting me to bed each night. Enough was enough, I didn't want to do this to them. Of course, my parents didn't want me thinking that way, but I was overcome with depression. I was at my lowest. I wanted to die.

As it turned out, having my parents there was what saved me. The reassurance of having them by my side eventually took over. Their attitude through another setback was unwavering. They handled it the same way they'd handled everything else; we'll find a way, we'll get through it. I think I even cracked a smile when Mum joked, 'Don't worry about us, mate, we're experts at wheelchairs.'

They continued the fight with the insurance company about paying for the surgery. One of the nurses was particularly nice and told us that, from what she could see, we were being ripped off. She even called the insurance company herself, which she probably got in strife for with the hospital. The company sent an assessor over to the hospital to interview me, but I barely remember it happening. According to Mum and Dad, it didn't go all that well. There were countless calls and emails and, in the end, the insurance company just stopped replying. They stopped calling back. They were happy to wipe their hands of me. It was devastating, but we didn't have the energy to keep fighting them. We had to come up with a solution.

Between dealing with the insurance company, Mum kept herself distracted by marvelling at how run down the hospital was. As a trained nurse, she knew a thing or two about hospitals and she couldn't believe what she was seeing. She couldn't believe the waste. As well as the three breaks in my neck I'd also broken my thumb. When Mum first walked in she thought I'd broken my whole arm. I was bandaged from the thumbnail to my armpit. At one point, after my arm was redressed, I complained the bandage was a bit tight – so they cut it down the middle, threw it in the bin and grabbed a new one. They could have just unwound the bandage and tried again. Mum was gobsmacked. I think it was her way of dealing with the grief. She took photos of everything she saw, from dead flies on the windowsill to dirty floors to whatever else was going on.

The hospital was ready to operate, but they weren't going to do a thing until they got their half a million bucks. They weren't trying to rush me out, so to speak, but if the surgery wasn't going to happen, they didn't want me taking up one of their rooms for too long. They just wanted to know what we wanted to do.

It didn't take us long to realise Australia was our best option. The moment I could get my feet on Aussie soil, everything would be taken care of. The healthcare system would kick in and I'd be able to get the surgery I needed to at least avoid ending up in a wheelchair. The problem was we were a 14-hour plane ride from home, and commercial airlines aren't set up to transport people with a life-threatening neck injury. We looked into my private health cover in Australia to see if they'd cover the cost of a private air ambulance back to the country but had no luck. And paying for that out of my own pocket was worse than paying for the surgery in the US; it was going to be well over a million bucks. We were between a rock and a hard place and we were getting more stressed by the day. Our only option was a commercial flight. Given that Mum was a nurse, or at least had been once upon a time, she would be able to provide me with some basic care on the way. The next step was finding an airline that would agree to this outrageous plan. CareFlight, an Australia charity that specialises in medical air transport, reached out to see if they could help. Luckily for me, they had some staff members who were into riding bikes and had heard what was going on. They started looking at ways to get me back home. Their first idea was to try and fund a private charter home, but the expense was huge. I didn't want to burden a charity that ran off donations with something like that. All I'd done was fall off a motorbike, I didn't deserve that kind of special treatment. I asked if they could just put me in contact with someone who could help get me onto a commercial flight. I was willing to take that risk; I was happy to sign as many indemnity forms as needed to get onto a normal plane and get me home to have this surgery. There was two days of solid work making calls and sorting out paperwork. In the end Qantas agreed to bring me home, as long as I signed my life away and they couldn't be held responsible for what happened if the plane hit turbulence or something like that and I was left in a wheelchair. I didn't care. I finally felt like people were trying to help me get home and get fixed up.

As part of the deal with Qantas we had to book business class tickets, which added to the expense but was still a lot better than our other options. Qantas agreed to assist getting me on and off the plane at each end, but for the flight itself it was going to be up to my mum to look after me. Dad took a different flight, as we were heading to Brisbane and he had to go to Sydney to pick up the car he and Mum had left at the airport.

Once the hospital in Palm Springs caught wind of the fact we weren't going ahead with the surgery in the US the clock started ticking on my stay. They weren't going to make any money out of me and it became clear they wanted to stabilise me and get me out of there as quickly as possible. The tipping point came when the traction mechanism tried to rip my head off. Dad had looked over it when they first fitted it and was a little concerned. He actually told the doctors, 'Gee this thing isn't all that flash. It's all worn out, it looks like it's going to collapse.' 'Nah, it's fine,' they told him. 'It's never collapsed on us before, it's perfectly safe.'

Every day, as they'd add more weight, Dad would talk about how clapped out this old thing was. The weight went up by 200 grams at a time and eventually there was a kilogram swinging off my neck. One day, as we were sorting out the flight home, a young doctor came in to add some weight. There was a huge bang, my head was pulled violently back and I was ripped clean up off the bed as the whole thing buckled in on itself. The doctor turned 20 shades of red and hit the distress button. It was panic stations. There were nurses grabbing my fingers and toes screaming, 'Can you feel this, can you feel that'. It hurt like hell, but I could still feel everything. I'd dodged another bullet. The young doctor who had started the whole commotion literally sprinted out of the room still wearing his gown, mask and all of the other intensive-care gear. He was gone and we never saw him again. He thought he'd killed me. Mum said, 'They'll have us out the door in twenty minutes.' The nurses wheeled me off for one more quick scan to make sure everything was okay and, a few minutes later, raced in and slammed a huge pile of files and CDs on the table. We were told that there was nothing more they could do for us and that we needed to leave. Clearly I'd become a risk they just weren't willing to take. They packed me in a wheelchair, stuck all those files and discs on my lap and rolled me out the door. The whole process took about 20 minutes, just as Mum had predicted. Dad snapped a few photos of the broken traction mechanism before we left, just in case we needed to get lawyers involved later on.

I spent the next two days lying flat on my back in a hotel room on the outskirts of Los Angeles as we waited for the flight home. All three of us were shitting ourselves, as one false move could have left me paralysed. We went to the airport and I vividly remember getting on the plane and trying to get comfortable. Everybody was looking at me like I was Frankenstein's monster because of the halo. I had to wear XXXXL shirts so they would fit over the top of the whole contraption, so I looked like a freak as I walked onto the plane. You could see the shock in people's eyes. They were all thinking,

This bloke shouldn't be getting onto a plane. Other than that, though, it was surprisingly easy. There was only one hiccup along the way. The seat was in the flatbed mode, and at some point I needed to go to the toilet. I pressed the button to fold the seat back up and, once it was almost upright, it just stopped moving. I pressed the button again, nothing. So I tried to stand up and I couldn't move. For a moment I panicked; had I lost feeling in my legs? I tried wriggling my toes and it worked. I called for assistance and the hostess took a look around the back of the seat. 'Whoops,' she said. 'You're tangled.' The halo had worked its way into the seating mechanism and I was pinned in position. I was lucky it didn't bend anything on either the halo or me.

We landed back in Brisbane on ANZAC Day morning. We grabbed our bags and then headed off to the cab rank. Given the whole ordeal had already been expensive enough, and we were spending money we didn't really have, the only way to get to the hospital from the airport was in a maxi taxi.

At the hospital we met with my surgeon Dr Paul Licina. He asked to see the files we'd brought back from the States. Mum handed over the big pile of stuff we'd been given at the hospital in Palm Springs and he took off to go through it all. A while later he came back with some good news.

'I can't quite believe it, but I think Toby is going to be okay,' he said. 'I'm a little worried about this other guy, though. He'll be dead in days.'

We were puzzled. What other guy? What was he talking about?

It turns out he'd thrown the first disc into his computer and an X-ray of a dislocated shoulder had come up. The next one was a knee. He ended up finding files for three or four different patients that were mixed in with my files. They'd obviously been accidentally given to us in the mad rush to throw us out of the hospital after the traction mechanism had broken.

It was a good laugh, but at the same time Dr Licina was gobsmacked by what he'd seen from the files that actually belonged to me. He told me that people who break just one of the vertebrae in that part of the neck end up in a wheelchair. Breaking three of them? A wheelchair is usually the least of your problems. I'd been told all of this in the States but, aside from the depressive episode I'd been through, I'd always wondered if they were being truthful about how serious it was. Part of me had suspected it might have been a shakedown to get us to pay the half million for the surgery. Turns out I was wrong. I had indeed got very, very close to being killed that day in Lucerne Valley. It was frightening, but at the same time it gave me a bit of perspective.

'Look, I've accepted I'm never going to ride a motorcycle again,' I told Dr Licina. 'I just want to get better and get on with my life.'

Dr Licina shrugged and said, 'Hey, it's going to be a long road, but I really think I can fix you up well enough that you'll live a long, happy, healthy life. And, honestly, I can't see why you won't be able to get back on a bike. If you can feel your arms and legs when you wake up from the surgery, there will be nothing stopping you from riding.'

Those words changed my whole mindset. I felt like I was on top of the world. It was as if the fog around my brain lifted, like I was coming out of the dark and back into the light. Life without bikes wasn't one I was really looking forward to, but that glimmer of hope made me feel like I had something to live for again.

Things were moving pretty quickly. We'd landed at six that morning, we were having this conversation with Dr Licina at around 10 am, and by 2.30 pm I was on an operating table getting prepped. Dr Licina gave up his ANZAC Day with his family and friends to get me sorted as quickly as possible, something I can never thank him enough for. Within hours of landing on Aussie soil I was in the middle of surgery. There were two options for the surgery – going through the back of my neck or my throat. If it had to be throat, I would have lost the use of my voice for the rest of my life. Luckily, he could get in through my neck and fit the metal work needed to the broken bones. I got out of theatre and back to the ward around midnight. Dr Licina called Mum and told her the surgery was a success. Mum wanted to come straight to the hospital, but he told her to let me sleep and to pop back in the morning.

Around 8 am, after I'd had a good rest, Dr Licina and his team came in to see how I was going. They tried sitting me up and I got light-headed straight away, so I laid down and rested for another half hour. Then we tried again. The nurses helped me up and onto this walking frame that had handlebars for me to rest my arms on. The halo was gone, all I had was a normal neck brace. Dad had driven through the night to get from Sydney to Brisbane, and he and Mum arrived at the hospital at the same time. They walked in just in time to watch me walk around the room.

In the days that followed the surgery I had some serious doubts about Dr Licina's theory that I'd be able to ride a motorcycle again. I was in agony. I had literally been knifed in the back and that's exactly how it felt. It was like there were two knives in my back spreading the flesh apart and another driving into my spine. I could still move and feel everything, so the surgery was a success – but as soon as I tried to lift my arms the pain through my back became excruciating. I couldn't move my arms up high enough to feed myself or brush my teeth. The promise of a normal life after surgery seemed so far-fetched.

It was a challenging time. I was in hospital for a week and then we moved into a house owned by some family friends close to Brisbane for another three weeks. I couldn't head back to Maitland, where I was living at the time, because I needed regular check-ups with Dr Licina. I had eight screws and three rods in my neck and four vertebrae that were fused together. My head had quite literally been screwed back on. It was hard going; each day my movement would improve a tiny bit, but I was still in constant pain. Crazy pain. I just wanted to lie down all day, but part of the rehab was getting moving as soon as possible, even if it hurt. And boy, did it hurt. After three or four weeks I could start to lift my arms up to my head. It meant I could finally brush my teeth and button up a shirt, basic things like that. I'd spent my life wearing T-shirts, but I had to switch to shirts with buttons because I couldn't get my arms over my head. After two or three months, the pain started to settle and I felt like there was light at the end of the tunnel.

8
Kurt

After a few weeks staying in Brisbane and having regular check-ups with Dr Licina, I was given the all-clear to head back home to New South Wales. I was still in a lot of pain and my movement was very limited, so initially I moved in with Mum and Dad. They'd left the caravan park and were looking after a property in Singleton, so it was a good place to lay low and let my body slowly heal. I'd been on an emotional rollercoaster since the crash and the initial part of my recovery was a bit of a downward slope. I was sore and had so many questions running through my head about my future. I didn't know if I'd be strong enough to hold a bike up. I didn't know if the rods in my neck would be strong enough to withstand another crash.

That was my biggest fear; crashing is an unavoidable part of being a professional motorcycle racer. You're going to fall at some point and you just hope your body can take the hit.

I didn't know if mine could anymore. The fact I was even thinking about crashing was a problem too. It's something that's usually so far from your mind, whether you're on a bike or not. You know it's going to happen, but you never actively think about it because thinking about it will slow you down. And here I was, obsessing about whether I could physically handle a fall . . . which put me at risk of losing the mental battle. I wondered if I'd used up all my luck; surely, if I had another serious crash I couldn't get that lucky again. There was a lot to think about, a lot of mental barriers to try and climb over. I genuinely considered hanging up my helmet. I'd had a decent run, I'd made an okay living and I'd won a few trophies. If that was it, I guess it was okay. I was happy. It was a dramatic turnaround from lying in a hospital bed, wishing my life would just end because I wouldn't be able to ride a bike again. Now, I didn't really know *if* I wanted to ride a bike again.

When I could lift my arms up high enough to pull on a T-shirt, I decided it was time to head to Maitland and move back in with Reggie. A key part of my physical recovery was low-impact, high-resistance exercise – and the best place to do that was the beach. Reggie and I spent hours at the beach. Sometimes we'd be there until the early hours of the morning, walking and talking about all sorts of things. Work came up a lot. I was genuinely considering what my options were if I couldn't go back to competing.

Along the way I started to get stronger and move better. And as I did, I began to think about bikes. How good would it be to get back on a bike? I missed the feeling of riding a motorcycle, and with every passing day I missed it more and more. I wasn't thinking about racing, I was just thinking about getting out there and riding for fun with my mates. Even if it was on a mini bike in a grass paddock, just to get that feeling of riding a bike again. As my fitness improved, my daydreaming got more and more ambitious. I'd catch myself thinking about being on a motocross track and that wonderful sensation of sailing over a jump. I imagined being back at Finke, ripping through the desert at 170 km/h again.

Even the negative things running through my brain began to have a positive effect. I felt like most of the industry had written me off – understandably, given what I'd been through. A lot of people seemed to think that even if I did make a comeback I'd never be the same as I was before the crash. At least, that's what I assumed they were thinking. Maybe I was projecting my own insecurities on what was happening around me. Wherever it was really coming from, the sense of doubt did me the world of good. Feeling written off was so familiar given the ups and downs I'd already faced and it lit a fire in my belly. It drove me to want to come back and prove these people wrong, show them that with drive and determination there's absolutely nothing that can keep you down. I wasn't just thinking about competing at Finke again, I was thinking about podiums. Wins. Titles. The mind is a powerful tool and once I started to think like that, things started moving quickly.

By the three-month mark since the crash my mind was made up. I was going back to racing, there were no ifs, buts or maybes. The countdown to getting back on a bike was on, and I was champing at the bit. I had regular check-ups in Brisbane and at the four-month check-up, things were looking great.

'It's coming back really strong and the healing is amazing,' Dr Licina told me. 'You look like you're doing everything like normal. Is anything causing you any pain?'

'Nope,' I said. 'It all feels good. I don't feel any different than I did before the crash.'

It was true. I felt like normal. Every now and then I'd wake up with a sore neck or something, but Dr Licina said that was to be expected and to just keep up the training to build more strength in my neck and shoulders. My next visit was booked in for the six-month mark.

'Are you still interested in getting back on a motorbike?' Dr Licina asked me before I left.

'That's all I'm thinking about,' I told him. 'All I want is that chance.'

'Well, it's looking very promising. When you come next time, if the scans look good, I'll give you the green light.'

I was ecstatic. I flew back to Newcastle from Brisbane and booked my flight north for the six-month check-up as soon as I got home. I spent the next eight weeks bursting with excitement. I couldn't believe it, I was within touching distance of being allowed to get back on a bike. It wasn't the green light to race, just to ride for fun. But I didn't care. It was something. I'd sat on a bike since the crash – I couldn't help myself – but I honestly hadn't ridden one. I hadn't even started one up. I'd followed the doctor's orders and avoided the temptation to go for a sneaky ride up and down the street.

After what felt like the longest eight weeks it was finally the night before the appointment. I had a 7 am flight out of Newcastle, which meant a 5 am alarm as it was a 40-minute drive from my place to the airport. I jumped into bed nice and early but I was way too excited to sleep. I laid there, staring at the ceiling until for hours and hours. The last time I looked at my phone it was 1 am. I must have fallen asleep at some point and when I woke up and grabbed my phone I was horrified by what I saw. It was 7.30 am. I was shattered. I'd slept through my alarm and the plane was on its way to Brisbane without me. I rang Dr Licina's office immediately. 'Shit, I'm so sorry I've missed my flight. Can I get an appointment tomorrow? I'll book another flight now . . .'

My desperate pleading couldn't change the fact that Dr Licina's dance card was full. 'Sorry,' said his receptionist. 'The next available slot is in two-and-a-half weeks.'

I blew up. It felt like I'd broken my neck again, but there was nothing I could do. Except wait a bit longer.

Second time around I didn't miss the flight. I was at the airport three hours early, waiting for boarding to start. When I got up there I received the news I wanted – I was free to jump back on a bike. To rub some salt in the wound, Dr Licina made sure I knew I would have been fit two-and-a-half weeks earlier too. I'd cost myself precious time in the saddle and I was kicking myself about it. I flew back to Newcastle and pinned it home, a bundle of nerves. The next morning I was going for a ride.

Knowing that the day was coming, I'd already been in touch with KTM. They were a little shocked at what they were hearing, but agreed to send me a brand new Freeride, which is an entry-level 350cc bike that's basically a cross between a trials bike and an enduro bike. Light and easy to handle, it was the perfect starting point for my comeback.

There were so many questions that were impossible to answer until I got back on a bike. Were there going to be any complications? Would I wake up the next day needing to start the whole recovery all over again? I went out to a mate's property in Newcastle and unloaded the Freeride. I put on my gear, sat on the bike and took a deep breath. I had the doctor's blessing, it was time for this to happen, but in that moment the nerves really kicked in. I was scared shitless. I'd worked so hard to get to this point and I was terrified that if I had one little fall, my neck wouldn't handle it and I'd be back to square one.

I kicked the bike into gear and slowly let the clutch out. Even once I was moving I didn't dare let the thing rip. The worry that I'd come into a corner, tuck the front end and fall over was at the forefront of my mind. I thought, maybe, there'd be this lightning bolt moment when the fear would drain away all at once and it'd be me and the bike, riding in harmony like we used to. But it didn't happen on that first day. Or the second. Or the third. I spent the next two or three weeks gently rolling around on that bike, worried about going too quick, making a mistake and having a crash. Of course, even without going silly, it still happened. After a few weeks, I was out riding and I clipped a stone and rolled over the front of the bike. As I came to a stop, lying on the ground, a mad panic-like heat came over my body. Can I feel everything? Can I move everything?

I could feel everything. I could move everything. I was 100 per cent fine.

It sounds stupid, but I was so happy to have that crash. It was the turning point, it lifted a blockage from my brain. I knew, from that moment on, my body could handle a crash like that. Then I'd start thinking about having a bigger, faster crash. And then I would have one and be fine. I went through these stages of self-discovery with my body and what it was now capable of dealing with. It's not that I went out there trying to throw myself down the track to see if I could walk afterwards; it was a long process of building trust in my body.

A month or so after getting back on a bike I decided to go to Mexico for the Baja 1000. I didn't want to race, I just wanted to be there with the KTM USA team. I wanted to show them that I was all back together, doing fine and could even ride a bike again. I called up the team and said, 'Hey, I'd love to see Kurt and Mike and Ivan. I just want to hang out with the crew.'

We agreed I'd be a spare back-up rider, but I needed to get clearance from Dr Licina. 'Honestly, I won't be needed in the race,' I told him. 'But let's say somebody crashed and I needed to get their bike to another place, will I be physically able to do it? The crashed bike will be beaten to hell, I'll just need to baby it to the next stop so it can be handed over to the next rider.'

He was okay with that, but made it very clear I couldn't go over there and race flat-out across the whole event. I promised him I wouldn't. As he was signing the forms he said, 'I'm going to be keeping an eye on the event, and if I see you on the start line getting ready to give it full gas, I'm not going to be a very happy doctor. I'll never sign you off to race again for as long as you live.'

I was pumped. I booked some flights and, around seven months after the crash, I found myself sitting on a plane heading back to North America.

The KTM USA guys were amazed when I got to the HQ in California. The last time they'd seen me it seemed imposs-ible I'd walk again, let alone be back on a motorcycle and talking about going racing. They had a bike I could use for some pre-running and training in Mexico. I didn't want to do anything crazy, I just wanted to have a bit of fun. I did some pre-running with Kurt, Ivan and Browny and it was fantastic. We were never wide-open, we'd just test out some lines and I tried to give the guys a hand. Sometimes Kurt would take one line and I'd take another, and we'd see which section was faster once we got back on the main track. It was nice to be back working with a team.

The race takes around 20 hours to complete, with four riders per bike. KTM had two factory bikes and they got off to the perfect start. I spent the day following the action from the helicopter, watching as the boys ran one-two for the first 1100-odd kilometres. You're not allowed to fly at night during the event, so we made plans for me to be dropped off at a checkpoint before it got dark. There was a bike waiting for me there so that I could cruise along behind the pack and help any of our guys if they needed it. Once my job was done I cruised back into town. My bike was loaded onto a truck and I wandered down to the finish to meet a few of the other guys and wait for Kurt. We were waiting and waiting and didn't really get much word about what was going on out on the track.

All of a sudden, word filtered through that the number 2x bike had come to a stop. We reasoned that it was probably a mechanical issue and Kurt was stuck out there somewhere. We tried to work out what was happening, but the Baja 1000 is one of those events where getting hold of information along the way is damn difficult. It's not easy to track the race, you've just got to sit and wait and hope. As more news floated in it seemed something was wrong with the bike, maybe the engine had blown up. We were devastated, we'd had such a good run and that would have been a cruel enough way to go out. Not long after, the story changed again. We were being told there'd been a crash, but there was still little in the way of reliable information.

We started to panic. Something wasn't right. Within ten minutes, we heard the news we were desperate not to hear. It was fatal. And it was Kurt.

I sat there at the finish line, feeling like I'd been kicked in the face. I was convinced it was a horrible dream, I thought that if I walked into the middle of the road and got hit by a car I'd wake up in a cold sweat. I pinched myself and nothing happened. It was real.

I was shattered. Everyone was shattered. Everyone knew Kurt and everyone loved Kurt. He treated everyone the same, whether it was a kid looking for an autograph or a national title winner he was racing against. He was just a kind, nice person who had time for everybody. There's always that risk when you're young that when you have the opportunity to meet someone you admire, they won't live up to your expectations. You'll feel like you've been fobbed off. That would never happen with Kurt. That's what drew me to him; I admired that more than anything. And he was super-fast on a motorcycle, you could see it when you rode with him. It looked so effortless, so smooth. If you could keep up with him, you knew you were doing something right. He was on another level to most of us. To this day, it still feels like a bad dream. Sometimes I find myself looking at my phone when it rings and wondering if it'll be Kurt's name on the screen.

The news of his death rattled the motorcycling world. He'd just got engaged to his girlfriend, Sarah, and his mum, Nancy, was so proud of him. The entire team was distraught; Kurt *was* KTM in the US and they took it hard. Watching his friends, family and teammates torn apart was hard in itself for me to see. It hit so close to home; that could've been me in April. That could've been my family, my friends, my team. It took me back to the mental place I'd been in hospital a few months earlier. This is the pain and torture I put my family at risk of every time I hop on a bike. Is it really worth it? What does it really mean, to hold a trophy above your head? Okay, you've just proved you're the fastest person at riding down that particular track. So what? Does anyone really care? Is it worth risking your life to hold a $35 trophy?

It was deflating. I thought I'd cleared all of these hurdles in my mind and I'd worked so hard to get back on a bike. To be faced with another tragedy so soon brought it all tumbling down. I thought about how getting back on a bike after my crash was an achievement in itself. Did I really need to go racing again? There was an element of fear to it, as well. If it could happen to Kurt, it could happen to anyone. After what I'd just been through, surely my next big crash would be my last.

I spent the next couple of weeks in a spiral. Kurt's death had pushed me closer to hanging up my helmet than my own crash did. I went so close to chucking the whole thing in. At one point I called Jeff at KTM back in Australia to talk through my reservations.

'Look, this is totally your decision,' he told me. 'We won't force you, we won't push you. We'd love to see you back racing bikes and trying to prove people wrong, but we get it. It's been a tough year. Not many people would consider coming back from that.'

I hung around in the States for two weeks for the Day in the Dirt at the end of November. Day in the Dirt is a fun, light-hearted moto event run annually by Red Bull. It's more of a party than a serious race meeting. I didn't exactly feel like partying, but there was plans to turn the 2013 event into a send-off for Kurt, a celebration of his life. So I felt obliged to stick around. Once I was there, it felt like a good place to make a 'soft' competitive comeback, so I entered a few of the races. They weren't all that serious, but I really enjoyed being back on the track, having fun with mates. I even finished second in the Coup de Grace, which is like the feature race.

Being back in that environment, watching people having fun on motorcycles – even against this backdrop of sadness – something clicked in my head. It made me remember why I loved riding bikes. At the end of the day, I thought, *Fuck, you only get one shot at this. Do you want to look back when you're fifty years old and wonder what might've happened if you'd got back on the bike?*

I'd finally accepted that there's a worst case scenario that comes with my job and there's nothing I can do about it. When my time's up and upstairs is calling, that'll be it. Between now and then, do what you love doing. It's funny how eventually my mind centres itself back to motorcycles. Maybe Min helps to push it there.

***

The comeback was back on. I flew to Newcastle and over the weeks and months that followed I pretty much rode every single day, I was so excited to be out there. By mid-February, still less than a year since the crash, I was in a really good place. My speed had returned and I was ready to go racing again.

With everything that had happened the year before it was nice to have some normality heading into the 2014 season. Just simple things, like getting our entry paperwork together for the Australian Off-Road Championship, felt really satisfying. And given I hadn't seriously competed for almost a year, I felt like that chance to prove myself had finally arrived. This was where I got to show everybody I was as good as I'd ever been, that I could still get out there and fight for titles. Of course, deep down, I didn't know if that was the case.

The AORC kicked off with two rounds in Bulahdelah in late March. I didn't know what to expect, but I quickly fell back into my own rhythm. I was relaxed on the bike and won the first round by over a minute. It was a feeling like nothing else. I was stoked, I couldn't believe it. Everyone was in shock – how can this happen? The guy broke his neck and here he is at his first off-road event blowing the field away. That lifted the monkey right off my back, and for the first time since the crash I felt 100 per cent like myself.

It didn't last long, though. Still flying high from the day before, the next morning for Round 2 I made a silly mistake. Midway through the tests I messed up a line and my front wheel clipped a stone on the edge of an off-camber bank. It tucked the front a little bit and then the rear wheel hit the stone and started to send me into a high-side. I kind of saved it, but it happened at a tricky part of the track where you had to split two trees that were almost exactly a handlebar-width apart. I couldn't straighten the bike in time and smashed into one of the trees at speed. It left me with a couple of broken ribs and a dislocated hip.

I couldn't believe it. Less than 24 hours earlier I'd been over the moon, feeling fit and back to my winning ways. And there I was in an ambulance again. Thankfully, my injuries weren't as bad as first thought. My hip was popped back into place and I was told I'd be fine for the rest of the season. Once I knew that, I could really reflect on what an incredible weekend it had been. I knew I was back, I knew I could do it. I was fired up for the rest of the 2014 season.

I was still a little ginger for the second event of the AORC season in Boylan, but I managed second outright on each day to keep the points ticking over. Daniel Milner, who left Queensland as the points leader, then crashed while training before the next event in Corner Inlet and hurt his ankle. He watched on from the sidelines as I grabbed two wins and took control of the championship.

From there, my season just kept getting better. In early June I dominated the Finke Desert Race, taking my third win by more than two minutes, before one of my more unusual wins to claim a fourth Hattah Desert Race crown. The Hattah race is run over seven or eight laps on a big sandy loop and you usually refuel on every second lap. I topped the prologue and made a good start, building a handy little lead over the first few laps. But, somehow, we miscalculated on fuel and I felt the bike start to splutter about two kilometres from the end of the third lap. I threw the bike around as much as I could to help it suck the tank dry and that got me to within about 50 metres of the pit area. But that was as far as the bike was going under its own steam. I had to push it as fast as I could through the sand for that last 50 metres so it would be refuelled. Fortunately, I had the speed to make up for the time I'd lost pushing the damn bike, and I got back out there and won the thing anyway.

I finished second to Daniel on both days of the AORC event in Coonawarra and then won both days in Kyogle at the penultimate event of the season. The final event of the season was in Heathcote, and I almost blew my chance to wrap up the title on the Saturday with a horrible start that dropped me like a stone through the field. I had to make up half a minute to get back to the front but, somehow, I did it with a couple of laps to go. That was all I needed to become the first person to win the AORC title four times. It was an amazing feeling, it felt like it justified my decision to go racing again after coming so close to throwing it all away.

I finished 2014 with a few successful trips overseas. I won the E3 class and finished second at the International Six Days Enduro in San Juan, Argentina, and went back to California to win the Coup de Grace at the Red Bull Day in the Dirt.

But the most interesting trip of all was to Morocco, where I dipped my toe into a whole new discipline of motorcycle racing.

9
Waypoints

Kurt Caselli was going to be the next big thing on the Dakar scene. He was called up by the factory KTM team when Dakar Rally legend Marc Coma was injured ahead of the 2013 event, and looked like a star on debut. He won a couple of stages and as soon as the event was over, before he'd even left South America, KTM's Dakar boss Alex Doringer signed him up on a full factory deal for 2014 and beyond. I didn't know it at the time, but as Kurt and Alex chatted about their plans for the future in some hotel lobby in Santiago, my name came up. Kurt wanted me on the Dakar team too, he wanted us to experience Dakar together. He showed Alex all these videos from Baja and Finke and told him: 'Alex, I think with his skills and talent and personality, Toby Price could be a Dakar winner.' Before they left that hotel lobby, Kurt asked Alex to make him a promise. 'One day, you have to get Toby on a bike at Dakar. I know it's not easy, I know you're running the factory team and it's expensive, but I know you'll find a way to do it.' Alex promised he'd make it happen someday, somehow. Kurt flew back to the States and, tragically, never returned to the Dakar. He was killed less than eight weeks out from the 2014 event.

I was already on Alex's radar from the overseas enduro stuff I'd been involved in and, once the dust had settled on Kurt's death and the 2014 Dakar was out of the way, Alex began to think about that promise to get me on a bike. His first call was to Ben Grabham. They were friends from Grabbo's Dakar days and at that stage Grabbo was in charge of KTM's desert racing program in Australia. Alex told Grabbo he was thinking about taking me to the Dakar Rally. 'That's a fantastic idea,' said Grabbo. I'd shown during the 2014 season that I was fully recovered and back to my best. Towards the end of the year the phone rang. It was Alex and he asked if I had any interest in navigation rallies.

For years I'd paid very little attention to rally racing. I knew of the Dakar because a) it's one of the most famous motorsport events in the world, and b) because I'd followed it when mates like Grabbo and Kurt were involved. But up until my crash it wasn't something I'd considered as a career path.

By the time Alex called me, however, I'd been giving it some serious thought. There was a lot of uncertainty about KTM's desert racing program in the US after Kurt's death, so Dakar started to emerge as the new challenge I could set for myself. I was keen to give it a go and that's exactly what I told Alex. 'Cool,' he said. 'First we have to see if you even like taking part in rallies. Let's get you on a bike for the Rallye du Maroc in Morocco in a month's time. If it goes well, we can chat about Dakar.'

It was an amazing opportunity, but it all happened so fast. The Rallye du Maroc was the final round of the FIM Cross-Country Rallies World Championship, so it was a big deal. And it was in October. The Dakar takes place in January each year, so if it was going to happen, it was all going to happen in a hurry.

Rally racing is completely different to desert racing. You're still out in the middle of nowhere, but desert courses are always either bunted or marked out by something. You don't have to worry about where the track goes. Rally racing, however, is all about finding your own way. There are no course markings, nothing to point you in the right direction. You work from a roadbook, which is a big roll of navigational notes on paper that is fed into a scrolling display called a roadbook tower. Some days it's so big that the roadbook doesn't fit in the tower; you have to cut it in half and start with the first half. Then, when you get a fuel stop, you grab the second part out of your kit bag and roll that into the tower.

Before each day, you go through all of the notes with highlighters and pens and pick out what you think is important information. You're effectively working on distances and CAP headings, digital directions based on compass readings. The roadbook is split into three boxes – the one on the left is your distance in kilometres; the middle one is a diagram of an arrow indicating direction or a rough drawing of something like an old building or a tree that acts as a landmark; the one on the right has a description of what you need to do at that point, written in abbreviated French. For example, it might say HP DS DN for *hors piste dans dunes* – head through the dunes. Or QT PP for *quitter piste principale* – leave main track. Everything is in French, whether it's a world championship round or Dakar. You very quickly learn a concentrated vocabulary. G means left, D means right, MVS means bad, IMP means imperative (don't miss that note) and so on. What you want is for the distance, diagram and instruction to all match up. You'll also be given a CAP heading to follow, so it might tell you to turn right and follow the piste (main track) at CAP 230 degrees. If you look down and your compass says 230 degrees, you know you're on the right track. If it doesn't, you're in trouble.

When those elements don't all line up you know you've gone wrong somewhere along the way. And it can take a while for you to come to that realisation. If you're lucky, you realise within a couple of kilometres. If you're not, you might be lost for 40 minutes. When you do make a mistake, you have to remember to reset your roadbook and tripmeter as well. Even if you only go 200 metres in the wrong direction, by the time you get back your tripmeter will be 400 metres out. If you don't hit reset, you're in for a long day.

To put it simply you're not only trying to ride a motorcycle as fast as it will go, but you're also trying to keep track of the roadbook and the things happening around you. It's like attempting to read the newspaper while driving your car to work. Actually, it's more like trying to do the sudoku and the crossword in the paper while driving your car to work as fast as possible. A rally bike is a completely different animal to a normal race bike too. A fully-loaded rally bike weighs in at around 170 kilograms, while your average motocross bike is less than 100 kilograms. When you add it all together it's a big, big challenge.

I flew out a few weeks before the Rallye du Maroc to do some training with Marc Coma. He'd already won four Dakars and five world championships at the time, so there was nobody better to learn from. We spent about a week testing and riding, and it all went pretty well. I felt I was riding the bike okay, but I had no idea how the roadbook system worked. I did as much study as I could in the short amount of time I had and worked through three roadbooks during testing. It was a lot to learn, but I at least got a basic handle on it before the rally started.

The rally itself went about as well as I could have hoped. At one point I made a rookie mistake and missed a waypoint, which cost me a lot of time. I still finished eighth and Marc won his sixth world title, so spirits were high in the KTM camp. Once the dust had settled in Morocco, Alex brought up Dakar again. 'Look, it's not a cheap exercise but I want to offer you a ride,' he said, 'if you're interested.'

Of course I agreed, and we started getting everything in place. Initially I thought KTM would be paying for the whole thing. But somewhere along the way Alex came clean; he was paying for it out of his own pocket. As he'd said at the start, tackling the Dakar isn't cheap. The entry fee alone is around 25,000 euros before you've even turned a wheel.

As KTM's main Dakar man, Alex was well-connected. The Dabrowski family, which ran the KTM customer Orlen Team, gave him a good deal to get me on one of their bikes. But even calling in those favours, Alex was still 40,000 euros out of pocket. He used the inheritance left to him by his grandfather who had passed away just before we lost Kurt. I actually felt more pressure than if it was a normal factory deal. I was used to manufacturers paying me to race bikes, but this guy was putting his own cash on the line. It made me a little nervous but Alex was adamant it was the right call. 'I have so much respect for Kurt, and he told me that I needed to give you a shot,' he told me. 'I promised him I would and I'm going to stay true to my word, whatever it takes.'

My first time at the International Six Days Enduro, I thought it was the most brutal thing I'd ever done. Then I was introduced to the Finke Desert Race and I felt like each day lasted a lifetime. But they're both nothing compared to the Dakar. Once you've done the Dakar, a Finke run feels like it's over in two blinks of an eyelid. There are liaison stages on Dakar that are as long as a Finke run – and that's just to get to the start of the timed stage, which could easily be another 400 kilometres. The Dakar is, quite literally, the same as doing two ISDEs in a row, with one rest day in between. It's the most remarkable test of mental and physical endurance. That's what makes it the mother of all two-wheeled adventures: there's nothing else like it. Ten thousand kilometres of riding over 12 or 13 days. To this day, I wonder if there's something wrong with me every time I sign the entry forms. All I'm doing is agreeing to two weeks of pain and torture. And that's when it goes well. You're putting yourself through a relentless hell that keeps getting harder and harder and harder.

The Dakar is based around a moving camp known as the Bivouac. That's both the service park and our accommodation. You leave the Bivouac each morning and you come back to it each night – except on most days it will be in a completely different place to where you started. Each day you take off from the Bivouac and complete what's called the liaison. That's quite simply a non-timed section that you ride to get to the start of the stage. It's not competitive but that doesn't mean it's not important. You have to get through it – you can DNF (Did Not Finish) because of a mechanical failure or crash on liaison – and for the morning liaison you have to be at the start of the stage on time. In my early Dakar days the liaison was part of the roadbook, so you had to navigate your way through it just like a competitive stage. In the last few years, they've started loading the liaison stage into the GPS we carry on the bike.

There's no such thing as a 'typical' day on the Dakar Rally, but here's what a day may well look like. Depending on your starting position your alarm will go off around 3 am. That gives you an hour to get yourself sorted and then you're on the bike by 4 am. You'll then head out for the liaison, which could be as far as 400 kilometres. You'll be given a time window to complete the liaison and you're governed by the normal road rules and a max speed of 120 km/h. Generally, you'll just cruise along at 100 km/h to be safe. By around 8.30 am you'll be at the start of the special stage, which will be another 400-odd kilometres of riding. And that's competitive riding with full navigation, which will take you anywhere from four to seven hours, depending on how fast the trails are. Then you'll have another 200 kilometres or so of liaison to get back to the Bivouac. If it's a technical timed stage, you might not get back until 5 pm. You can easily be out and on the bike for more than 12 hours. You then spend a few hours getting yourself sorted – debriefing with the team, cleaning and repacking your gear, eating dinner and working out your schedule for the next day. We also have two physios on the team so you can get your aches and pains looked at. If all goes well, you'll be in bed by 9 pm and asleep by 10 pm, ready to do the same thing again the next day.

The sleep part sounds easy but it's not. I've been blessed across my Dakar career to have a motorhome to rest in, which helps, but it's still bloody noisy in the Bivouac. There are guys working on cars and bikes until all hours, revving engines and blasting around doing test runs. You'll be in a deep, exhausted sleep and at 1 am someone in a V8 buggy will go flying past your window, full gas. The trucks are the last to finish the stage and the crews work on them all night. When you get up at around 3 to 4 am to get ready some of those guys haven't been to bed yet. Between the talking, the clanking of tools, and motors running constantly, getting a good night's sleep is impossible. It catches up with you, too.

You can prepare all you like for your first Dakar, but there's one thing that you just can't envisage before you experience it – the fatigue. On the really long days, we cover 1100 kilometres. The average distance per day across the Dakar is at least 600 kilometres. If you jumped on a bike and tried to cover that many kays in a single day, cruising along the open roads, you'd be both physically and mentally drained. With the Dakar you need to factor in that it's a competition. There's the added mental and physical exhaustion that comes from trying to haul that heavy bike through some of the toughest terrain in the world, as fast as it will go. More often than not it is brutally hot. And then there's the mental gymnastics of navigation. When you get through a day of that, you feel like you could sleep for a week. But all you get is some disrupted sleep among the madness of the Bivouac. Then you get up the next morning and do it again. For 12, 13 days with one rest day in between.

The rest day follows the first six or seven stages, depending on how long the event is. When you're coming off a week of waking up at 3 am, you get so excited about having an epic sleep-in on the rest day . . . but it never happens. Without fail your body clock betrays you and, even without an alarm, you'll be wide awake at 3 am again. By the time your brain processes the fact that you don't need to get up and dressed, you're well beyond the point of going back to sleep. The adrenaline is pumping. I've had years where I've eventually been able to doze off for another hour or so, but then you wake up feeling ten times worse anyway. It's better to stay awake.

The Dakar-spec KTM 450 is an absolute beast – it weighs an extra 70-odd kilograms compared to a moto or road-going bike. Most of that additional weight comes in liquid form. A normal motocross bike would have one 8.5-litre fuel tank at the front and the rear end is basically an air filter and a mud guard. The Dakar bike has two 8.5-litre tanks on the front, one on the left and one on the right, and a rear tank that holds another 17 litres. The rear end is all fuel tank. When I leave the Bivouac for a Dakar stage, I'm carrying the best part of 34 litres of fuel. We're also required to carry three litres of water, which sits in a tank that's moulded into the bash plate at the front of the bike. The main reason for having the water is to help fix the bike if you end up with a hole in the radiator. The second reason is human survival; if your bike can't be fixed and you're facing a six-hour wait in the desert to be rescued, you've got something to keep you hydrated. You can't drink it straight away, though; it's usually close to boiling after sitting under the motor for however long. If you had some tea bags you'd be able to make a nice cuppa. Between the fuel and the water, there's around 35 kilograms right there.

Remarkably, given the weight the KTM 450 has to haul through the desert for two weeks, it's basically the same engine as the 450 SX-F, but with some upgraded internals. The swing-arm is a bit heavier and more rigid than in a standard bike, so it can deal with the extra weight without snapping in half. The frame has a lot of bracing as well, which adds strength but also increases the weight. The second biggest contributor to the weight behind the fuel and water is the carbon-fibre roadbook tower, which hangs off the front of the bike frame. In a way, it's worse than the fuel and water because it's so high. Whether you're racing bikes or cars, you always want a low centre of gravity. Ideally you wouldn't have this huge tower over the top of the handlebars – but it's got to be where you can see it. It's a bit of a catch 22 and the engineers are always trying to find ways to shift the majority of the weight as low as possible. Then there's the GPS tracker, the Iritrack safety tracker and all the sensors the organisers fit to the bike. The Iritrack system is the only point of contact with the outside world that you have when you're out on a stage – and it can only be used in emergencies. In reality, when you're on the stage, you're on your own. There's absolutely no radio contact with your team or other competitors. You have no idea who is where. You're flying blind; you have to make your own way.

For that reason we also have a toolbox that's filled with as many multifunctional tools to try and cover all the bolts and screws and plugs that are on the motorcycle. You usually take spare gear, clutch and front brake levers with you, the sort of things that easily snap off if you take a tumble. There's also spark plugs and metal putty that you can use to try and patch up bits and pieces to help you get through the day. You'll have a fuel injector and some cabling so that you can do things like reroute fuel pumps if needed. Then there's a tow rope, just in case you get stuck badly enough to need some help from another car or bike. If you can't find someone to give you a tow and you can't fix the bike yourself, you're in for a long old wait. There's a truck that sweeps the stage after all of the competitors are through to pick up the broken bikes and stranded riders. But it might take five or six hours to get there.

I try not to carry too much on myself when I head out to a stage, because I worry about getting hurt by something in my jacket if I have a crash. So all I really have is a spare goggle lens – I start the day with a clear lens before the sun comes up and then switch to a tinted lens – and a food pack with some lollies, power gel, a power bar, little things to give me an energy boost along the way. And we all have a hat with us. Not for sun protection, but for post-stage interviews. You better be wearing the right hat when you're on camera or you'll be in trouble with the sponsors. There's some paperwork that comes along for the ride too, like my passport and any parts of the roadbook that don't fit in the tower at the start of the day. My jacket is also designed to hold a three-litre camel pack, which I use for drinking water. It all adds up and you're left trying to manhandle 170 kilograms of motorcycle.

***

Heading into my first Dakar, the thing that struck me was the scale. We started in Argentina and while I knew the race had a big following, seeing it with my own eyes was something else. In the last couple of days before the start, Buenos Aires was buzzing. On one particular day, we had to go to two separate places to do a bit of pre-race paper-work. It should have taken us an hour but it took all day. We couldn't get anywhere without being mobbed by fans. I got a lot more attention than I expected, given I was a newbie, but it was nothing compared to what Marc had to put up with. Everyone was desperate to get a piece of him. It was amazing how the fans would track us down. They even knew which hotel we were staying at and left presents for us.

For the opening ceremony, we rode across the start/finish ramp in the middle of town. They closed this whole street down and there were literally tens of thousands of fans there. It was a 20-kilometre ride from the Bivouac to the ramp and there were people five deep the entire way, screaming like mad. I couldn't believe what I was seeing, it was a sea of spectators. I was shocked by it, to be honest. It was at that moment I started to think, *What the hell have I signed up for here?*

Because Alex was paying my way, I was riding this plain white bike with no sponsor stickers on it. At the ceremonial start it stuck out like a sore thumb next to all the other bikes covered in graphics. It perfectly summed up how I was feeling at that point. I was a fish out of water, with no idea what I was doing there. I didn't even know if I'd packed enough gear to get through 13 days of racing. The bike was a stock standard 450 Rally that anybody could buy, I had none of the trick factory bits and pieces.

I was given the very specific brief of what's known as 'the water boy' for that 2015 event. To put it simply, I was out there to be a mobile spare-parts service for the full-blown factory riders. It's not that I wasn't allowed to beat them; it was more that if they hit trouble, I was expected to sacrifice my own race. If Marc needed a wheel or a fuel tank or even a motor somewhere out on the stage, I had to hand mine over. It was all about experience, not results, which suited me just fine. There was no pressure – I could feel my way into the Dakar world. My only job was to survive. The team told me that if I made it to the rest day, I'd be doing all right. Then we could get into the second week and see what happens.

The event kicked off on 4 January and, while I didn't set the world on fire with my pace I went pretty well over the first few stages. I was fifth on the second day and fourth on the third day as I settled into the Top 10.

Given I was still so new to rallies, I was surprised at how comfortable I felt from the word go. One of my real strengths as a rider is going fast. I don't mean riding a bike as fast as it will go through any particular corner, I mean sitting there with the throttle wide open for long stretches. It's a skill that you don't necessarily need for moto and supercross, but it's important when it comes to desert racing – particularly on the Finke – and critical on the Dakar. For me it comes naturally, thanks to all those years of flogging across paddocks in Roto with the bike maxed out in top gear. I then honed that skill over the years at Finke. So when I got to the Dakar the speed didn't worry me at all. I felt I could ride the bike at full throttle and feel comfortable watching my roadbook and compass and tripmeter and everything else I had to keep an eye on. I still had the available brain space to do all the math needed to stay on track.

What I was less comfortable with was the local traffic on the liaison stages. My first impression of Argentina was the dry, fast roads. The second was how little the road rules seemed to matter when we were coming in and out of towns.

By the midway point in the event, as we moved from Argentina to Chile and its soft sand dunes, I felt like I really had a handle on the navigation. I started to get some better bits on my bike too. Sam Sunderland crashed out of the event on Stage 4 and whatever was left of his bike was up for grabs. I was riding on this stock suspension and my wrists were getting beaten to hell, flogged all day long. So Alex talked KTM into letting me grab some bits off Sam's bike. We swapped out the forks and clutch basket to improve the bike, and boy, did it make a big difference. On Day 6, the last stage before the rest day, I finished second, just over a minute behind stage winner Hélder Rodrigues. And that was despite nearly missing a waypoint and needing to backtrack a bit during the stage.

After the rest day, I got my first taste of a Dakar marathon stage doing an overnight trip from Chile into Bolivia and back. A marathon stage is basically two days of fending for yourself. The first day starts like any other on the Dakar, leaving the Bivouac, liaison stage, timed stage etc. but when you're done you don't head back to the relative comfort of the service park. You camp somewhere, completely separated from the team. You might be 200 kilometres away from your mechanics and engineers and all the spare parts. It means you have to be a bit more conservative on that first day of the marathon stage. If you have a crash and bend your handlebars or something like that, you're stuck with it for two days.

The night before the marathon you pack a bag with some clothes, a towel, food, things like that. When you get to the designated camp area at the end of the first day, you get the bag you've packed and another bag that has a yoga mat and a thin blanket in it. That's it. I've slept on a concrete floor in a hall. I've slept in the seating area of a stadium. It's crazy. You spend all day on the bike, your brain is completely fried, and then you lay down on a thin piece of rubber on a concrete floor and you're expected to get some rest. Then, you get up and do another six, seven, eight hundred kilometres on the bike.

The Dakar is hard enough without the marathon stage, but at the same time it's a critical part of the event. The whole point of the event is to try to break both man and machine. When it comes to the marathon, it's the man that usually breaks before the machine.

My first marathon was eye-opening but mostly due to the weather. We copped rain on both days but the second was extreme. We had to ride across a salt pan that had something like 35 times the salt content of beach water. You could park a car there for two days and it would almost rust completely away. Once it was drowned in water, the salt pan became a corrosive mud bath that we had to ride through. It was virtually eating our bikes as we went; the wiring copped a hammering and the bikes kept stalling and then not starting.

I had to help push-start Marc a couple of times as we battled our way through. Despite that, it was a very positive couple of days for the KTM team; Honda rider Joan Barreda damaged his bike on Stage 7 and by the time he got to the end of Stage 8 he'd forfeited his long-held lead to Marc.

Meanwhile, I'd worked my way up to fourth, as more and more factory parts were taken off Sam's crashed bike and fitted to mine. It was like I was playing a video game, collecting coins on a stage that I could then swap for go-fast parts from the KTM truck back in the Bivouac. An air filter here, a shock there. My bike just kept getting better.

I lost a bit of time on Stage 9, our last full day in Chile, but held on to fourth in the overall standings. We crossed back into Argentina as part of a second marathon stage on Day 10 and I found myself closing the gap to third-placed Pablo Quintanilla to around 20 seconds. It was at that point I realised that I wasn't just enjoying a very, very solid Dakar debut . . . I was in genuine contention for a podium finish. Things got even better on the second day of the marathon when I finished third for the stage and moved into third for the rally.

I never considered for a single moment that I'd be a stage winner at my first Dakar, but on the penultimate day everything came together. On the blast from Termas de Rio Hondo to Rosario I ended up nearly two minutes clear of Joan. Man, it was perfect. I was on the verge of a podium with an 11-minute gap back to Pablo, and Marc was leading by nearly 18 minutes.

All we needed was a nice, clean run through the final day . . . but of course the Dakar gods had a curveball waiting for us. About 40 kilometres into the final stage, we reached a stretch of track that had been hit by a storm and turned into a bog hole. We run what's basically a road tyre on a Dakar bike because a normal motocross tyre just doesn't have the mileage. We'd started in reverse order that day and, by the time I got there, there were stranded bikes as far as the eye could see. There I was, blown away that I was in contention for a podium at my first Dakar, only to come across this scene of muddy madness. There were people that had slid off the track and ended up stuck in trenches and ditches. It was like another world. I somehow managed to battle my way through and took off to the finish line, but even when I got there I couldn't just blast over the line. I had to sit there and wait for Marc to come through; after all, even when I was fighting for a podium my priority was to ensure Marc won the race. Once he safely crossed the line to secure his fifth Dakar crown, my job was done and I could finally cross the finish line. In third place. At my first ever Dakar. It was the best finish for a Dakar rookie in 17 years. By the time we finished, the top car competitors weren't that far behind us, and I remember a few of the drivers coming up and saying, 'Who the hell are you? Where did you come from?' I'm telling these blokes that I'm just some Aussie who came over for a first crack at the Dakar and they're all going, 'What? It's your first time here?'

No one seemed to know how this nobody on his plain white bike had finished on the podium. They probably wouldn't have believed me if I'd told them that Alex had paid for it out of his own pocket. It was the ultimate fairytale, not just for me but for Alex as well.

Unsurprisingly, he was ecstatic. Considering the job I was given was to survive and support the factory riders, just making the finish would have been declared a success. If I'd finished 15th, for example, Alex would have been thrilled. I think the complete lack of expectation really helped me along the way. At no point did I feel like I had to push hard to impress anyone. I kind of treated it as a fun experience, where I had nothing to lose and everything to gain. If I'd gone there saying I wanted to finish on the podium, two things would have happened; one, everyone would have laughed at me, and two, it would never have happened. I would have thrown it away somewhere. To give the whole thing some context, Marc didn't win his first Dakar stage until his fourth attempt. To finish third overall in my second rally and first Dakar . . . you can't make that happen yourself. It has to happen around you while you mind your own business.

I left South America having earned the respect of some top Dakar competitors, both on two wheels and four. When I landed back in Australia, I was both shocked with what had happened and absolutely exhausted. I had gone into the event completely unprepared for the fatigue. I lost something like nine kilograms in 13 days of racing. When I got to the finish, I felt a whole new kind of terrible I'd never felt before. I was a zombie for days. I remember shortly after arriving Australia I was at a friend's house trying to recover. We were watching an AMA Supercross event on TV and one minute I was watching what was happening, the next I zoned out. At the end of one of the heats Erin Bates, who is part of the Supercross TV team, popped up on screen and started interviewing one of the riders. She said something like, 'How did that race go for you, it looks like you made a really good start' . . . and I just started answering the question. I was off in my own little world, my brain thought I was being interviewed in the Bivouac at the end of a Dakar stage. It took me a good three months to get any energy back. For the first month I just didn't want to get out of bed, I could barely lift my head off the pillow. It's crazy what your body goes through on the Dakar.

10
Victory

The 2015 Dakar result cemented my place as a rally rider, but it didn't mean I was done with enduro and desert racing. I still had commitments with KTM Australia, including one final tilt at the Australian Off-Road Championship. I wanted to go out with a bang and made a perfect start with a couple of wins in Kilkivan. Rounds 3 and 4 were in Corner Inlet, and on the Saturday I got caught up in a second-corner pile-up and dropped to the back of the field. I still managed to work my way back up to fourth and that was as bad as my season got. I won on the Sunday in Corner Inlet, and then took four more wins on the bounce at Wanbi and Aratula. My winning streak ended with a second place on the Saturday in Kyogle, but I already had a hand on a record fifth AORC title. A win the next day wrapped it up with two rounds to spare. In August I bowed out of the AORC with a second place and one last win in Monkerai. It was an emotional rollercoaster;

I was stoked to win another title and I was excited about the rally stuff overseas, but I was sad to see my time in the AORC come to an end. It's the series that saved my career when it was hanging by a thread in 2009, and the success I enjoyed over the years that followed set me on the path to the Dakar.

The biggest threat to my 2015 AORC campaign came at the Finke Desert Race in early June. In the lead-up to Finke I flew out to Alice Springs a few times to do some pre-running and testing. My last trip was about a week-and-a-half before the event and I wanted to pick up the pace a little to see where I was at in terms of fitness. It may not be as gruelling as Dakar but Finke still beats you up. If you don't prepare, you'll find muscles that you didn't know existed – and the only way to prepare is to ride that track. I took off on one last test run from Alice to Finke and everything was going well. I felt comfortable and, while I was pushing, I was nowhere near my limit. I was just clocking off the kilometres to try and get my body into shape. I got to the 150-kilometre mark, about ten kays short of the fuel stop, and I was running all the same lines I'd been running for the past couple of days. So I really wasn't expecting there to be a huge stick protruding backwards out of the windrow on the side of the track. I had no idea it was there. I'm not sure if I ran a little wide or if it had been dug up overnight somehow, but all of a sudden my foot got ripped off the peg. The force was unbelievable. It threw my right leg over the seat and almost threw me completely off the bike. I side-saddled the thing for a moment before I got it back under control. Not knowing what was there at the time I thought, *What the fuck was that?*

I looked down and there was a massive stick hanging out of my boot. My first thought was, *Shit, this thing has gone straight through my foot.* It really didn't look good. I slowed down the bike and came to a gentle stop, and as soon as I did it started to really hurt. When I say it was a stick, I'm not talking about a twig. This thing was basically a tree branch, it was huge. And there it was going straight through my boot. Between taking in the size of the stick and the pain, I was convinced it had annihilated my ankle. I genuinely thought it might have cut my foot off. I pushed the bike over to the service road as I knew the crew were following me in a car and I didn't want them to not see me and drive on past.

I laid down on the side of the service road and my foot started thumping with pain, getting worse by the millisecond. I took another look at my boot; I was never going to get my foot out while that stick was through it. I didn't know whether to pull it out or leave it in. I had no idea what was going on under that boot. What I did notice, however, was that there was no blood. If it had cut my foot off, surely there would be blood pouring out.

At that point, the stick had been in there for three or four minutes. It was getting weird and I wasn't sure how long I'd be waiting for the crew; I'd been ripping along at 150 km/h so I'd pulled a fair gap over the service car. I decided it had to come out.

So I gritted my teeth and just ripped it out of my boot. I looked at the stick and there was hardly any blood on the end that had been stuck in my foot. That sent me into an even bigger panic; the thing must have snapped off in the boot and the rest of it was still lodged in my ankle. The next step was to try and get the boot off, but I was worried that if I pulled my leg out, my ankle and foot wouldn't come with it. I was terrified. I stuck my hand down there to have a feel around and there was still no blood. *What if my foot swells up so much I'll never get the boot off?* I thought, freaking out.

So I gritted my teeth again and this time ripped off my boot. In hindsight that was a bad call; as the team physio later told me, the pressure from the boot was actually good for the swelling. But I wasn't thinking clearly, I was in a state of sheer panic. I couldn't see any blood, but I had no way of being sure the stick hadn't hit an artery and I was bleeding to death.

Once I got my foot out I took a look at it and it started to swell up in front of my eyes. But there was still no blood. I was confused. *How did that stick go through a tight-fitting motocross boot and miss my ankle?* When I took a closer look, I could see it had sliced up the side of the foot and ripped it open rather than pierced through it. There wasn't a lot of blood because it was basically a big scratch. The pain was coming from the two outside bones in my foot that the stick had clearly broken on its way through. When the crew arrived, I explained what had happened and they chucked me in the car so we could head back to Alice.

Growing up on a working farm, bikes were part of life at Roto – it was only a matter of time before I took that need for speed to the track.

Dad was unfazed about me competing in the youngest category – four to seven: 'He knows how to dodge sheep, so he'll be right.'

For a long time, winning wasn't all that important. I just loved riding bikes. I wanted to be on two wheels, either on my BMX or my motorbike.

Roto was the perfect place to breed a love of anything with a motor. I was into everything that had an engine strapped to it.

I quickly became very comfortable hammering across a paddock at full throttle. Thanks to the jumps and tracks Dad and my uncle would carve out, I also grew comfortable in the air.

Winning a holiday to the Gold Coast on the longest ever Plucka Duck segment earned me some serious cred when I went back to school at Hillston.

To this day if the word 'race' comes up, it flicks a switch in my brain. But to me, it was always riding first, winning second.

Early on a club president told Dad, 'I reckon you've got a bit of a speed demon on your hands there. You need to take him to a big meeting, see how he goes.' Turns out, I went well.

Top left: It was a huge leap to bikes with a clutch – more gears, more power, and more travel to bigger state and national meetings.

Right and bottom left: With great power comes great responsibility . . . and I didn't always come out in one piece. Two broken wrists in 1997 wasn't the best Mother's Day gift. It was the beginning of a long relationship with emergency wards around the world.

Winning multiple, consecutive NSW motocross titles was all leading me to the goal of representing Australia overseas.

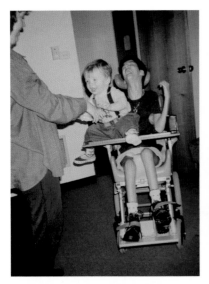

Min was six years old when I came on the scene, so having a disabled sister was always completely normal. I didn't see her that way. I loved her from the word go, and she loved me. It was an unbreakable bond. She accomplished the things that she wanted to do in life. If she could do that, what was my excuse?

Toby Price shows his delight after winning last year's Finke Desert Race
Picture: JUSTIN BRIERTY

PRICE WANTS FINKE PRIZE

Dale Fletcher

DEFENDING Finke bike champion Toby Price is striving for back-to-back titles this weekend and his motto is all about repeating the process.

The Singleton flyer won on his first attempt at Finke last year and has come into this weekend's

Price scorched the field on day one last year, being the only rider to get to Finke in under two hours, and he hopes to do the same on Sunday.

He said: "Hopefully, all the prep-arations have been

"There is no point changing something that obviously works." and I can't wait to get out there and get it all happening."

Price will again just worry about

> Being the hunted is going to be the hard part, with a target on your back. But I can't put any more pressure on myself

TOBY PRICE
DEFENDING FINKE DESERT RACE CHAMPION

He said: "Fingers crossed we get down and back safely. That is my main goal and we will go with it from there.

"Being the hunted is going to be the hard part, with a target on your back. But I can't put any more pressure on myself."

collected and go out and have some fun with it.

"That is the thought process I had last year and it worked, so I'm going to stick with that I reckon."

Price is hoping for some rain to juice the track up come Sunday.

He said: "We didn't have too much rain on the track last year and I have done a bit of pre-running down on the track and it is pretty dusty, so the forecast of

With one Finke bike crown in my pocket, I was gunning for back-to-back titles – it wasn't to be that year, but I would go on to win another six across the two- and four-wheel categories.

Toby's on fire

Price dominates world race circuit

Price pushing for an upset

The Price is right

Prayers for Toby

Aussie champ

The headlines pretty much summed up my rise from local champ to getting traction on the world stage (including some much-needed prayers I'd need all too soon and often). Here I am, bright-eyed and wanting to take on all comers in the 2011 Hattah Desert Race, which I went on to win for the second time.

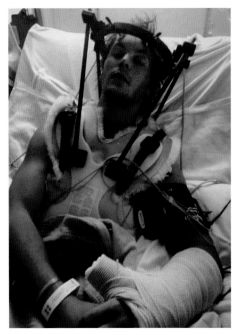

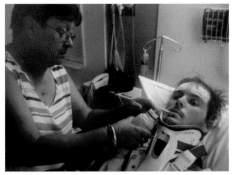

Above and left: It all came unstuck when I crashed out spectacularly at a 2013 AMA Hare and Hound National Championship event in California. I woke up in Palm Springs, my neck broken in three places and a halo bolted into my head. Thankfully, Mum and Dad flew over to sort me out.

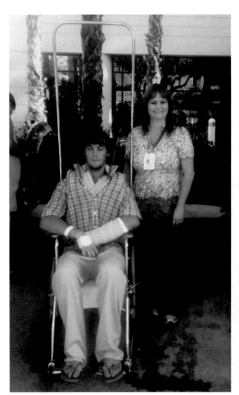

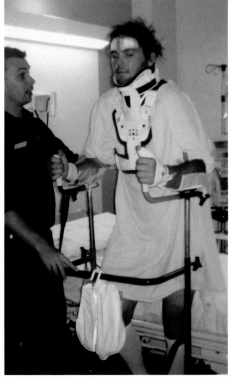

Faced with the prospect of never walking again – let alone riding – the first order of business was getting back on a Qantas flight to Australia for a surgery that wouldn't send my family broke. The second order was getting back on my feet and, ultimately, back in the saddle.

I never would have made it through my accident without my parents. Here we are in 2016 at the premier of my doco *Paying the Price*. (Red Bull Content Pool)

Kurt Caselli, a great mate and true inspiration. Gone too soon. (Red Bull Content Pool)

I'll never forget the moment when KTM's Dakar boss Alex Doringer let me know I'd be replacing a retiring Marc Coma at the Red Bull KTM Factory Racing Team for 2014.

I wanted to make the most of every world enduro event I entered, with all eyes on Dakar. Me working up some dust devils, Igualada, Spain, 2015. (Amanda West/FourOhFour Films)

The 2016 Dakar starting podium ceremony in Buenos Aires, Argentina. There's no telling where the Aussie flag will fly when I'm overseas. (Red Bull Content Pool)

Stage 5 of the 2016 Dakar Rally – from Jujuy, Argentina, to Uyuni, Bolivia. (Red Bull Content Pool)

Celebrating my first Dakar victory on the podium after Stage 13 between Villa Carlos Paz and Rosario, Argentina. (Franck Fife/AFP via Getty Images)

After crashing out while leading Stage 4 of the 2017 Dakar and breaking my femur, it was a long and painful road back to Dakar 2018 in Cordoba, Argentina. I (along with the titanium rod screwed into my bone) came away with a hard-won third place. (Red Bull Content Pool)

It's always good to catch up with the next generation and sign some autographs – in this case at the Tatts Finke Desert Race, 2018. (Owlpine Group)

Above: Relaxing with my mechanics prior to the prologue during the 2018 Finke. Life's easier when you're surrounded by the best in the business. (Owlpine Group)

Right: Highlighting a road book at the KTM Factory Racing Team HQ in preparation for the World Championships in Igualada, Spain, 2018. (Red Bull Content Pool)

The quest for Iron Man glory – winning Finke on both two and four wheels on the same weekend – begins in 2018. (Owlpine Group)

I'd only run the trophy truck at Finke in 2017 as the broken femur kept me off the bike. And, 100 kilometres out from the finish, it was all looking good . . . (Owlpine Group)

Aside from the two gruelling legs, another reason we called it the Iron Man is the commute from the finish line of one event to the start line of the next. (Owlpine Group)

Kicking up dust in the desert, Dakar 2019 in Peru. (Red Bull Content Pool)

Closing out my second Dakar victory, 2019 – not even a broken wrist could dull the celebrations. (Red Bull Content Pool)

My mullet shave/kiss contract with Laia Sanz, Queen of the Dakar. (Red Bull Content Pool)

Racing my Red Bull trophy truck on day one of the Finke Desert Race in 2019, and collecting my thoughts the next day after suffering a race-ending mechanical 150 kilometres from the finish. That was a tough one to swallow. (Owlpine Group)

Matthias Walkner, Sam Sunderland and me during the pre-race test at the Atacama Rally in Copiapó, Chile, 2019. (Red Bull Content Pool)

Making serious tracks during the first stage of the Atacama Rally in Terra Amarilla, Chile, 2019. (Red Bull Content Pool)

There's nothing like coming home to recharge in the Australian bush and get ready for another Dakar campaign, Maleny, Queensland, 2020. (Red Bull Content Pool)

A little friendly race with my mate Jack Miller, showing some style over the finish line tabletop in Rockhampton, 2020. (Red Bull Content Pool)

My third-place podium at Dakar 2020 in Qiddiya, Saudi Arabia, was bittersweet. We lost a true legend in Paulo Gonçalves. (Red Bull Content Pool)

Carving some shapes in the dunes, Dubai, 2020. *Bottom:* Sam Sunderland, Matthias Walkner, me and Daniel Sanders during the Red Bull Dakar line-up, 2020. (Both photos Red Bull Content Pool)

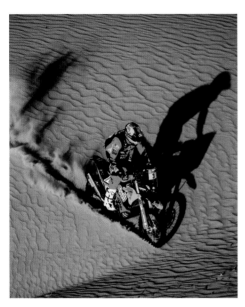

Racing through the shadows during Stage 2 of Dakar 2021, between Bisha and Wadi Al Dawasir, Saudi Arabia. (Eric Vargiolu/DPPI)

During the 'marathon' Stage 7, unable to use mechanics, I relied on my trusty duct tape and zip-ties to fix a slashed rear tyre. And the legend of the Bush Mechanic was born.

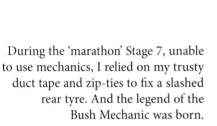

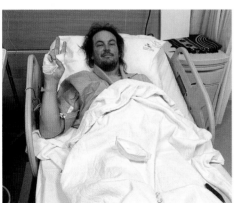

Oops, I did it again – recuperating in Tabuk, Saudi Arabia, after crashing out on Stage 9 of Dakar 2021 and suffering a broken collarbone and a busted hand.

I was speechless after receiving my Order of Australia medal at Government House.

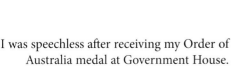

Finally! After several stabs at the trophy truck class at Finke, I tasted victory in 2021. (Owlpine Group)

I felt immensely proud that we could get the win for our amazing team and reward them for all their hard work. Nothing like a sip from the gold cup. (Owlpine Group)

It was great to take a break from the COVID madness and get back out on the bike at the Rallye du Maroc in October, 2021. All stops to Dakar in January. (Red Bull Content Pool)

I was dejected. It was a week out from Finke and, while I hadn't quite been amputated at the ankle as I'd first feared, I was in so much pain. My hopes of a fourth Finke win had been dashed.

Word spreads quickly in the Finke world, particularly when it comes to injuries. We didn't want to give too much away, so when we got back to Alice Springs we snuck into the motorhome and the physio checked out my foot. He could tell by the swelling that there was some serious damage and every time I tried to put weight on it, it would click, so we knew something was cracked. But I didn't want to go to the hospital. I was the pre-race favourite and there were already whispers doing the rounds that I'd sliced my foot off. And that was before I'd left the motorhome. If somebody had seen me going off to hospital, my competitors would have been licking their lips. The last thing I wanted was anybody sensing any weakness and thinking this might be their year.

Everyone who looked at my foot was convinced I wouldn't be able to ride, but I wasn't ready to give up on the race. I still had six days to recover and I wanted to wait it out, rather than throwing in the towel early. I switched off all my social media, everything, so I didn't give anything away . . . but that in itself fuelled the rumour mill. People knew something was going on, but the extent of the injury was a mystery. The theories ranged from my foot being amputated to me having sliced myself in half on a barbed-wire fence. We just kept our mouths shut and cancelled all public appearances we had planned in the lead-up to the race.

Staying off the foot was pretty easy because I didn't have a choice. I couldn't walk, even to the shower, I had to hop everywhere. Eventually we reached the crunch point, I had to make a decision. When the boys asked what I wanted to do I said, 'Well, I just spent a month out here training. I've done five thousand kilometres up and down this track . . . I can't let it all go to waste. I've got to try something.'

The team was usually very optimistic but even they thought I was nuts. The physio didn't know how I'd get this huge swollen foot into a boot in the first place, and the mechanics were worried about how the bike would handle if I couldn't put any weight on the right-hand side. They were fair points to make when you're about to jump on a bike for a 170 km/h blast through the middle of nowhere. But I had to try. I decided I'd rather go out there and crash, than just give up and go home. So we pulled the padding out of a boot and made a metal plate to fit in the bottom that would stop it from flexing or folding. We made a new footrest that was more comfortable for me, and wrapped and taped my ankle as much as we could so it wouldn't move. The rest was up to me and whether I could deal with 470-odd kilometres of sheer torture.

The pain was every bit as bad as I'd expected, but at least I got a little morale boost when I won the prologue. All of my competitors, meanwhile, were convinced there wasn't actually anything wrong me with. Of course, that wasn't the case. I had to be helped onto the bike and, once I was on it, I was stuck there. We didn't have a wheelchair on hand so my only way of getting anywhere was on the motorcycle.

Next up was the 230-kilometre blast from Alice to Finke and it was pure anguish. It wasn't just the broken foot that hurt, it was the whole left side of my body as well. I couldn't put weight on the side of the injury so I was compensating through my left leg. Every now and then, there was a four- to five-kilometre stretch where I could rest for a minute. I'd sit down on the seat, which took the weight off my left leg, and hold my right foot in the air to get some relief from the vibration that was constantly rattling through those broken bones. But those reprieves were few and far between. I know the Finke track very well so I could tell when I was coming up to sections that were going to punish my body. All I could do was grit my teeth and tell myself, 'Right, this next thirty kilometres is going to hurt. Don't whinge, don't bitch, get it done.' But as painful as it was, I never at any point really thought about quitting. If my mind began to stray towards those areas I would think about Kurt, think about Min, think about how I never know if there will even be a tomorrow. That helped me to refocus on the job at hand. My body was battered and bruised but it was still working.

Another distraction tactic I developed over the years of riding through injuries was thinking about the story. Thinking about what a badarse story it will be when you're in a nursing home, and the only race you're in is the race to the biscuit tin at morning tea. It's a weird, but effective, motivation strategy for me.

I got to Finke and my foot had gone beyond being purple with bruising. It was pitch back. Not only could I not walk,

I couldn't stand up. But, somehow, I ended with a five-minute lead for the run back to Alice. I couldn't believe it.

That little advantage gave my confidence a huge boost. I'd had the shit beaten out of me on the first leg, but I didn't need to punish myself on the way back. I could manage the gap and look after my body a bit more. That's not to say it was pleasant – I still had to wedge my foot into that boot and carry all my weight on the left leg – but I made it back to Alice. And even increased my lead to win a fourth Finke crown. Once I was home, I could actually get it properly seen to by a doctor. X-rays proved what he had thought: there were two broken bones, and I needed surgery to get them pinned back into place.

To this day, I don't know how that stick didn't go straight through my ankle. I've still got the boot and the stick sitting in my office, and every now and then I look at it, shocked at how I got away with that one.

Nursing that broken foot, I won those two AORC rounds at Aratula two weeks later and then set off to the Hattah Desert Race on the first weekend in July. I was still in pain but nothing like what I'd felt at Finke. The biggest issue was that I couldn't do much training in the lead-up to Hattah, which isn't ideal heading into a four-hour endurance race. I'd already won the race four times but, like with the Finke, I really wanted another win. It would've been easy to sit it out and let my foot heal, but I'd forged a reputation as the King of the Desert in Australia and I wanted to add as many big desert race wins as I could, just in case this overseas thing really took off. I wanted to break records.

I won the prologue and then rode through the discomfort to win a record-breaking fifth Hattah at what ended up being my last attempt. Job done.

As I was claiming victory in desert races and dealing with this busted foot in Australia, there were a lot of balls in the air regarding my overseas program. Just before Finke, I agreed to a deal that would see me compete in both the FIM Cross-Country Rallies World Championship and the Dakar Rally . . . but not with KTM. There was no space in the packed KTM line-up, so I signed on with the Husqvarna factory team instead. KTM owned Husqvarna, so there was a link there, but I had to keep the deal very quiet because I was still under contract with KTM Australia and, technically, it was a different brand. Jeff Liesk was one of the very few people who knew about it and, while he wasn't thrilled, I had his blessing. We just needed to keep it under wraps until the Australian season was done and dusted.

I was stoked, this was my big break in rally racing. Of course, I would have loved a full-works KTM ride; I was so closely aligned with the brand and KTM had been an unstoppable Dakar force for more than a decade. It felt weird to think I wouldn't be on a KTM anymore. But this was still a great factory ride.

The night before the prologue for Hattah I was having dinner in the main street of Mildura. My phone rang and it was Alex Doringer. I figured he was just calling to wish me luck on the race and that's exactly how the conversation started. But once those pleasantries were out of the way, the whole thing took an unexpected turn.

'Look, I've got some news for you,' he said. 'Marc Coma is retiring.'

'Shit,' I said. 'That's no good . . . why?'

'He feels that it's time to get out. That's it.'

'Bummer, I was looking forward to racing against him at Dakar next year. And he promised he'd do some training with me when I start work with Husqvarna.'

'Well, that's the reason I'm calling. You won't be riding a Husqvarna. We've changed your contract and you'll be replacing Marc at KTM.'

I couldn't believe it. Not only was I going to be riding for the best team in the Dakar field, but I was able to stay true to KTM. I was always a loyal rider, all I'd ever raced were Kawasakis and KTMs. I was bursting inside but I couldn't tell anyone. Nobody knew about the Husqvarna deal, nobody knew that Marc was retiring and nobody knew that I was going to replace him. It gave my patience a real workout, that one.

The good thing was that, once I was staying on at KTM, we could get the news out there quite quickly without worrying about brand clashes and stuff like that. The next day news started to break that Marc was hanging up his helmet, and by the end of the following week the big announcement dropped. I was officially joining the Red Bull KTM Factory Racing Team.

When it went public it finally felt real. On one hand I felt like at last I'd made it on what had been this crazy one step forward, three steps back adventure. I thought back to when I was racing juniors and how I would never, in my wildest dreams, have imagined signing a deal like this. Not because I thought it was unattainable, but because rally racing was the furthermost thing from my mind. It took the gnarliest series of twists and turns, some great and some terrible, to lead me to a destiny that I never even knew existed. But on the other hand, I didn't let myself get too carried away; I'd signed what I thought were life-changing deals before – Kawasaki in 2004, the Baja stuff with KTM in 2013 – only to have fate knock me down on my arse, literally in some cases, and take it all away.

I decided the best thing to do was, perhaps for the first time in my life, take a methodical approach. I'd had my breakthrough Dakar performance in 2015 and, despite having a shiny new factory deal, I decided I wasn't going to carry any pressure into the 2016 Dakar Rally. Marc won Dakar for the first time on his fifth attempt, so I didn't need to go and win the thing on my second attempt. The slow and steady approach had worked for me in 2015, so I decided to do the same thing in 2016 – with the benefit of a little more knowledge and better preparation.

The fatigue I went through after my Dakar debut in 2015 was a painful, but valuable, lesson in what I needed in terms of physical preparation. I'd gone into that event at around 95 kilograms – which is right where I feel at my strongest – and by the end of it I weighed 85 kilos. I hadn't weighed that little since I was a kid, and my body was basically eating itself alive. I knew I had to start the race heavier and let my body work down to its peak weight. The thing about the Dakar is that it's not a weight-critical event. The bike itself is heavy and any additional weight you carry on your body will be burnt off so quickly, anyway. You win Dakar in the second week, not the first. I needed to be as fit as humanly possible at the end, if I wanted any chance of winning. So I didn't train all that much in the lead-up to the second Dakar, I didn't see the point of punishing myself before going into an event that had the very intention of punishing me.

There was some method to my madness. At the Hattah Desert Race one year a physio fitted me and a couple of other riders with a chest strap that monitored everything from g-forces to heart rate to calories burned. When you stood the three of us together I was the odd one out, no doubt about it. They were trim, fit-looking blokes. If I take my shirt off, let's just say my body shape doesn't exactly scream 'professional athlete'. So we all wore this monitor for the four-hour race through the desert, and when we were done the trainer downloaded all the data. He was shocked with what he saw. My body was working something like 25 per cent less than the others. Their heart rates peaked somewhere around 198 beats per minute and mine was only 173. My body had been through half the g-forces the others went through. Those two were like high-performance race engines and I was like an old diesel tractor motor just chugging its way through the race.

My approach was – and still is – a bit of an eye-opener for my more fitness-conscious Dakar teammates, but at the end of the day it's a deeply personal, unique thing. The 'train less, start heavy' theory was what I came up with after that first Dakar and it has served me very well ever since. Guys like Matthias Walkner and Sam Sunderland, they can't tackle the race that way. They have to train like mad in the lead-up and hit all their marks or they don't feel organised or ready for the event. Whichever way you go, it's as much about your mental preparation as it is your physical preparation. There's no right or wrong way, it's what works for you. These days I keep myself fit and strong before a Dakar, but I'm perfectly happy going in tipping the scales at 100 kilograms knowing that I'll hit that magic 95 by the second week.

That new (lack of) fitness regime meant I travelled to the 2016 Dakar feeling significantly better prepared physically, and I was way better mentally prepared purely through knowing what was coming. I knew what to pack, I knew what to expect in the days leading up to the race and I knew the challenge that was waiting for me across Argentina and Bolivia. But, hand on heart, I didn't get on the plane to South America thinking I really had a chance of winning the thing. It was as far from my mind as it had been the year before. I wanted to consolidate this opportunity with the KTM factory squad, not squander it by doing something stupid. Yes, the team had won the last 14 Dakars in a row, but there were guys in our line-up like Jordi Viladoms, Olivier Pain and Sam, who had a lot more experience than me. They could go out and fight for victory and I would just cruise along and continue the learning process. That was at least until I got to Buenos Aires and poked my head into the garage tent. There was my bike with #3 on the windscreen. It hit me that it was the lowest number on our team; with Marc gone I was our best-placed rider from the previous year. Was I the team leader? Was I about to oversee a 14-year winning streak come to an end? I'll admit that right then I had one of those 'have I bitten off more than I can chew?' moments. I'd worked so hard to block out the pressure, but the closer we got to the start, the more weight I felt on my shoulders.

The pressure is real, too. This is a professional sport. Bike manufacturers are spending a lot of money on their factory Dakar programs, and they need to see a return on that spend. For KTM, that comes from beating its big rivals in the two-wheel market, particularly Honda and Yamaha. Even beating brands owned by the KTM Group, like Husqvarna, is important to the factory KTM team. It's all about retaining top spot on the pecking order.

The team rivalries are bigger than the personal rivalries between the riders, at least from my perspective. I've never been one for personal rivalries with other riders. I don't like losing, but there's nobody I hate losing to more than anybody else. I've had a few disagreements with rivals, and even teammates, over the years – usually after you've been stuck in somebody's dust. But it's never blossomed into a long-lasting rivalry. I think the sheer challenge of Dakar creates a camaraderie between the riders you don't see in other sports, or even other motorsports. We're all pushing ourselves to the physical and mental limits. We're all risking our lives. Beating Dakar comes first, beating the other riders comes second. You don't have the time and energy to have an arch-rival. And if you do happen to crash out on a stage, it's a competitor who will be first on the scene, so it helps to have friends rather than enemies.

Weather played a big part in the 2016 event, and after battling through a soggy prologue the first stage was cancelled. We finally got going on the second day, although the stage was shortened, and I really didn't want to run at the front. I wanted to be cool, calm and collected, just cruise in the mid-pack for the first few days as I warmed into a rhythm. Leading is hard at the Dakar, particularly in the first week. You've got no wheel tracks to follow, so you're always at risk of making a navigational mistake, and at the same time you're showing everyone behind you where to go. The very last thing I wanted was to win that second stage and have to lead the field the next day. I thought I was taking it easy but when I crossed the finish line, bang, a number one showed up next to my name.

My approach clearly didn't work, I was leading the Dakar Rally. The race is tricky like that; there are days you wake up and decide to go for broke and, inevitably, you end up making a heap of navigation mistakes and dump a heap of time. There are other days you decide to concentrate on the navigation, spend the whole day cruising like you're out on a Sunday ride and you win the stage. You're walking this fine line between going too slow and pushing too hard and, particularly early in the event, it can be as hard to lose a stage as it is to win it.

As expected, leading was difficult on Stage 3 and, after a few close calls with people and wildlife along the way, I decided to back off. I dropped some time and slipped to ninth in the standings, but I wasn't too worried. I was actually happy to drop back a bit, that way I could focus on the task at hand – finding a rhythm, limiting mistakes and setting myself up for a proper crack in the second week. Stages 4 and 5 were marathon stages that took us into Bolivia, and on the second day I hit my stride. The long, fast climb up to 4600 metres above sea level suited my riding style nicely and a second stage win helped me jump from seventh to third in the standings and cut Paulo Gonçalves' lead from nearly ten minutes to less than two minutes. But boy it was tough on both my body and bike. Bolivia always is, because of the altitudes we often ride at. As spectacular as the scenery can be, the bikes struggle for power in the thin air. It's not much fun for your lungs either. Of all the places I've ever ridden, Bolivia is about as hard as it gets.

I was within striking distance of the Hondas and I was ready to start putting some pressure on them. I did exactly that on Stage 6 and it worked. Despite a close call with a car early in the stage, I took another win to close within 35 seconds of Paulo, while Joan Barreda tumbled down the order after his bike stopped out.

Stage 7 was a complete mess thanks to overnight flooding. Matthias had a big crash and broke his femur, and Paulo dropped a heap of time after stopping to help him. It left the results a little unclear at the end of the day, but they eventually neutralised the stage back to Waypoint 5 and rightly gave Paulo more than ten minutes back for stopping on the stage. Once it all shook out, Paulo took a three-minute lead into the rest day. That chance to catch my breath made me realise how much better my body was holding up than the year before. I was exhausted, there's no getting around that on the Dakar, but I felt much better prepared for the second week. Not only was I benefitting from a heavier starting weight, but I was limiting my weight loss along the way by eating as much food each night as possible. Literally eating until I made myself sick. It was another little lesson I'd taken from my rookie campaign in 2015.

The second week got off to a perfect start. I won Stage 8, a long blast from Salta to Belén, as Paulo took a spectacular tumble. He was bloody lucky he didn't break himself or his bike. He got going again but the delay helped me grab the overall lead back by two minutes. It was the second week, I was feeling fit and fast and I was leading the Dakar Rally. Maybe I had a shot at winning this thing after all.

If Stage 7 was a mess, then Stage 9 was a debacle. The rain felt like a distant memory as the weather laid down its next brutal challenge – the heat. It was a 45-degree scorcher and, to make matters even worse, the first leg of a marathon. In those conditions it was a critical test for bikes and riders. As the reigning stage winner I was first out and, despite how uncomfortably hot it was, I had a good run over to Check Point 2 (Cp2). That was a compulsory 15-minute fuel stop, so once I was there I started to fuel up the bike and kept an eye on my watch. We were running at two-minute intervals that year, so after two minutes had past I knew that, at the very least, the front group wasn't catching me. Then it was four minutes and nobody was there. Six minutes, still no one.

I started to panic a bit; had I made a mistake? Had I missed a waypoint and stumbled across the fuel stop by accident? I checked the GPS and everything was ticked off, it all made sense. It was really strange. The clock kept ticking and with about two minutes of the compulsory stop left, I got my helmet and gear on, ready to complete the rest of the stage.

Once I was back on the bike and about to pull up to the start boards I heard a bike arrive behind me. I swung around to see who it was and saw Paulo, who'd started behind me. *This is pretty good*, I thought. *I've pulled 13 minutes on the guy*. I fired up and hit the rest of the stage.

After a bit the heat really started to get to me. I'd drunk as much as I could during the stop but it was brutal. All I could think about was riding as fast as I could so that this nightmare would be over. The last 40-odd kilometres were particularly difficult, very soft sand dunes, just shitty snot to ride through. By then I'd ran out of water in my camelback, so I was suffering big time.

As I was out there baking myself under the sun on the stage, there was a lot going on behind me that I didn't know about. Firstly, Paulo had serious problems back in CP2. A branch had punctured his radiator and his motor had seized. He wasn't going anywhere and, had the stage played out normally, he would have been out of the race and I would have had one hand on the trophy. But it wasn't to be. As soon as I reached the end of the stage and pulled my helmet off, the media team rolled up with cameras and microphones to get my thoughts on the day.

'You do know that the stage was cut short at CP2, right?' the reporter asked me.

'Wait, what? Why?'

'The heat. There were riders getting dehydrated and lost, and the ACO decided to end the stage at CP2.'

I sat there for a second or two and then it hit me. This decision had obviously been made after I'd already taken off from CP2 to finish the stage. I'd spent hours flogging myself and my bike unnecessarily across the wilderness. I'd covered well over 100 kilometres, in debilitating heat, for nothing . . . while most of the riders were hanging out at the check point. As it was a marathon stage, I couldn't change my rear tyre for the next day either.

I was furious. With those cameras in my face and microphones under my nose and I had to bite my tongue like never before. I was baffled at how it had happened. There were helicopters buzzing above us during the stage, couldn't the organisers have radioed one of the crew and told them to land in front of me, flag me down and tell me to stop? I was angry and I was hot, hot like I was about to burst into flames. I needed to cool off and process what had happened, so I climbed in the back of this refrigerated truck that was parked there. I found a drum filled with water, which I splashed all over myself.

After I'd cooled and calmed down I hopped out of the truck to try and find some answers. But there was more bad news coming. Because Paulo had made it to CP2 on his broken bike, and that's where the stage was cancelled, he was given a nominal time like everyone else. Instead of being out of the race, he was still third overall. One of Paulo's teammates towed him to the Bivouac and, as it was a marathon stage, the Honda riders had to pitch in and fix the bikes themselves overnight. The water boy donated a heap of parts, which put him out of the race, and they got Paulo's bike going again. He was more than half an hour behind me, but at the Dakar even that's too close for comfort – particularly as I'd done all those unnecessary kilometres.

I went to bed that night feeling completely wronged by what had happened. To be honest, I didn't care that Paulo was still in the race; on the Dakar you take your breaks when they come, so I didn't begrudge him anything. I was more upset that nobody had stopped me during the second part of the stage. By the time I woke up, the anger was gone and I was feeling determined to go and win the whole fucking thing. The officials weren't going to take it away from me. I wanted to throw it back in their faces.

On Stage 10 Paulo and I pretty much matched each other, leaving me with that half-hour advantage . . . until the organisers intervened again. This time the ruling went my way, as Paulo was served a 40-minute penalty for the time he'd lost trying to repair his bike before Stage 9 was cancelled. It still didn't fix the extra kilometres I'd covered, but I guess it was better than nothing. And it gave me some breathing space. As much as I'd had my troubles over the marathon stage, it had ruined Paulo's race. He'd gone from leading the thing at the rest day to being more than an hour behind after three more stages. Things went from bad to worse for the bloke on Stage 11. He took a second tumble off the bike and this time managed to knock himself out cold. He was airlifted to hospital but, thankfully, it was just a nasty concussion.

My teammate Štefan Svitko had been in second since the end of Stage 9, and by the end of Stage 11 I had a handy 35-minute lead. I pulled another couple of minutes on Stefan across Stage 12, which put me in the box seat for the final stage. I had to cover a total of 700 kilometres on the last day but only 180 of them were timed. Everything was stacked in my favour; a short timed stage and a 37-minute lead. It was mine to lose. And I hated every bit of it. That timed stage felt like it was 500 kilometres long. It felt like it was never going to end. Every time I looked down, I swore the tripmeter hadn't moved a single kilometre. We started in reverse order, so I had to be really careful with traffic as I came across slower bikes. You never know on the Dakar, someone can pop out of a bush and T-bone you at any second. I was scared shitless the whole time. Considering my lead, I'd already had people congratulating me on winning the Dakar the last two days, but I honestly didn't believe it was going to happen until I got within a kilometre of the finish line of that last time stage. At that point I knew that, even if the bike stopped, I could push the bike over the line and then someone would give me a tow to the Bivouac.

I was going to win the Dakar Rally. Nobody had ever won the Dakar Rally on just their second attempt. No Australian had ever won the Dakar Rally, full stop. And here I was breaking those records, about to claim victory. The tears were flowing under my goggles as I cruised to the finish.

I wish I had more clarity on what I was thinking when I crossed the line. I wish I could say I was thinking about Min or Kurt or what my parents had sacrificed to get me there . . . but in all honesty I have no idea. It was so overwhelming. I remember the sensation – I still get goosebumps when I think about pulling up after the stage and seeing my teammates and crew – but it was such a blur. And when I did start to see through the noise and colour going on around me, what I felt more than anything was relief.

What I didn't know until I got to the finish was that my manager-slash-mate Matty Macalpine and a mutual friend Judd were waiting for me in Rosario. They'd been watching on from Australia, and on the third-last day they made the crazy decision to jump on a plane and head to South America. I was leading the race when they left Brisbane, but anything could have happened by the time they got to Buenos Aires. They jumped in a tiny hire car and drove up to Rosario, to the ceremonial finish.

As I rode through the crowd coming into town, there were all these people cheering and chanting my name. At some point I saw an Aussie flag, so I pulled over to say g'day to the bloke holding it. He wanted a photo and as I turned around to pose with him, I swore I saw Matty and Judd in the crowd. I actually panicked for a second; was I seeing things? Was this just a dream, after all? As I sat there in a daze, they jumped the fence and grabbed me.

Shit, it was real. It was so special to have two good mates there to enjoy the moment, to see me cross the finish line and get the trophy.

The team calls the trophy Felix. I don't know why, but boy, were they happy to have another Felix in their hands. The 15th Dakar win in a row for KTM, what an achievement. Once the formalities were done, me, Judd and Matty wandered back towards the hotel. They got sidetracked by a small pub somewhere along the way and disappeared for a few hours before we met back up at the Red Bull afterparty in Rosario. Matty and Judd had been at it for hours, but it didn't take me long to catch up. After two weeks of slaving away in the desert, I reckon I was off my trolley after two beers.

As the night wore, on the celebrations got a little rowdy and the glass clinking between us boys got a bit out of control. We smashed a few beer bottles and ended up with cuts on our hands and arms. When the bouncer saw us standing there surrounded by broken glass, blood all over our shirts, he kicked us and the girl who had organised the party – who was an innocent bystander – out of the bar. I somehow made my way back to my hotel room and passed out, cradling Felix with blood all over me and the sheets. I forgot to close the door, too. It must have been a hell of a sight for anybody who walked past.

During those Saturday night celebrations in Rosario, Alex told me that, as a reward for winning the Dakar, KTM would pay for a holiday anywhere in the world. There was an AMA Supercross round in Anaheim, California, the following weekend, so I decided I'd spend a few days in Buenos Aires with Matty and Judd and then fly to the States to catch up with the KTM guys over there. 'Are you sure?' asked Alex. 'Why don't you just get away from bikes and racing for a while, have a proper break?' I didn't want a break. The KTM USA team had played a big part in getting me to Dakar in the first place and I was itching to visit, say thanks and let them get their hands on Felix.

I woke up the morning after the party with a thumping headache; *shit, so this is what winning the Dakar really feels like*. Once the fog cleared I went looking for some breakfast in the hotel restaurant, and when I got there I couldn't see anybody from the team hanging around. It was a three-and-a-half hour drive to Buenos Aires and I was meant to be getting a lift – but everyone was long gone. Except Matty and Judd.

'Boys, you're going to have to give me a lift,' I said.

Matty cracked up. 'Mate, there's no way we'll get you and all your bags into our tiny piece of shit rental.'

He was right. I had a couple of huge kit bags and Judd, no offence, is a big lad. I'm not exactly small myself. We weren't all fitting in this tiny bubble car without some serious MacGyver work. The first idea was to throw my essentials in a smaller bag and bin everything that I didn't really need. But I just couldn't bring myself to throw out all the kit I'd just used to win the Dakar. I wanted to take this stuff home and get it framed. We had a poke around this tiny car, and the only way it was going to work was if we tied my bags onto the roof. There weren't any roof racks, but we really didn't have a choice.

I went to reception and asked them to point me in the direction of a hardware store where I could buy some ratchet straps. 'It's Sunday,' the girl behind the desk told me. 'There's nothing open here on a Sunday.' Buried deep in my kit bag I found some sheets I'd been given for one of the marathon stages. *This'll have to do*, I thought.

We cut them up and tied them together like a rope, threw my bags – and Felix – on the roof and wrapped the sheet rope through the top of the doors and over the luggage. It was flimsy as all hell, only held on by the door hinges. None of us thought it would keep all the way to Buenos Aires. We crammed Matty, who's pretty slim, in the back seat and Judd and I sat up front, more bags between our legs, like two big gorillas. We gently took off down the road, literally holding onto the luggage with our hands out the windows.

We hadn't been on the road long when we hit a speed bump. There was a loud creak and the roof of our little car bowed inwards. Well, the damage was down now, I figured. We may as well keep going. We hit the highway and the next thing we were screaming along at 115 km/h, pissing ourselves laughing the whole way. When we got to the next hotel, we pulled off the bags and there was a huge dent in the roof. We did our best to punch it back ourselves, but I think we made it worse. We took it back to the hire-car place, expecting to have to pay for the damage, but they didn't give two shits. We hightailed it out of there and never heard about it again. The next few days, we ate and drank our way through Buenos Aires before I jetted off to the US.

When I got back to Australia there was one last surprise waiting for me. I landed in Sydney and had a connecting flight to Brisbane, where I was going to meet my parents. But when I walked through passport control at Sydney Airport, there was Mum and Dad waiting for me, huge smiles on their faces. Might have been a few tears as well.

The whirlwind didn't stop once I was home. I spent a solid week doing media calls and parading the trophy around, which was very special. It helped me take in that I was the first Australian to win the Dakar Rally and what that achievement meant. But the media circus was exhausting, too; I'd spend all day doing interviews with Aussie media before Europe began to wake up in the evening. So I'd do a couple of hours of calls with European media before the US started their mornings. It'd be well past midnight before I was done each day.

Once the media rounds were finished it was back on a plane. My Dakar win coincided with KTM exceeding one billion euros in revenue, a milestone in the company's history, so they put on this incredible joint celebration at Kitzbühel, a ski resort in Austria. Me, Jeff Liesk and Bronte Howson, who ran KTM's Aussie distributor AHG at the time, were all invited – and there was no expense spared. For the first time in my life I had a first-class air ticket and I was blown away. My cabin had its own shower and toilet, it was fancier than the caravan I'd been living in a couple of years earlier. And for what that ticket cost, I could have paid three years' worth of site fees. The contrast between a caravan and a first-class cabin on an Emirates plane was a smack in the face. In reality it had been a long, hard slog to get to where I was, but as I stepped on that plane it didn't feel like it. Things were changing so fast, it was like my head was spinning, I was on this rapid climb. Bronte and Jeff had a lot to celebrate, given they'd had a hands-on role in helping KTM hit its billion-euro milestone, and they drank the plane out of champagne. I was absolutely knackered from the event and all the media stuff, so I was excited to have a cabin to myself and a proper bed. Finally, I had a chance to get some sleep. As soon as we were in the sky, I shut the door and dozed off . . . only to wake up a few minutes later feeling like I was in a sticky swimming pool. Jeff and Bronte had snuck into my cabin and poured an entire bottle of top-shelf champagne all over me. Lucky I had a shower available so I could rinse off, although I did spend the rest of the flight expecting the air marshals to arrest us when we landed in Europe.

There were no police waiting for us at Munich Airport, but the boys were still a mess. Jeff had one carry-on bag, the thing was tiny, but in his drunken state he was convinced he couldn't carry it so he grabbed a luggage trolley. That was fine until we came to a ramp near some escalators and Jeff decided to jump on the trolley and see how fast he could go. He ripped down this ramp until the front wheels hit this tiny lip where the floor levelled out at the bottom. The trolley pulled a huge wheelie before he ended up face-first on the tiled floor in the hire-car pick-up area. The hire car was in Jeff's name, so it was a hell of a job to get the staff to believe he was sober enough to give us the keys. We finally talked them round, got the keys and walked out to the car park – at which point Jeff and Bronte both, wisely, declared they were too drunk to drive. So I became their chauffeur as we drove east into Austria, stopping at the KTM factory in Mattig-hofen and then continuing on to Kitzbühel. It was an epic location and an equally epic party.

Six days later I was back at home and could finally catch my breath. I remember dropping my bags, sitting on the couch and thinking, *What the fuck just happened?* I'd processed bits and pieces of the Dakar win, but it took me a few days of normal life for it to really sink in.

11
Four Wheels

I may be a life long bike man, but I've always had a soft spot for cars and trucks. I've been driving cars for almost as long as I've been riding bikes. My fascination with four-wheeled motorsport goes all the way back to my dad and my uncle competing in the national off-road championship in a buggy. I used to watch them and go through old photos and wonder what it must've been like. Maybe if I hadn't taken up PeeWee racing when I was so young I would've found my way into go-karts instead, and had a completely different career. Who knows?

At the 2015 Dakar Rally I met former NASCAR driver Robby Gordon who, after his stock car career, took up racing trucks both on and off road. Robby started up a category called Stadium Super Trucks which, basically, is for life-sized versions of remote-control trucks powered by a big V8 engine. They go on normal car racing tracks, except there are ramps all over the place for them to jump over. It's all a bit of fun, more spectacular than it is serious. Anyway, Robby was about to take the series to Australia for the first time to race at the Adelaide 500 and asked if I wanted to compete. It was heaps of fun and I ended up going back a year later, right after I'd won the Dakar, for another go.

Given things were cranking along on two wheels, I started to think about expanding my horizons. I'd won the Finke Desert Race four times on a bike, how cool would it be to win it in a trophy truck as well? I still had a deal in place with KTM Australia to race the bike at Finke, so that was the priority, but the more I looked at the schedule, the more I was convinced I could do both. Nobody else seemed to share my optimism. Every time I told somebody about this ambitious plan they said I was crazy. I'm not all that good at taking no for an answer and the more people said it wasn't possible, the more determined I was to make it happen.

The way I saw it, it was all a matter of timing. The cars ran before the bikes on both days. If I could set a decent prologue time in the truck and get a nice early starting slot, I could race from Alice to Finke, jump straight in a helicopter and fly back to Alice, and then have 20 minutes or so to get ready, jump on the bike and ride to Finke again. Then on the second day I'd do the exact same thing, but in reverse. Against a lot of people's better judgement, I did a deal to rent a trophy truck for the Finke weekend and went public with this batshit crazy plan.

Once I had the Finke stuff in place, I had to switch back to two-wheel mode. My new KTM deal included a number of rounds at the FIM Cross-Country Rallies World Championship, which is a series of five- and six-day rallies spread across the globe. As much as a world championship carries some prestige, the harsh reality is that the rounds primarily serve as preparation for the following year's Dakar. Given how expensive racing is, it's normal for the factory teams to pick and choose between the five rounds in a season, which means you generally only end up doing four of them. It is usually coordinated around being able to transport the gear via sea freight to help limit costs. Air freight is so expensive when you're talking about four motorcycles, which need a case each, and then three or four cases of spare parts to get through six days of racing. That's a lot of freight to stick inside a cargo plane, and it'll easily run up a $100,000-plus bill. Even for a factory team, there's no such thing as an unlimited budget. Another contributing factor is the conditions; a world-championship round held on smooth tracks won't do much for our Dakar prep, so we'll usually sit it out. That can cost you a world championship, because if you're not there, you can't score points. But that's just where the world championship sits in terms of importance compared to the Dakar.

For 2016, KTM decided to kick things off with a Middle Eastern swing in April, racing world-championship rounds in Abu Dhabi and Qatar. Flying over there I was genuinely nervous, more than I thought I would be. I felt like I needed to go and claim a world championship round to show everyone that my win in Dakar wasn't a fluke. There was no external pressure, it all just existed in my head. Anyway, the campaign got off to a perfect start with a win in Abu Dhabi after a close three-way battle with my teammate Sam Sunderland and Husqvarna's Pablo Quintanilla. The only issue was a pinched nerve in my back that was giving me some grief. In the couple of weeks between the Abu Dhabi and Qatar rounds, I did everything I could to try to fix it. I saw all sorts of doctors and had every treatment from secret remedies to hyperbaric chambers. I thought I'd sorted it out by the time Qatar rolled around and I was pain-free for the first day or so. Then I hit a hole out on a stage and, bang, the pain came back. I was keen to keep going but, even though it was only April, the team was already thinking about Dakar for January the next year. They didn't want to take any risks in terms of long-term damage, so they pulled out of the race and sent me home for more treatment. For once in my life I decided not to argue about it.

I got my back sorted out and then my focus turned to Finke in early June. We only got hold of the truck a few days before we took off to Alice Springs and, when we got there, I literally hadn't driven the thing. So we decided to head out to a test track on the outskirts of town to give it a run. I asked my crew if we should take off the panels so I could get a feel for the truck and not be worried about scratching up the bodywork. But the journalist Charles Wooley from the show *60 Minutes* was out there with a film crew to do a story on me, and we needed to make sure the sponsors were getting maximum exposure. So the panels stayed on.

My experience driving trophy trucks to that point was half a day of testing in a similar, but not identical, truck. I was an amateur, and this was all the practice I was getting in this truck before Finke kicked off. I went out for a few laps and I was just building up to it. They are such unique things to drive, because you've got 700-odd horsepower under your right foot, and almost 80 centimetres of rear-suspension travel, and 60 centimetres of front-wheel travel. You hit these massive bumps but it feels like you're cruising down the freeway. Obviously I wasn't going quick enough because off-road racer Brad Gallard, who owned the truck, told me to jump in the passenger seat and he'd show me how to drive it. He did a couple of runs and it really opened my eyes to what this thing was capable of. If I didn't pull my finger out, I was going to be miles off the pace. I was starting to shit myself.

The plan was to stick Charles in the truck with me for a ride for his TV piece but, before that, I wanted to do one more run with my navigator Kyle Pfitzner to try out a few things I'd picked up from Brad. We left Charles waiting, already wearing a race suit, and took off down the track. It all began to come together for me, I finally felt like I knew what I was doing. I radioed the crew and said, 'Give me one more lap and then Charles can jump in.'

I came belting through a high-speed section of whoops, a series of rolling, consecutive jumps, on my way back, got to the third-last bump and it pulled the heim joint out of the rear trailing arm. The whole rear end, diff housing and all, pulled away from the rear suspension and turned into a big, expensive handbrake. It sagged in the right rear corner, and then as I hit a jump that was right behind the whoops, the suspension went to full extension. When I landed it basically jack-knifed as the frame landed on the wheels, picked the truck up and tipped it into a rollover at around 110 km/h. It must have rolled five or six times up the track, I felt like I was in a violent washing machine.

The truck came to a rest on its side and I was in shock. I was used to going flying off bikes, but this was something completely different. I'd never even crashed a road car, let alone something like this. Both me and Kyle were fine and he shut the engine down before we climbed through the side window that was facing upwards. Once we were out, I just stood there and stared at this destroyed truck. Charles wandered over and he looked as shocked as I was; he could have so easily been in the passenger seat.

We only had one set of panels stickered up and they'd been torn to shreds. The rear end housing was long gone, the shock shafts were bent, the brackets that held the body on were done for. The only good news was that the cockpit area wasn't damaged and we'd saved the engine by shutting it down before it lost oil pressure. I knew getting through the Finke double unscathed was unlikely, but I'd expected to at least make it to the start line. It was devastating, I was completely deflated. This wasn't an arrive-and-drive factory deal, this was something me and my guys had put together ourselves. We'd sourced the truck, found the sponsors to pay for it, and were the ones who would wear the consequences of the crash. We pushed the truck back on its wheels and skull-dragged it onto a trailer. I left the guys to it and took off to Alice for a media appearance with KTM.

As I've said before, the rumour mill is brutal during Finke week. We hadn't told a soul what had happened, but by the time I got to Alice Springs everyone was talking about how I'd written this truck off, I was badly hurt, all this stuff. I was fine, I didn't have a scratch on me, but I couldn't say the same about the poor old truck.

The crew towed the wreckage back to town and sweet-talked a local garage owner into leaving his doors open for the night. The crash happened at around 1 pm and the crew worked until 2 am bolting it all back together. We missed scrutineering on the Friday night, so we had to get the truck signed off on Saturday morning, right before prologue. I was already burning the candle at both ends enough trying to do cars and bikes – this was the last thing I needed. But, somehow, we were still in the race.

I really struggled in the prologue, but that was to be expected. I was inexperienced enough as it was, and the crash destroyed the little confidence I had. When I rolled out onto the stage the thing hadn't turned a wheel since the rollover, and we'd been up the entire night fixing it. All I could do was hope we'd tightened every nut and bolt properly.

I had to feel my way back into it, but I couldn't dawdle around too much; I'd worked out that I couldn't qualify any worse than 28th if I was going to have time to get to Finke and back before the start of the bike race. I ended up 18th, good enough but far from ideal. At least the truck was working. It ran faultlessly through the prologue, which gave me a much-needed boost ahead of the first leg. I then jumped on the bike, back in my comfort zone, and went quickest in the two-wheeled prologue.

There were a few butterflies in my stomach when Kyle and I took off towards Finke in the truck on the Sunday morning, but once we got going I fell into a pretty good groove. By the 30-kilometre mark we'd started to pick off a few of the guys that were in front of us. By then I was feeling good, so I decided to start pushing. That's when we began hauling the rest of the blokes in. It was an absolute blast. We were catching up to cars and nerfing them, which means to give their rear bumper a tap to let them know you're sitting in their dust. Usually they'll get out of the way and let you through. By the time we got to Finke, we'd worked our way up to fifth place and we were only about three minutes off the lead. I was over the moon.

I raced over to the airstrip and jumped on a plane – we'd ditched the chopper idea because the plane was faster – and flew back to Alice Springs. I jumped on the bike and had a clean run through to Finke, pulling a nice little two-minute lead. By the end of the day, I was exhausted but ecstatic. The crazy plan was actually coming together.

On the Monday Kyle and I jumped in the truck for the run back to Alice. We were about three kilometres out of Finke before the truck started to misfire and make a few weird noises. I looked over at Kyle, who was watching the gauges, and he told me that the motor wasn't running hot and we should just press on. We powered on for another 40-odd kilometres and the noises started getting worse. There was oil smoke coming through the air cleaner and the big V8 dropped a cylinder. I looked over at Kyle again. 'Mate, it needs a rebuild anyway,' he said. 'So as long as it keeps running, we may as well keep going.'

I don't know how but the motor held on. What we didn't know was that a couple of buggies that started ahead of us had problems on the way back to Alice. We eventually caught up to the only truck left in front of us. I gave it a nerf and enjoyed an awesome battle for a few kilometres. We eventually got clear and crossed the line, thinking we'd won the truck class and finished third overall. I had to get to the airport ASAP to fly back to Finke, so I left all the post-race formalities to Kyle. It wasn't until later I found out we'd actually finished second overall. I had another clean run back on the bike to take out a fifth title on two wheels. But all I could really think about was the truck and how close we'd come. Not only was the double logistically possible, it was winnable. I left determined to return and win the Finke on four wheels.

My world championship campaign continued with the Atacama Rally in Chile in late August, where I finished third, followed by a win on the Rallye du Maroc in early October. I ended up as the only driver with multiple round wins, but was only third in the points. If it wasn't for the retirement in Qatar, I may have won the title.

I made one more start on four wheels before the 2016 season was over. Over the years I'd become good mates with

Jesse Jones and Bryce Menzies, a couple of legends of the US desert racing scene. It all began when I met Bryce at one of the Red Bull Day in the Dirt events and we'd kept in touch. After the International Six Days Enduro in Argentina in 2014 I wanted to go and hang out at the Baja 1000 but, with KTM pulling out after Kurt's death, I didn't really have anything to do there. I knew Jesse and Bryce were teaming up in Jesse's trophy truck, so I called Bryce to see if they needed a hand. He was down for it, so I jumped on a plane and flew straight to Mexico. I was literally a gopher for the team, doing grocery shopping, servicing the pre-run cars, washing windscreens, things like that. At some point I was chatting to Jesse and he said, 'What are you doing here, anyway?' I told him I was at a loose end now that KTM had pulled out and I just wanted to help and be involved in the Baja 1000. 'So, you've just finished second at a world enduro event and you're happy to change our wheels and do all the other crappy jobs? That's pretty random.'

'I don't give a shit,' I said. 'I'm just happy to be here, I love this stuff.'

I think it left an impression on Jesse.

Fast forward a couple of years and Jesse was chatting to Rick Geiser, who builds the Geiser Brothers trophy trucks. Jesse told Rick that Bryce was injured and he needed a new co-driver for the Baja 1000. Rick explained how he'd just got back from the Finke Desert Race in Australia, and that this Aussie bloke called Toby Price looked pretty quick in a truck. He'd never raced one before and beat heaps of the best off-road racers in the country to finish second. 'Yeah, I know Toby,' said Jesse.

'Well, why don't you give him a call and see if he wants to race?' said Rick.

I had no idea that conversation had taken place until Jesse's name flashed up on my phone a few weeks later. 'Want to come to Baja again this year?' he asked.

'Yeah, mate,' I said. 'I'm happy to come and give you guys a hand. Whatever you need, I'll do it.'

'I need a driver. You and me are going to team up for the race.'

I thought he was taking the piss, but he was serious. He's just had Rick build him a brand new truck and he wanted me to race it with him at the Baja 1000. I was blown away, but I didn't need to be asked twice.

In November me, Matty Macalpine and Dave Ellis, who's also part of my management team, flew out to Mexico. Matty and Dave caught their first glimpse of the trophy truck world at Finke and I was pumped for them to experience the Baja 1000. The adventure started with pre-running, which involves taking the pre-runner trucks, as they are known, out on sections of the actual track to make notes and get a feel for what's out there. We were using two pre-runners, and while they're not quite full-blown race trucks, they're not far off. They're basically a race truck with a production cab, so you've got a few creature comforts like power windows, air-conditioning, stereo, things you don't have on the race truck. They aren't cheap, either; each pre-runner build costs around $700,000.

When we got to the coastal city of Ensenada for that first Baja, I realised that Jesse's pre-running system is pretty loose. Once the pre-runners were prepped he walked over and threw me a pencil case full of cash – I'm talking $20,000 – and told me to head off, check out my parts of the loop and have some fun. I was shitting myself. A bag full of cash, in a $700,000 truck, driving around remote parts of Mexico? Surely that's just asking to be robbed. 'No, no, you'll be fine,' he said. 'Just don't leave that pencil case in the truck if you park somewhere, they always get broken into.'

There was a local guide by the name of René, who jumped in to help out with translating, and Jesse told me the fuel stations I needed to go to, to make sure I filled up my gas or else I'd get stuck. Then he said things like, 'If you get bored of pre-running and want a day or two off, there's a great surf spot here, and the tacos are amazing there . . .' Excited, I jumped in this crazy expensive truck and took off. It was like something out of a dream. And let me tell you, there are no tacos on earth that taste as good as the ones you find in these tiny stands in the back blocks of Mexico.

There were other times during the pre-running that the whole crew and the two cars would cruise around together. Matty and Dave came out for a few days too, but we learned the hard way that Dave's stomach wasn't quite up to bouncing through the desert. I'll never forget one night when we were following the other truck and it came to a screeching halt ahead of us. I pulled up behind just in time to see Dave launch himself out of the window of the truck ahead and start throwing his guts up. Once he emptied his stomach, he looked back at me, blood pouring down his face. Turned out he hadn't seen a cactus that was right outside the window. He headbutted it at full force and copped a face full of thorns. We were pissing ourselves laughing. It was an absolute blast – until we got to the race.

At Baja, we had a two-man driver team – me and Jesse – and a navigator who stayed on board for all 1000 miles. The plan was for Jesse to jump out at a fuel stop at the 300-mile mark, and then I'd take over. Unfortunately we were only about 200 miles into the race before the mechanical problems started. First the truck threw a drive shaft, then a tail shaft not long before I was due to hop in. We were carrying a spare tail shaft, so we put that in the truck and off I went. But I didn't get far before it blew another tail shaft. Obviously something was out of whack in the drive line, but all we could do was patch it up and keep going. Next it threw a power steering belt, which left me stuck on top of a mountain somewhere. We put a new belt on and got it going again, but we'd dumped a lot of time and we were really chasing our tails.

I was just trying to get through the night, but it was really foggy and I couldn't see too far ahead. Somebody had dragged a stone out onto the track and I ran into it, which split the power steering pump in half. Once more, we repaired it the best we could and I wrestled the thing to the next fuel stop, where Jesse was meant to get back behind the wheel. By that point, we'd lost so much time Jesse said, 'Right, shut it down. We're done. There's no use continuing, it's going to keep breaking down. I'm better off keeping the miles off the engine.'

I understood why he made that decision; it was an $800,000 truck powered by a $110,000 engine. You don't want to blow things to bits for no real reason. But I was disappointed. I felt like a failure for hitting that rock. I ended up sitting in the driver's seat, all on my own, having a sulk for a half-hour or so.

12
Bolivia

I didn't feel like I'd made the big time because I'd won the Dakar. I never felt like that was an achievement that I could rest on. And boy, did I feel the pressure in the lead-up to the 2017 event. There were no excuses anymore; I knew the recipe, I'd shown I could win it. At least, that's what I thought heading back to South America as the reigning Dakar winner.

The thing is, the closer to the top you are, the harder it is to find the improvement you need to keep climbing. I contemplated long and hard about my preparation for Dakar 2017 and decided, despite the pressure I was piling on myself, not to change anything. I was feeling physically fit, probably as injury-free as I'd been at any point in my career, and the world championship rounds were proof that the bike was fast. What I needed to focus on was keeping my head in the game.

The first test was going to be arriving in Paraguay for the start. Two years ago, I started my Dakar as a nobody. I was in awe of how the fans flocked around Marc Coma but nobody gave two shits about who I was. When I returned a year later, after finishing third in 2015, people began to take notice; I started getting recognised by fans as we went about the pre-race formalities. When I arrived at Asunción as the reigning winner in early 2017, the intensity from the fans was on a whole other level.

It all felt very different and at times it was a little overwhelming. But, a few days out from the start, I pulled myself up. 'Nothing's changed,' I told myself. 'Yes, there's more pressure but you know how to ride a motorcycle, you know how to do your job properly. It's really no different to last year, or the year before, or what you've been doing your whole life. Concentrate on what's in front of you and go out and back that win up.'

As the reigning winner, I was first on the road for the opening stage that ran from Asunción to Resistencia, across the Argentinian border. I was surprised at how green it was as the stage wound its way through farming country. But it was hard going as first on the road, and there were people and cows all over the place, so I decided to back off and just make sure I got through the stage in one piece. I was only 17th quickest, but at the same time I was barely a minute off the lead, so I wasn't worried. Being further down the order then made life a lot easier for Stage 2; there were still a few cows around but at least I wasn't always first on the scene.

There were plenty of really fast roads, too, which suited me. I felt I could switch off from the pressure a bit and just ride. I ended up winning the stage by more than three minutes, which put me in the overall lead.

But that feeling of self-assuredness was short-lived. I made a complete mess of Stage 3, getting lost early in the stage and dropping 20 minutes before the first check point. By the end I was fifth overall and 17-odd minutes behind Honda's Joan Barreda. I was filthy with myself; I was the reigning winner, I was KTM's team leader, we were trying to keep a 15-year winning streak alive and here I was making mistakes and handing a huge early advantage to Honda. I was shaken by it, and by the prospect of losing the race for KTM. When I rolled out for Stage 4, I wasn't necessarily in the best frame of mind.

The competitive stage was basically split with a transport in between. I pushed like mad on the first part and thought I'd be making up ground on the Hondas. But I heard a very different story from a marshal, when I got to the start of the second part of the competitive stage. 'Wow, the Honda guys are on the move today,' he told me. 'They're long gone. By my calculations they're about six minutes in front of you.'

'Righto . . . shit,' was all I could say. It didn't make sense.

Maybe he got his wires crossed. Maybe he was playing games to make me push even harder – which worked. I didn't listen to my own instincts, I listened to what this guy was telling me. I was distracted and I was trying way too hard. It was only a matter of time before it caught me out.

At the 371-kilometre-long fast stretch – it was pretty much wide open throttle – I clipped a rock that had been dug out of the road. It kicked me forward and sent me soaring over the handlebars in front of the bike. My very last memory is of seeing rocks flying underneath me as I hurtled towards the ground. That's it, instant blackout. When I came to the first thing I saw was Paulo Gonçalves, who'd stopped to help me. I didn't know what had happened or where I was, but I knew my left leg was in a lot of pain. When the rescue helicopter arrived, it didn't take the medicos long to work out that my left femur was broken.

It felt like I'd walked out on the street and been hit by a bus. From the massive highs of the previous years to the lowest of lows. Things got a little hazy once the medicos gave me some pain relief and got to work. I vaguely remember arriving at a Bolivian hospital, but passed out as soon as I got there. When I woke up the next morning there was a doctor waiting for me. 'Right,' he said. 'We decided to operate on you straight away. We've put a rod in, and it all went well.'

I looked up and there was a bag of blood swinging from an IV pole. It didn't seem like it had gone too well, I'd clearly lost a lot of blood. And where did this bag of blood come from? It was hugely confronting, to be lying in hospital in a developing country, that I didn't know or understand at all, with a bag of blood swinging over my head. I started to ask a few questions and worked out that, yeah, I had lost a lot of blood in theatre – to the point that I'd had clotting around my lungs and went into a seizure. I was lucky to be alive.

I spent the next day or so catching my breath. They had me on really good pain medication, so every now and then I'd just black out unexpectedly. When I was awake and kind of with it, I'd jump straight on the phone to my mates and managers, losing my mind. 'Get me the fuck out of this place, I'm going to wake up one day and have no kidneys left. They're going to harvest my organs. It looks like the worst hospital in the world, you've got to figure a way out. I don't care what it costs, grab my credit card and book me a personal jet. Send me broke but get me out of here, I'm scared for my life.' But at that stage there was nothing anyone could really do.

I didn't know the half of it, either. The hospital was somewhere near La Paz, which is where the Bivouac was located for the rest day after Stage 6. My teammates Sam Sunderland, Matthias Walkner and Laia Sanz decided to come and say g'day, and when they walked into the room all three of them were as white as a ghost. *Shit, how bad do I look? Was there something the doctors weren't telling me?* I thought. They didn't say much, just asked me how I was and if I remembered what had happened. Then they took off.

It was only later I found out their reaction was pure shock at the conditions in the hospital. They'd walked into reception and the floor tiles were filthy. Even worse, there were cats wandering around inside. When they saw me lying there, fresh from serious surgery, they were convinced I was going to die from an infection or something. It was gnarly. It wasn't until a few days after, when I was feeling a bit better and could start organising how I was going to get back to Australia, that they dared to message me some of the photos they'd taken of the place. I was still in the hospital and was shocked by the things I saw that were going on a few metres from me. In that moment I really couldn't believe I was alive, not because of the crash but because of this third-world hospital.

As I waited there, I slipped back into a familiar frame of mind – why do I do this to myself? Here I was cheating death again, and for what? Trying to win a big, brass trophy? Isn't my life worth more than that? I could be a doctor or a policeman, making a difference to other people's lives. But instead, I'm flying around the world beating the shit out of myself on motorcycles, riding with my mullet flapping out the back of my helmet trying to have fun. In those tough times, when you're faced with how quickly your life could end, it all seems so trivial.

As it turned out, the Honda riders were later penalised for illegal refuelling during the transport part of the very stage that I crashed on. Perhaps being able to carry less weight explained why they were so fast on the first part of the stage and why I had to push so hard to catch them. Joan and Paulo were both handed a one-hour time penalty, which took them out of the running. Sam went on to dominate the rest of the event and keep KTM's streak alive.

By the time the race was finished I was back on Aussie soil. A few days after my surgery we did some more X-rays and, despite my scepticism of the Bolivian medical system, the job on my leg looked pretty good. Everything was in the right position and, while it didn't appear perfectly aligned, it wasn't bad. Given the situation I was in, I definitely couldn't complain. We decided I was well enough to get in a wheelchair and on a plane back to Australia. All I needed was some blood-thinners for the flight to avoid any clots and I was good to go.

About a month after I arrived home I started doing some light recovery work, things like stretching my body to try and free everything up. The muscle around my leg still had a lot of haematoma, so I was getting plenty of massage and dry needling work done. The muscles had stretched so much and then retracted and were stiff as a board. It was tough and it was slow, but it was a path I knew well. With treatment and patience, the pain would disappear. I spent time in hyperbaric chambers, I was strict with my diet, I was basically doing everything I could to help myself heal.

But I didn't. By the middle of the year, I had hit a road block. I wasn't getting better, my leg wasn't improving at all. It was constantly sore, I couldn't walk properly let alone even think about riding a motorcycle. I had heaps of check-ups and X-rays with my doctors and everything looked good, there was bone growth and healing, the screws were in place, the rod was in place. It wasn't actually my femur that hurt, it was my knee. So we started investigating that, but it was perfect. Every doctor or physio I spoke to said the same thing: 'Your knees are solid, they are the only half-decent joints in your whole body.' If my left knee was so solid, why couldn't it support any weight? Why did it always feel like it was going to collapse under me?

We spent another two months working on my knee and eventually, finally, it started to improve. I began to get impatient. It was already August and I still hadn't ridden a bike since the crash. I hadn't taken part in a single world championship round. Although it was still five months away, I could feel any chance of winning the 2018 Dakar Rally slipping through my fingers. I had to get back on a bike, I had to learn to adjust my riding style to the pain. I didn't have any other choice. I couldn't just tell the team and all the sponsors I wasn't going to return to the Dakar. It was time to grit my teeth and start riding. Maybe, I thought, it will help click things back into place and the pain will disappear.

That was wishful thinking. When I got on a bike my left-hand cornering was terrible. I was so scared of leaning on my left leg, there was no way it could carry the weight of the bike. Landing off jumps was painful. One day I was out trying my best to get through a test session, and I came off the bike and undid the very small bit of progress I'd made.

I just couldn't figure it out. I'd ridden with injuries so many times before, but this was different. This time I wasn't trying to ride through a new injury. I was simply running out of recovery options. Maybe this wasn't something that was ever going to get better. I started to wonder if I'd finally done it, if I'd permanently broken myself. I began to consider that not only might my riding career be over, but that I might be forced to live with this jarring pain in my left knee forever. I'd already come back from a broken right femur earlier in the year. Hell, I'd come back from a broken neck. How had this relatively straightforward injury done me in?

I couldn't shake the feeling that something had happened in that hospital in Bolivia, but every doctor I showed the X-rays to said they looked fine. The team decided to get the Red Bull guys involved and they were very confident they could fix me up. About three months out from Dakar, I flew to Austria to visit the Red Bull Athlete Performance Centre. I spent two weeks there, training and trying to get my body realigned and repositioned. The staff were monitoring everything. They would tape computer diagnostic sensors all over me, and I would walk around this 3D-room so they could scan my entire body and measure the temperature of each muscle. But even with all the technology there was no smoking gun. Yes, I was walking crooked as hell, but that's because I'd been favouring my right leg for nine months. They tried to straighten me up, but it was just too painful to try and change my gait. They stuck me on a bike to see if I was any better but, after half a day of riding, I woke up the next morning feeling like I was right back where I'd been in February. I wanted to just pack it in, I told the Red Bull guys I was done. But they had one more Hail Mary to try.

They sent me to a doctor that had a good track record of thinking outside the box. He took an X-ray of my femur, had a look and said, 'Yeah, it all looks fine . . . but I wonder if there's something wrong with that rod in your leg. It's got to be that.' The problem was, the only way to know was to go back under the knife, pull that rod out and stick a new one in. It was a lot to go through based on some random doctor's gut feeling, but I was at the end of my tether. I just didn't care anymore. A week of pain lying in a hospital bed? Who cares. I was living in agony day in, day out. 'Let's do it right now,' I said.

A day or two later I was back on the operating table. It turned out to be a mission to get the thing out, as there's no universal tooling in the world of medicine. Some of the bits and pieces they'd used in Bolivia were a little old-fashioned. But finally the doctor was able to remove the 10-millimetre rod, drill out the bone slightly to make a bigger gap and fitted a 12.5 millimetre rod back in. As part of the operation they dislocate your hip, so when I woke up my hip was destroyed. I felt like I did the morning after my Dakar crash, which was a massive downer. I was convinced there was no way I was going back to the Dakar in a few months.

Then I started moving my leg. The stabbing pain in my knee was completely gone. I couldn't walk because of my hip, but there was no doubt it felt different. The next day the doctors got me out of bed and standing up with a walking frame. I couldn't feel . . . anything. I was told to try without the frame. I could hold my weight just fine. Then they asked me to take a few steps. My leg felt perfect. I walked around, waiting for the pain to kick in. 'How much morphine am I on?' I asked the docs.

'Minimal dose,' I was told. 'You'd feel any pain that was there.'

I didn't know what the hell was going on. I'd become a completely new person overnight. It turned out that the original rod just wasn't quite long enough. All I needed was a slightly thicker, longer titanium rod screwed into the femur. Immediately I could walk down the hallway without a limp, without any pain. I was blown away by it. If we'd done this back in February, I would have been racing again by March, April at the latest. Instead, I was a couple of months out from the Dakar, about as unprepared as you can possibly get.

13
Survival

After the surgery, I had to wait a few weeks for the external wounds to heal up and the stitches to come out. As soon as that was done I was back on a bike. It was a real race against time; by that stage it was early November, two months out from the Dakar.

I flew back to Australia, packed some bags and then took off again to Morocco to join the team for some training. Man, I felt completely unready. The event was weeks away and I could only now actually go out for a jog. And I could barely make two kilometres, I was so out of shape. I may like being a little heavy going into the Dakar, but normally I'm still in good form. And my race fitness was nowhere; I'd hardly done any kilometres on a bike and hadn't ridden a competitive stage since I took off from Jujuy in Argentina on the morning of the crash.

To add to the uncertainty there was a brand new KTM 450 Rally that I had to get my head around. I felt bad for the team, showing up in this sort of condition. It was embarrassing. I tried to compensate by spending as much time on the bike as possible, but I also had to be careful of not overdoing it. My body was still recovering from surgery. It wasn't until December, three weeks from rolling down the start ramp in Lima, Peru, that I could really start putting some effort in on the bike.

I did my best in those few weeks, but it was a drop in the ocean. When I jumped on the plane to Peru all I could do was laugh – I wasn't fit, I wasn't ready, I'd almost forgotten how to ride a motorcycle . . . I felt like I was wasting everybody's time. There was no way I was going to get through two weeks of the Dakar. But on the flip side, I couldn't just stay home. I had a contract with the team. I had obligations to sponsors to think about. If I didn't race at Dakar it was going to cost me a lot of money, and like everyone, I had a normal life with bills to worry about. I wasn't in any pain, I was just unprepared – so all I could do was give it a go.

As I sat on the plane to Lima I started to map out my approach to the race. Given where my body and mind were at, there was no point trying to win the thing. The next fortnight was going to be all about survival, just getting to the finish and seeing where I shook out. It was almost like going back to my first year: focus on the finish, not the result. The difference to 2015 was that now I was a former Dakar winner. I wasn't flying under the radar anymore. But I had to shut out the external expectations and worry about nursing myself through the race. Stick to survival mode.

Survival was how it felt for the first two days as we charged along the stunning Peruvian coastline. On Stage 1 I was bloody slow, on Stage 2 I at least managed to climb into the Top 10. After those first two days I was physically wrecked, the finish line felt a long, long way away. We spent the next couple of days in the dunes, one of the Dakar's toughest and most unique challenges. You have no reference points when you're out in serious dune sections. There are times you climb up on top of a dune, come to a stop and all you have around you is more dunes. Three hundred and sixty degrees, as far as the eye can see. So if you don't meticulously follow the CAP, you can get stuck for hours. Literally. That caught plenty of people out on Stage 3, including Joan Barreda, who lost a heap of time after getting lost. For the first time since the race started, I actually felt in the game as I cruised through the dunes. I was among the front-runners all stage and may have won it if I didn't take a tumble late in the day. I didn't hurt myself, but I filled my roadbook with sand and broke my camelback, which meant I was pretty thirsty by the end of the stage. Still, I finished third for the day and moved into fourth outright. Maybe a win wasn't completely out of the question. On Stage 4 it was my turn to get a bit lost and dump some time, although I managed to limit the damage. The same couldn't be said for Sam Sunderland, who crashed out of the lead.

For the next couple of days, I just battled on as best I could and by the time we got to La Paz for the rest day I was sixth outright, ten minutes off the overall lead. To be honest, it was better than I had expected. And it was a wide open race with heaps of riders still in contention. If the second week went my way, another Dakar win would definitely be within reach.

We kicked off the second week with a marathon stage, and a couple of little falls in these baths of mud we had to navigate through the first day meant I had to call on my mechanic skills overnight. But I got the bike reasonably sorted and reached the end sitting fourth outright, seven minutes and 35 seconds off the overall lead. I was well-placed in terms of position, but the marathon really punished me physically. By the time I got back to the Bivouac, I was struggling big time.

Luckily, Mother Nature decided to do me a favour. Thanks to heavy rain the race organisers decided to cancel Stage 9, giving me a much-needed additional rest day.

I woke on the morning of Stage 10 feeling great. It was a long day, nearly 800 kilometres, and the competitive stage was split into two sections and two roadbooks. In between there was a transport stage and a service stop with the team, where we could refuel the bike, eat some lunch, things like that. I was among the frontrunners up until the break, but a quirk in the navigation caught me out heading into the second leg. The team was set up down a short road, maybe 40 or 50 metres long, which I rode in and out of before starting the second part of the competitive stage. That threw my roadbook out by about 100 metres, and I completely forgot to reset the trip meter at the start of the stage.

I was riding in a group with my teammate Antoine Méo and Honda's Kevin Benavides, and they had done exactly the same thing. A few kays down the road there was an instruction to turn right into a dry riverbed and, right on cue, there it was. A riverbed that matched the roadbook, the trip meter and the CAP heading perfectly.

What we didn't know was that 100 metres further down the road there was an identical riverbed running in the same direction. We were meant to turn into the second one but, with our tripmeters slightly out, we turned into the first one.

Because the two riverbeds were parallel to each other, there was nothing in the CAP heading to tip us off to the blunder. All three of us just kept ripping along, none the wiser. It wasn't until we'd gone 20 kilometres down this river that the CAP heading started to head left, which I thought was a little strange. But we'd all gone so far; we were only six kilometres from the next waypoint, it didn't make sense to turn around. We charged on to what should have been the next waypoint but the validation point didn't open. We were super confused because we felt like we'd done the right thing, but it wouldn't validate the waypoint.

All of a sudden a helicopter landed in front of us and another ten, 11 bikes arrived behind us. We weren't the only ones who had made the mistake, so the organisers sent the chopper out to tell us to head back. We had to ride all the way to the initial turn-off into the wrong wash, recalibrate, and turn back into the right wash 100 metres down the road. Another 20 kilometres later, there was the waypoint. Only one rider from the group of frontrunners got the note right, my teammate Matthias Walkner. He ended up with a huge lead of almost 40 minutes, while I dropped to fifth with a 50-minute deficit.

I arrived in the Bivouac to complete chaos, people running around trying to work out what had happened. I was still trying to figure it out myself, but the one thing I knew was that I'd fucked up. I was furious with myself. When the media team rolled up with its cameras, asking me what had happened, I was holding back tears. I couldn't talk, I couldn't bring myself to relive what had gone on. I gave a couple of short, one-word answers until the reporter got the hint and moved off.

I was so scared about talking to the team about what had happened. I wanted to hide from them, but that's not how this sport works. You have to debrief everything, good and bad. It wasn't until I sat down with the team and we pulled up the section on Google Maps that I could see where we'd gone wrong. Two riverbeds running side by side. It was clear as day on a map, but very hard to spot at eye level. At the same time I couldn't blame the roadbook. Yes, it was a difficult note, but it wasn't impossible. I wasn't the only one to make the mistake, but I still made it. When I'm out on the bike, the buck stops with me. I had to take it on the chin, as much as it hurt.

I ended up winning two of the last three stages and cutting the gap to Matthias down to 23 minutes, good enough for third overall. Matthias was definitely managing his huge lead over the last few stages but, given I dropped 43 minutes in that riverbed, I couldn't help but think about what might have been. There's every chance that one note, 100 metres, cost me a Dakar win. At least Matthias kept KTM's winning streak going for a 17th straight Dakar.

Third wasn't an ideal result, and I was filthy about that wrong note, but at least I left South America feeling like I gave it 100 per cent on all 12 stages. There wasn't a single day that I backed off; I pushed my tired, unprepared body as hard as it would go. As a sportsperson, that's all you can really ask of yourself. In one way I was satisfied, in another I was bitterly disappointed. When you win the Dakar, you tick off a massive career goal. Whatever happens in the future, nobody can take that away from you. But it's addictive. Winning one made me want to win a second one even more. Between the crash in 2017, having nearly a year off the bike and then the navigational fuck-up in 2018, I'd missed two great opportunities to claim the Dakar crown.

14
Iron Man

The best thing about the 2018 Dakar Rally was that I'd ridden myself back to fitness. I'd spent two weeks in the toughest conditions there were for a rider, working all the right muscles and joints. It was a tough way to get back to full fitness, I would've much preferred to build up to it, but it worked.

Before I knew it, we were at the opening round of the FIM Cross-Country Rallies World Championship in Abu Dhabi. I got off to a good start with a win on the first day. Then on Day 2 it all turned to shit; I came off the bike in a big way, bent the bash plate right back and damaged the fuel line. It took me half an hour to fix it up and get going again. Luckily I wasn't seriously injured, although I did jar my back a bit and was sore the next few days. I pretty much wrote off any chance of winning the world championship right there and then.

I was a little down in the mouth overnight, but on the third day I got a timely reminder that there's more to life than riding bikes. After the fuel stop I was running with Mohammed Balooshi, an Emirati rider, until he had a huge crash in front of me. In cross-country racing you're not just a rider, you're a makeshift mechanic and paramedic as well. Even if I'd been leading the rally I would've stopped straight away to help. It's just what we do. I jumped on the brakes, dropped my bike and ran over to see if he was hurt.

All rally motorcycles are fitted with an Iritrack system, which can sense when you've stopped via a satellite connection to a control centre in France. If you come to a rapid stop, and the bike is lying on its side, the Iritrack will automatically send a distress signal to the control centre, which will then relay the GPS coordinates to the medical crews at the event and get a helicopter in the air as soon as possible. On the bike we have three buttons: one green, one red and one blue. If you've just stopped to fix something and you don't need medical assistance, you hit the green button to let the control centre know you're okay. The red button is a manual version of the SOS system, so if you come across someone who's crashed, you hit the red button on both your bike and their bike. There's also an EPIRB (emergency position indicating radio beacons) system you activate. The more information the chopper crew has, the better. The blue button on the Iritrack is a radio to speak to the control centre; they keep you updated on how far away the chopper is. It's an intricate system but the response is pretty fast. You can be in the middle of nowhere and there will usually be a chopper on site within ten minutes. In saying that, ten minutes can feel like ten hours when someone is badly hurt. You never want to find yourself in that makeshift paramedic role, it's a frightening, frantic experience that you never feel prepared for. At the same time, you can't leave someone for dead in the desert.

When I got to Mohammed he was out cold. I hit the red buttons on our bikes, set off the EPIRBs and took a closer look at him. The good news was that he was breathing and all his airways were nice and open, but you know if someone is unconscious that their head has taken a big knock. It's always a critical situation. His body didn't seem too bashed up, but I didn't want to shake him in case there was something going on with his neck or spine. So I just kept calling his name to see if he would wake up. He eventually did, but only four or five minutes after the helicopter had arrived. Thankfully it turned out his only injury was a nasty concussion.

When he was loaded up and on his way to hospital, I jumped on my bike and finished the stage. I got most of the time I'd lost helping Mohammed back, but still went on to finish the rally a pretty underwhelming seventh overall.

KTM sat out the second round of the world champ-ionship in Qatar, so my focus turned to Finke Desert Race and my second shot at the double – winning on both two and four wheels on the same weekend. The Iron Man, we called it. I'd only run the trophy truck at Finke in 2017 as the broken femur kept me off the bike. We went close to another podium too, before an engine sensor failure took us out of the running.

It was a little risky going for the Iron Man in 2018, because it was also my shot at a record sixth Finke title on the bike. If something went wrong in the truck, I could feasibly end up stranded in the desert and not get back to either Alice or Finke in time to start the two-wheel section. I'm sure KTM Australia would have preferred I'd not bothered with the truck. A lot of people thought I was nuts. I was, really. I was getting paid to race the motorcycle, but paying, out of my own pocket, to race the truck. That thing costs roughly $110 per kilometre to run, so it isn't cheap by a long shot. If you want to race a bike at Finke, you can rock up with a mate to help out and off you go, but with the trophy truck you need a navigator and at least four more people on your crew. The total cost for the few days in Finke comes to about $110,000. Getting it all together, and finding the money to pay for it all, is a lot of work. And that's before you even get to the start line in Alice Springs.

But I did it in 2018, and still do it to this day, for two reasons. One, I just can't help myself. I love a challenge, and I love it even more when people tell me it won't work. Secondly, and much more importantly, I do it because it's what my dad used to do. It's not about trying to emulate him, it's about giving something back to him. Something that I took away. My parents did so much for me through-out my junior career. Without me racing bikes, they'd be on easy street by now. But they chose to help me do something

I loved to do. They sacrificed so much, they lived day-to-day, week-to-week, to pay for me to race bikes. I've seen the financial pressures of motorsport – people re-mortgaging houses and so on – tear families to bits over the years. But we got through it and my parents never complained about what they gave up. But they did give things up, like Dad and his off-road racing. Now I'm in a financial position to give it back to him. He's very involved in the trophy truck and he's fascinated by the modern technology. I love watching him go through the truck and marvel at how things have changed. I love seeing his face after he comes for a ride when we're out testing. That's what I really get out of it.

Our second crack at the Iron Man got off to a perfect start. In prologue I was quickest on the bike and fourth quickest in the car, which gave me a little more breathing room in terms of getting the plane back to Alice Springs. The next day we kicked off with the run out to Finke in the truck. My time limit was two hours and six minutes. If I couldn't get to the finish line within then, I'd have to park the truck on the side of the road, jump in the helicopter that was following me, and either fly to the finish in Finke to get a plane back to Alice, or chopper it back to the start line directly. Whichever was going to be fastest. Anyway, the time limit wasn't a problem. I had a great run out to Finke in the truck, picking up a couple of places to end up second overall – just three minutes off the lead. I was right in the game and the truck felt awesome. I had a five-minute debrief with the crew, then went straight to the airstrip and flew back to Alice. I switched my brain into motorcycle mode and blasted up that same stretch of road. I had a bit of an off along the way and grazed my arm on some branches, but I was comfortably quickest with a lead of about four minutes. I couldn't have been happier with how things were going.

Once I finished the debrief with KTM I went back to check on the truck guys. I expected it all to be pretty quiet in the tent; I'd only asked for a few small set-up changes to deal with the fuel load as it lightens along the run. But, in the course of routine checks, the guys had discovered metal filings in a filter – never a good sign. Something was broken somewhere. The transmission was the primary suspect, but we didn't have a spare with us. Even though I'd thought about it in the lead-up to the event, with a $48,000 price tag I decided we could do without it. Whoops. I asked the guys if they thought that the gearbox would make it back to Alice, and the answer was a resounding 'Who knows?' It may have been fine, but it was a huge risk to take when we had one hand on the double.

We really needed another transmission, and it wasn't until well after dark that we hatched a plan to get one. Our only hope was a phone call to my good mate Billy Geddes. He was running the same sort of truck, with the same transmission, but was already out of the race. About 40 kilometres out of Finke he'd landed awkwardly off a bump and pitched his truck into a roll. If the transmission wasn't damaged, maybe he'd loan it to me. All I could do was ask. 'You've got every right to say no, and I'm not going to pressure you into anything, but can I please borrow your gearbox?'

He didn't hesitate for a second. 'Mate, I'll start pulling the gearbox out of my truck now.'

The next challenge was that Billy's truck was in Alice Springs. It was already 7 pm, pitch black, and in the car it would have been a ten-hour round trip to go and get it. The only option was to bite the bullet and fork out for a chopper to fly back to Alice and pick up the gearbox. When Billy's gearbox arrived, it was quite literally just sitting on the back seat of the chopper. As part of the deal, I'd promised Billy I'd rebuild his box, so between that and the helicopter trip, the whole thing added about $12,000 to my bill. That's more than you get for winning the Finke. But at least I was still in the race.

The boys didn't finish working on the truck until 2 am. They had a few plumbing issues and had to fabricate bits and pieces, but eventually got there. Three-and-a-half hours later, me and my navigator Jason Duncan were jumping back in to get ready for the run to Alice Springs.

We took off from Finke just after 7 am, feeling like we had a huge chance of winning. I was absolutely pumped. I was ready to make Finke Desert Race history. But within 100 kilometres, the dream was over. We were belting down the track when, all of a sudden, the steering wheel felt like it had seized. 'Fuck, the wheel's gone!' I screamed at Jason. 'Something's broken in the steering.'

I wrangled the truck off the track and onto the service road, and we both jumped out to have a look. As soon as I undid my belts, I knew any hope of winning was gone. The power-steering pump had busted and we didn't have a spare with us, so we couldn't even limp to the finish. After all that money, all that time, we were screwed over by a $300 part.

The chopper picked me up from where we'd parked the truck and took me back to Finke. I was dejected, but my day wasn't done. I had a couple of hours to push the disappointment to the furthest part of my mind and focus on the next job at hand – winning that sixth bike title. But I couldn't get it out of my head. Sitting around waiting just made me stress about what might go wrong on the motorcycle. What if I crash? What if something breaks? Did the guys replace the chain? Is the chain tension right? Did they do the nut up on the rear axle?

What if I end up going home with nothing?

The anxiety quickly disappeared when I was back on the bike and heading towards Alice . . . at least until I clipped a square-edged hole in a corner and the bike kicked sideways. I couldn't quite catch it, and I realised if I tried to hang onto the bike I was going to end up in the bush. The safest option was to accept my fate and lay the bike down in the middle of the track. I hit my head pretty hard, but once I got up it seemed like nothing was broken on me or the bike.

I got away with it, which was insanely lucky. It probably took me about 20 seconds to dust myself off, pick up the bike, hit the starter and get going again – but it felt like a lifetime. I thought my lead must have evaporated. I rode the last 100-odd kilometres in a panic, convinced someone was going to catch and pass me. When I got to the last fuel stop, 80 kays from Alice, I was screaming at the crew. 'I've crashed, I've crashed, check the bike!'

I was frantic, nothing like my usual cool, calm self. It wasn't me, that's not who I am, but I was so scared of failing twice on one day. I was frightened that, if I didn't win on the bikes, the critics who said I shouldn't even be driving the truck would be proven right. I could hear them in my head – 'Wake up to yourself. Stop being an idiot. You're not a four-wheel person, stick to riding bikes.' I needed to win the race, so I could shut the haters up. I needed to win the race, so KTM wouldn't see the truck as a distraction and ban me from racing it next year. I needed to win the race so badly it destroyed my composure.

The tricky thing is, when you're out on the bike you don't know what's happening behind you. I thought the crash had cost me all this time, but it hadn't. I'd actually pulled time on the field. I was ten minutes down the road and could have cruised to the finish as cool as you like. At the fuel stop, the boys assured me that the bike was fine and that I had a good lead. That helped me focus just enough to get through the last 80 kilometres unscathed. I failed at the Iron Man, but I still put my name in the Finke Desert Race history books with a record sixth win on the bike.

***

During the celebrations back in Alice, Danny Apro, one of the KTM mechanics, said, 'Dude, I'm going to have the best souvenir from your sixth Finke win.' He pulled up his sleeve and showed me this gnarly burn. The rear brake caliper had roasted his arm while he was looking over the bike during that last fuel stop. I felt terrible. He'd only done it because I was in that mad, rushed frame of mind, shouting at the poor blokes. 'I'm so sorry . . .' I started to say.

'Don't apologise! That's a memory I'll have for the rest of my life, it's fucking cool.'

There aren't many times in your life when someone would be amped that you'd given them a third-degree burn. Motorcycle racing is a weird old sport. But it showed me, once again, how awesome that Aussie KTM team was and why we'd had so much success. Everyone was always pulling in the same direction, everyone just wanted to get a result whatever it took. It was a bittersweet evening in Alice because I'd wanted that truck win so badly. But that little exchange with Danny gave me some perspective about what me and those Aussie KTM guys achieved not just on that day, but over the years.

The world championship season continued with a two-event swing in South America in August. Given I'd finished so far down the order in Abu Dhabi, I didn't have any pressure on me in terms of the title fight; it was all about Dakar preparation. At the Atacama Rally in Chile, I just eased my way back into things. It was a tricky rally in terms of navigation so I was pretty conservative but, apart from a missed CAP on the fourth stage, I managed to avoid any serious mistakes.

I was top three on all five days and banked a decent haul of points with second overall.

The following week we travelled to Argentina for the Desafío Ruta 40, where I felt like I yo-yoed up and down the timesheet over the five days. I had a decent enough start on the first morning until I got past the first fuel stop and my GPS decided to lose its signal. It cost me about five minutes and put me on the backfoot. Stage 2 was mostly off-piste and, driven by a bit of the frustration from the GPS drama, I just went for it. I got those five minutes back at the midway point of the stage, and ended the day leading the rally by more than two minutes. I then lost time running first on Stage 3 and dropped to third overall, before a better day on Stage 4 put me back in second. On the final day, I had three minutes and 28 seconds to make up on Paulo Gonçalves, so I decided to just go for it. I didn't back off once all day, it was heaps of fun. I won the stage and went so close to catching Paulo to win the rally. He only hung on by six seconds.

The two second places had helped me close the gap to series leader Pablo Quintanilla, but Pablo had been consistent and had an eight-point margin going into the Rallye du Maroc in October. There was no point playing it safe, I had to finish in front of Pablo. I had another GPS drama on the first stage – it wouldn't register a waypoint even though I was on the course – but I still finished the day with a three-minute lead. Even better for me was that Pablo got lost a couple of times and dropped about 20 minutes. I had to lead the way on Stage 2 which was tough, but I limited the damage, finished second to my teammate Matthias Walkner and still pulled another minute over Pablo. Stage 3 was the first leg of a marathon, and it was my turn to make a few navigational errors. It cost me nearly eight minutes and handed the lead of the rally to Matthias. I was still ahead of Pablo, but the points haul for a win was my best shot at the title.

Finishing sixth on the first leg of the marathon was a blessing for the second leg. It was nice starting a bit further down the pack, and I could just work my way through the stage and pick off the guys in front of me. I passed everyone except Sam Sunderland, who started first and won the stage by seven minutes. That gave me a lead of seven minutes and 27 seconds heading into the last day and nearly half a minute up my sleeve over Pablo. The title I'd written off after Abu Dhabi was suddenly very much within reach. I was pipped to the post by Ricky Brabec on the final stage, but that didn't matter. I won the Rallye du Maroc by more than seven-and-a-half minutes and, with Pablo back in fourth, the world championship by six points.

It was an awesome feeling. Every time you jump on the bike you want to win, whether it's the stage, the race or the championship. It was my first world championship in any discipline and, I have to admit, it was cool to see the words 'Price World Rally Champion' printed on the T-shirts the team had waiting at the finish.

But . . . it wasn't like winning the Dakar. It sounds harsh, but to be brutally honest, winning that title didn't compare to a Dakar stage win. In isolation, becoming world champion was a massive achievement. But in our sport there's only one prize that really matters. What I was happiest about when we wrapped up in Morocco was that I was fit, healthy, happy and prepared to finally go and win a second Dakar Rally.

15
One-handed

With the world championship won and done, focus turned to the 2019 Dakar Rally. Four weeks out from the event, the whole team travelled to the Emirates to do some testing around Dubai and Abu Dhabi in the sand dunes.

Dakar is all about endurance fitness. When you're out on a long run, your heart rate will be quite consistent over the eight hours or so you're on the bike. But a bit of strength and conditioning doesn't hurt either, so on one particular day during testing the team wanted to give us a bit of a workout. They found some hard-pack ground and set up what was basically a big moto track. We were then told to head over there and punch out some hard, fast laps to get our heart rates up. We'd done a heap of laps on this loop and the ground began to get pretty rough. At one stage I was riding through the pack, blasting past my teammates. Then I got to Matthias Walkner, and we reached a tough section together. He was on the right, I was on the left, and then we both cross-rutted and collided in the middle. He lost the front end and tucked onto the ground, which was lucky. He dusted himself straight off and he was fine. But I got ejected from the bike, took off through the air and landed on my wrist.

Initially I thought I was okay, and my first instinct was to go and give Matthias a mouthful. He had the same idea, so there was a bit of yelling and finger-pointing for a while. It wasn't until the team dragged us over to the tent and showed us a replay that we could see we'd actually both fucked up. We'd both got a bit loose and, somehow, ended up on the same bit of dirt. It's amazing, really, we had 1000 acres to ride on but still managed to crash into each other.

I had a bit of a sore wrist on my right hand, but it just felt like a sprain. I could move it fine, so I really wasn't worried. I figured I'd ice it up that afternoon and I'd wake up a little bruised, but ready to get back on the bike the next day. Worst case scenario, I'd need a day or two to rest. The next morning it was still painful, but nothing crazy. I was still convinced it was a light sprain and was happy to press on, but the team decided it was worth jumping in a car and heading to hospital in Dubai for a quick check-up. Just so we knew that everything was okay.

I went in for an X-ray and when the doctor came back he wasn't entirely sure what was going on. 'Look, you've got a broken scaphoid . . . it's one of the bones that sits below your thumb, where your wrist is. But it doesn't seem like a brand new break to me,' he said. 'I reckon it's been there a while so it shouldn't be a problem.' Phew.

I was meant to head back to Australia a few days later, but between me and the team we thought it better to play it safe and get a second opinion. We wanted reassurance that everything was in order and that it wouldn't be an issue on the Dakar. So I flew straight to Barcelona to see famous trauma specialist Dr Xavier Mir. My wrist felt okay and I wasn't anticipating bad news. But Dr Mir took one look and said, 'This is a fresh break. I don't think you're going to the Dakar.'

It was a bitter pill to swallow. I'd just gone through the injury wringer and came out the other side. I'd had this amazing 2018 season, I was the world champion. Everything was perfectly set up for me to win another Dakar title. And now I wasn't even going to make the start line, let alone the finish. All I could do was try and convince Dr Mir to at least give me a shot at getting on a bike for Dakar. 'I just don't see it happening, it's not possible,' he told me. 'It's a complicated bone.'

I kept pushing. Begging. Pleading for him to do whatever it took, screw it back together, wrap something around it, anything. 'I don't care if it's a dodgy fix that will only hold on for two weeks,' I said. 'Just do it.'

'Well, you definitely need surgery to screw and pin it back together,' he explained. 'But it's going to be tender. You're not going to be able to hold onto a motorcycle for twelve days.'

I wasn't worried about pain, I just wanted to get on with it. 'Fine, can we do the surgery right now? Every second we sit here talking about it is a second less I have to try and recover.'

Dr Mir shook his head. 'Forget about January,' he said. 'Let's fix your wrist properly, put it back together and go from there.'

I was being bullish about it, but deep down I was shaken by Dr Mir's reaction. He's the surgeon to the MotoGP stars, famous for his ability to patch riders up in inconceivably short amounts of time. When the best doctor in the world at stitching bike riders back together is telling you it's not going to happen, that's difficult to ignore. And sure he'd got MotoGP riders back on a bike just weeks after breaking a scaphoid, but grand prix racing is very different to rally racing. That's not to downplay how hard it would be to wrestle a 200 horsepower GP bike at speeds of up to 330 km/h for 40 minutes with a busted wrist, but it's not the Dakar. A grand prix doesn't go for two weeks. There's no rocks and ledges and drops and jumps that your body has to absorb. Even with the sophisticated suspension on our Dakar bikes, your wrists cop a belting when you're out on a Dakar stage. Dr Mir wasn't being a pessimist when he said I wouldn't be ready for Dakar, he was just being honest.

He got me into surgery as quickly as possible, put in a screw and stuck my arm in a brace. As impossible as it all looked, I couldn't give up on the idea of going to Dakar. I went back to Australia so I could be in my own world and to recover comfortably at home. I kept up my fitness with stationary cycling and things like that, which was all I could really do. That and just wait.

Five days out from my flight to Peru I decided to get on a bike. I'd been putting it off, but I figured that whether I tried to ride five days before the flight, or a day before the flight, it probably wouldn't make a big difference. I had to bite the bullet, take off the brace and give it a go. Queensland Moto Park has some flat areas of grass, so I thought that was a good starting point. My wrist was a little sore, but it didn't feel too bad. Then I went out on the motocross track. I didn't do any of the jumps, but I made sure I hit a few bumps and ruts to see how the wrist would react. It hurt a bit more but it was manageable. So then I decided to try a few jumps. I rode around for a few hours and when I was done it was sore but still moveable. What I was nervous about was the next morning. If I woke up and my wrist was locked solid, that would mean I'd done more damage to it. Either way, I felt it was worth the risk. If I turned a six-month recovery into an eight-month recovery, who cares? I woke up the next day and the wrist was a bit tender, but it wasn't swollen or overly aggravated. Maybe I had a shot at the Dakar, after all.

I put the brace back on and spent the next three days to-ing and fro-ing about what to do. Should I get on the plane or not? The team kept telling me it didn't matter, that they didn't mind if I waited until I got to the airport to make a decision. 'The ball's in your court,' I was told. 'We're not telling you to ride, we're not telling you not to ride. Just let us know if you don't get on the plane.'

On the morning of the flight, I decided I'd at least go to the airport. I packed my bags, chucked them in the car and off

I went. Once I was at the airport, I slipped into autopilot mode: checked in, looked at the boarding time, wandered to the lounge to hang out, all the usual stuff. It wasn't until I arrived at the lounge that it really hit me. Was I seriously going to fly all the way to South America and try and ride this bike? Am I just wasting the team's time and money? Am I doing the wrong thing? Then my brain would swing the other way and tell me I had to get on the plane and give it a go.

I was all over the shop. I tried to weigh up the pros and cons, but the list of cons was three times longer than the list of pros. It didn't make any sense for me to get on the plane. I thought about when I started out in seniors and how I almost ruined my career by trying to ride through injuries rather than giving my body the time it needed to heal. I thought about how the Dakar pushes you to your absolute physical limits, even when you're completely fit and healthy. It also pushes you to the limit of your mental strength, even when you're properly prepared for it. You finish the Dakar feeling like you've been dragged around the world behind a car at the very best of times. This was a lost cause, a complete waste of time. I was about to get up, walk over to the desk and ask if they could get my bags off the plane so I could go home. But I couldn't bring myself to do it.

It wasn't until a few minutes before boarding that I made a choice. *Stuff it*, I thought. *I'm going to go. Two or three days, that's my goal. I'll try and win one of the first couple of stages, then I'll call it quits and come home. The team will be happy I gave it a go.*

It was a solid plan. I felt like my wrist could make it through a few stages, as long as I didn't do anything stupid like drop off a big ledge. It would be fine for normal riding, but I couldn't afford any heavy landings. It was a split-second decision and I made it right as we were being called to board the flight over the PA. I thought my mind would stop swimming once I got on the plane, but it didn't. The whole way to Lima I'd have moments of thinking, *What the fuck are you doing, mate?* At least once we were in the air there was no turning back.

Once I got to Lima there really was no turning back. The Dakar hype train left the station the second my feet hit the ground and I immediately realised this was happening whether I liked it or not. I actually felt good about it. It was easy to overthink everything on the plane, but once I was with the team, hanging out, I was happy to be there. I stopped obsessing over my wrist and started getting swept up in the distractions of prepping for the event. I still didn't plan on going beyond the first two or three stages, but those thoughts that I shouldn't be there at all disappeared. I threw myself into everything I could in the days leading up to the event.

Usually you try to avoid the pre-race media appearances, but I was volunteering for all of them. Anything to keep my mind busy. The only drawback with doing interview after interview was that the first question was always the same – 'So, how's the wrist?' I ended up with a standard response: 'Look it's not great, but we'll see what happens. We'll take it day by day; if it feels good, I'll keep going, if it doesn't, I'll stop. But Dakar only comes around once a year, so I've got to give it a crack.' Then I'd deflect any questions about my wrist and talk about how excited I was to see the team again and how cool it was to see my bike for the first time. It doesn't matter how long you've been involved in racing, you never lose that sense of awe when you see a brand new bike someone has built for you before an event. It's magical.

We had a shakedown test a few days out and I took it easy, minimising the kilometres and just doing what we needed to do. The wrist felt good, I was pretty comfortable. Stephen Gall from CTi braces made me a carbon-fibre brace that would help stop my wrist from overextending. That was the biggest danger. If I dropped off something and hit the bottom of the suspension travel, I didn't want my wrist to fold back too far.

The next thing I knew we were at the opening ceremony.

The first day was a blur and the adrenaline of the build-up really carried me through. I was in some pain, but I was just thrilled to be out there on the bike, at the biggest race in the world. I finished the stage sixth, about three minutes off the lead, which I was pretty happy with. I was sharing a motorhome with my good mate Sam Sunderland in the Bivouac, and that night spirits were high. Unfortunately, the good times were short-lived. On Stage 2 the pain started to set in and on Stage 3 it became even worse. Because of the World Anti-Doping Agency rules, I was basically limited to paracetamol to try to manage the pain. Adding insult to my injury was that the weather conditions on the third stage were shocking and I dumped 15-odd minutes with a few navigation issues. I remember at some point during the stage, Sam and I were lost together and I had a bit of a tantrum. 'Fuck this, fuck my wrist, I'm going home!' I was shouting as we sat there in the middle of nowhere. It was all heat-of-the-moment stuff.

Getting through the third stage was my initial goal, so that night, once I'd calmed down, I reassessed where things were at. There was no getting around it, my wrist wasn't great. If I'd won one of the first three stages, I probably would have called it quits. But I hadn't, and I was only two stages out from the rest day. With a bit of encouragement from Sam, I decided to stick it out until then. By then I wasn't even thinking about where I was in the results. To be honest, that's pretty normal in the first week; you always have winning on the bottom of your list of priorities until you get to the rest day. But it wasn't on my list at all. I didn't consider myself in the hunt to finish the race, let alone win it.

Even to get to the rest day I knew I needed some help. The paracetamol wasn't cutting it, I needed to find non-medical pain relief. Given it was my throttle wrist, I figured if I could find a way to give it a rest on the liaison stages that would be a huge benefit. I'd already tried constructing a makeshift cruise control by wrapping race tape around the inside of the handlebar between the grip and the handguard. It made the throttle hard to twist, but once I got it to a certain point it would hold itself in place. It worked, but a little too well. I had a couple of hairy moments where I couldn't wind the throttle off. If I wanted to slow down I had to grab the clutch, let the engine rev its head off and then dump the clutch again. After a couple of very close calls with cliffs and cars, I decided enough was enough. I was genuinely putting my life at risk trying to hold the throttle with tape, I needed a better solution.

So I had a poke around the bike and noticed there was a rubber band that held the battery in its plastic cage. I went to the parts truck, grabbed a spare band and wrapped it around the grip and the guard. I pulled it tight and voila, it held the throttle in place. And because it was rubber, I could pull back against it and wind off the throttle. It was perfect. I didn't use it on the competitive stages, I couldn't afford to take that risk. But to be able to give my wrist a break on those long liaison stages was a godsend. When I was on the open road, I could pull my right arm completely off the handlebars and spare my wrist from all the painful bumps and jars that you just can't avoid on a motorcycle. Instead of having to tough out the entire day, it gave me an extra two or three hours of peace in the morning, and an extra two or three hours of healing time on the way back to the Bivouac after the stage. It made an amazing difference. A five-dollar piece of rubber, which comes standard on every single KTM motorcycle, held my race together.

I battled my way through the next two stages and made it to Arequipa for the rest day. I was worried about how the screw in my wrist was holding up, so I spoke to the KTM team doctor and we decided we'd go to the local hospital for an X-ray the next day. After a much-needed proper night's sleep in a comfy hotel room bed. We probably should have walked to the hospital the following morning because the taxi ride was one of the wildest experiences I've had in my entire life. I was convinced we were going to die a number of times. It was way scarier than riding a motorcycle through the desert.

The hospital itself was a much nicer experience. The doctors knew the event, knew who I was and were pumped that I was there. There was no queuing or waiting, they took me straight through for an X-ray. It wasn't the latest and greatest medical equipment, but it was good enough to see what was going on with that screw. I decided that if it was bad news, if the bone had split again, I was going to cut my losses and call it quits. When the doctor put the image up in front of the lightbox I was frightened to look. I told the team doctor that I was just going to stare at the floor and wait for him to say something.

'Hey, check this out,' he said once he'd reviewed the X-ray. 'It's actually not too bad.' I took a look at the screen and, yeah, it looked quite promising. The scaphoid wasn't healed, you could see the crack, but the screw was still in place and holding the bone together. It was really comforting to know my wrist was still intact and it completely changed my mindset. If the wrist was holding up okay, and I could grit my way through the pain, why not keep going? I was already a few stages down, with five left to go. Sure, five stages still meant thousands more kilometres, but thanks to that X-ray it didn't feel impossible. I decided to stop setting goals. No more 'just get to this day' or 'just focus on the finish', I'd just take the old-fashioned day-at-a-time approach. I'd get through as many days as possible, and if the day came that I had to quit, then so be it.

The mental boost I'd got from the X-ray quickly disappeared when the second week kicked off. The pain had been manageable up to that point, but I felt like I was beginning to lose control of it. The whole thing was like a terrible rollercoaster. I'd wake up each day and my wrist would be fine after a night's rest. Maybe today it will be okay, I'd think. I'd feel all right during the morning liaison with the makeshift cruise control on, but once I was in the competitive stage it was agony. After half an hour, my fingers would start to go numb and I'd worry about carpal tunnel and intersection syndrome. Fast forward to the evening and I'd be in absolute pain, questioning what the hell I was doing to myself.

Stage 7 was a real challenge. The timed section was long (323 kilometres), fast and rough. I didn't help myself by taking a bit of a tumble off the bike and landing on my wrist. It was the sort of silly mistake I just couldn't afford to make.

The worst part of the injury was that it was my throttle hand. In the choppy sections I was literally riding one-handed; I'd have to take my hand off the throttle and roll over bumps and whoops. The riskiest thing you can do in whoops and choppy bumps is back off, because that's when the bike gets messy and you can very rapidly lose control of it.

And when you lose control, the only way to fix it is to wind on some throttle. I couldn't do that, my wrist just wasn't up to it. It was bloody dangerous.

By the time I got to the end of that stage, I was done. I couldn't take it anymore. Forget about what the X-ray had looked like on the rest day, I could feel that I was doing serious damage to myself. It just wasn't worth it. And the less throttle control I had, the more I was worried about having a big crash. On the liaison back to the Bivouac I decided it was over, I couldn't put up with it any longer. It was a huge call because, despite having not won a stage, I'd worked my way into the top three and I was only eight-and-a-half minutes off the lead.

When I arrived at the Bivouac I was honest with the team. 'I think I'm done, I reckon this is my last day.' The crew understood completely. They hadn't expected me to make the start, let alone reach Stage 7. For them it was a win I'd made it that far. We agreed that the team would prep the bike for the next day, and I'd go and get treated by the doctor and then get some rest. We'd make a final decision in the morning. I went back to the camper and the doctor gave my wrist a light massage to try and get some blood moving. That's about everything we could do, that and take some paracetamol, which was doing fuck all.

When Sam returned to the camper I was sitting there pretty despondent, in a hell of a lot of pain and over the whole thing. I was sick of it. I felt stupid for even being there in the first place.

'Mate, you've done seven days,' said Sam. 'I don't want to tell you to man up, but . . . you've only got three days left to go. You're in third place. The finish line is coming, it's almost here. If you really can't do it, fine, pull the pin. That works for me, I'll have the camper to myself. But fuck, man, you're so close.'

I thought about it for a while. I physically couldn't keep up the same pace I'd been running for the past two days, but maybe if I backed off a bit I could get to the finish. Sam and Matthias were only a couple of minutes behind me, so they were right in contention for a win. I could even give those guys a hand, make sure they had a good run to the finish so that one of them keeps the KTM winning streak alive. I felt confident about the decision. I went back out to see the boys. 'You know what?' I told them. 'Stuff what I said. Sammy's given me a spray and I've pulled my head out of my arse. I'll stop being a sook. Get the bike ready and we'll sack up and go again tomorrow.' In two hours I'd gone from a firm decision to quit, to committing myself to another three days of torture.

I got through Stage 8 and when Ricky Brabec's Honda blew its motor to bits, I found myself leading the rally by a minute over Pablo. Which was great, except for the fact I felt like there was a flaming sword sticking out of my right wrist. But what could I do? There was no way I was going to quit now that I was in the lead.

Before we even got on the road for Stage 9, the race took a complex turn. At the end of Stage 8 there were basically six riders right in contention. I was leading over Pablo, and

Matthias and Sam were third and fourth, both six minutes behind. Adrien van Beveren from Yamaha was fifth, ten minutes behind me; Kevin Benavides from Honda, 20. But there were some big penalties at the end of the stage. Kevin had three hours added to his time after race officials found he was carrying additional notes with him on the stage. That took him out of the running. And poor Sam copped an hour on his time because the officials thought he'd been messing with his Iritrack system when it wouldn't work at the start of the stage. There was a theory that he'd purposely broken it so he didn't have to be first out. Of course that was bullshit, he'd just blown a fuse. But the officials weren't buying it and he was penalised.

That left four of us in contention. It was up to me and Matthias to keep KTM's streak alive, and Pablo and Adrien to try and end it. It was more important than ever that I stuck with it, so Matthias wasn't left on his own in this battle at the front.

I expected the others to easily overhaul me on the ninth stage but, amazingly, it didn't happen. We started in groups of ten for the 313-kilometre loop in and out of Pisco, so I could just kind of keep pace and hang with the others. Adrien retired late in the stage with an engine failure, while Sam, Pablo and I basically finished where we started.

It set up an incredible final stage. I was one minute ahead of Pablo. *One.* You can lose a minute by backing off to check on a note. You can lose a minute by overshooting a corner. Any mistake you make out on a stage will cost you at least

60 seconds. Matthias was only six minutes behind me as well, so it was a three-way fight . . . if I made it to the start of the Stage 10. I was still on the absolute edge of throwing in the towel. I was in excruciating pain. Again, Sam came to my rescue with some stern words in the motorhome. 'Dude, you already know you're going to need more surgery. Whether you leave today or battle through to the end. The damage is done. Your wrist is fucked. But if you keep going, you might win. You'll definitely end on the podium. At least you'll have something cool to talk about while you're recovering. Just finish the damn race.'

He was right. Stopping wasn't going to fix my wrist. Once I got home this thing was going to be pinned, plated, the whole deal. I was facing a lengthy stint off the bike, anyway, so I might as well make it count and try to win this rally.

The good news was that the blast from Pisco to the finish in Lima was relatively short. I only had to get through 112 kilometres of competitive stage. I was certain I could physically make it to the end, but I was convinced Pablo would run me down. A one-minute lead just wasn't enough. The six minutes to Matthias I might manage, but one minute? No way. It was a reverse start for that final stage, so we were the three last bikes out. The rest of the field would leave tracks for us to follow, so I knew we wouldn't be looking at our roadbooks. I couldn't take it easy and hope that Pablo would make a mistake and got lost along the way. The pace would be high and the scope for a navigational blunder was very low. I didn't stand a chance.

The bikes all took off one by one until, eventually, it was just me and Pablo left at the start. I was sitting right behind him, watching him, as he waited to head out into the stage. I couldn't believe how fresh he seemed, how much energy he had. He was bouncing around on the seat, jumping up and down, revving the shit out of the bike. It was like he was at the starting gate of a motocross race, looking for the holeshot in a 40-bike field. He looked like someone who was on Day 1 of the Dakar Rally, not Day 10.

He looked ready to go out there and rip me a new one. Destroy me.

It was no accident. Pablo knew I had my eye on him, and I have no doubt his antics were to try and get under my skin. And it worked a treat. I was beyond my physical and mental limits, I could barely move my wrist enough to twist the throttle. He'd beaten me right there and then on the start line. As he blasted off into the stage at a million kilometres an hour, I sat there completely resigned to finishing second. And to be honest I was fine with it. I still couldn't quite believe I'd got that far.

I pulled up the line and watched the clock count down. Five, four, three, two, one, GO. Once I dropped the clutch and took off, all my concerns about the result vanished. I was in my own little world, not thinking about anything except riding the bike and the pain from my wrist. All I could do was follow the tracks in front of me and keep focussed on the dunes. The last thing I could afford to do was take the wrong line and have a hard drop off a ledge somewhere. My wrist was hanging on by a thread and a big landing would finish me off.

I got about ten kilometres into the stage and there was a long stretch of sand. It looked completely flat and boy, was I happy to see it. I needed that opportunity to relax a bit and rest my arm. As I was ripping across this stretch, I noticed there was a helicopter parked on the ground up ahead of me. That was weird. The media helicopters were usually in the air filming while the stage was underway. The only other possibility was that it was a medical helicopter.

From what I could see on the roadbook the track went straight towards the helicopter, so I just kept going. As I approached it, I started to veer to the right of the track so I could ride around where it had landed. I got closer and closer when suddenly an alarm went off on my Iritrack. It scared the shit out of me! I thought I'd gone into a speed zone without realising and I was about to throw the race away with a penalty. I slammed on the brakes and looked at the roadbook, but there was nothing about a speed zone. I rolled over a gentle crest and then it hit me. This stretch wasn't as flat as it appeared from the bike. By moving to the right to avoid the helicopter, I'd missed a steep ledge over a dune.

There, at the bottom of the ledge, was a crashed bike. It looked like a nasty accident, so I immediately headed that way to see if I could help. Given the helicopter was already there and there were medicos on the ground, I was under no sporting obligation to stop, but it's human nature. I couldn't just keep going knowing someone was hurt. I could see from a distance that it was a white bike, but it wasn't until I got much closer that I realised it was Pablo. I looked back and I could see what had happened. He'd thought the ground was flat, dropped off that bank at full speed, bottomed-out the suspension on landing and gone flying off the bike. It could have so easily been me. I thought it was a flat stretch with no ledges too, and there was nothing in the roadbook to suggest otherwise. That's the danger of riding through dunes. They change shape so quickly, literally overnight. The roadbook can only tell you so much. If I'd ridden over that ledge and landed like Pablo did, who knows what sort of permanent, life-changing damage it would have done to my wrist. The only thing that saved me was the fact that Pablo did it first.

When I got to the crash scene, I wasn't thinking about what this meant for the rally. I was in shock, and I was desperately hoping Pablo was all right. I pulled up in a cloud of sand and asked the medicos what was going on. 'He's fine,' one of them told me. 'You don't need to stop, we've got it sorted.'

It wasn't until I got going again that it actually dawned on me. That was the bloke I was racing against. He's out. If I make it to the finish, I'm going to win the Dakar Rally. I was 100 kilometres from the end, and for the very first time I started to think about winning. I'd been leading for two days, but I'd never thought about actually taking the crown. I felt like I was going to burst with excitement, but it was too early for that. I was barely ten kilometres into the stage, there was plenty of time to make a mistake. I shut the excitement out and refocussed on the task at hand – getting to the finish.

The rest of the stage went well. I hit all of my waypoints and I looked after my wrist. When I was close to the finish, I had a moment of panic. I thought I'd missed a waypoint somewhere, but I had no idea why. I hadn't seen the arrow that shows up on the GPS when you miss a waypoint, but I was convinced something was wrong. I stopped and scrolled back through the GPS. Every waypoint was checked off. And the next waypoint was the finish line. I continued the route, which wound its way through a valley, where there was about eight kilometres of fast, wide-open track. At the end of the valley, I turned left to go back into the dunes. I looked at the roadbook and I was two kilometres from the finish. I had the same feeling I'd had at the end of the 2016 Dakar – another few hundred metres and I'd be close enough to push the bike if I had to.

Now was the time to get excited. I was going to win the Dakar. I could see the Bivouac. I could see the crowd. I could see the finish line. What the hell is about to happen?

I went through the two panels at the finish, and I felt like all the emotion was immediately sucked out of me. I felt nothing, it was like a dream. I had a real-life moment where I thought I was about to wake up and it would have all been in my head. It was impossible to comprehend that I'd won the Dakar Rally with a broken scaphoid.

Everything was a blur. I did a couple of interviews and then walked over to the team. The crew were all just standing there, looking at me in complete shock. None of us could work out how it had happened. They were speechless. I was speechless. It was the 18th consecutive Dakar win for KTM and, even better, we locked out the podium. Matthias finished second and, after having his penalty reversed on the last day, Sam was classified in third. It was particularly important to me to share the podium with Sam. He had pushed me through the rally. There were times when I was broken and he would put me back together. I owed my win to those nights in the camper when he kept my spirits up. At the finish he grabbed me and said, 'See, I told you to keep pushing. You're not human, dude'.

Once the initial excitement wore off, I felt human. I was in so much pain. When we were on the podium they handed me the latest Felix, and I couldn't even hold it above my head. I just wasn't strong enough.

It was a shame Pablo wasn't on the podium with me. He broke his ankle badly in that crash, but hats off to him, he got back on the bike and rode the last 100 kilometres to the finish. He dropped to fourth overall but, man, he could hold his head up high. He was going for his first Dakar win and he didn't leave anything on the table. He gave it everything he had, and you have to admire that.

As we rode off the ramp I looked at Felix and thought about how I could barely hold the trophy. How did I get through an entire Dakar Rally like this? The mind can make the body do extraordinary things if it focuses hard enough on an outcome.

***

During the rally, just after the rest day, I'd made a bet with my teammate and friend Laia Sanz. She's a one of a kind, Laia, and it's amazing what she can do on a bike. She gets out there and hands it to the boys on the Dakar, it's incredible. Laia goes to me, 'You know, I reckon you can win this, even with a broken wrist.'

'There's no way in the world,' I said. 'It's not possible.'

'Well, if you do win the race . . . I get to give you a haircut. And I'm going to shave off your mullet.'

Sometimes I feel like I'm known better for my mullet than riding bikes, so the stakes were pretty high. But at that point I genuinely believed I didn't have a hope in hell of winning the race.

'Yeah, go for it. It ain't going to happen, so that's perfectly fine.'

Laia wasn't done there, either.

'I'll make a bet too. If I finish in the Top Fifteen, you can kiss me.'

'What? For real?'

'Yep. I'll even put it in writing.'

The next thing, there was a napkin out and we were working through a 'contract'. To be totally clear, Laia had a boyfriend. She made that bet because she didn't think there was any chance she would be one of the Top 15 riders. Looking back on it, it was a weird bet. I guess we were all sleep deprived and going a bit loopy.

It was meant to be an inside joke, but the Red Bull Media House guys were there when we were writing the napkin contract and joking around about the terms and conditions. The whole thing blew up. There was real media hype about this stupid joke we'd made sitting around the Bivouac one night.

Once the genie was out of the bottle, there was no getting it back in. Fast forward to the finish and not only did I win, but Laia finished 11th. We'd both lost our bets. I'd just won the Dakar Rally with a broken scaphoid, and the first question I got when I crossed the line was, 'When is the haircut? And when are you two going to make out?'

I didn't actually think I'd have to go through with it, but I soon realised I didn't have much choice. The napkin was a binding contract and the mullet was coming off, whether I liked it or not. Even worse, Laia's boyfriend was there at the finish line. *Great*, I thought. *I'm going to lose my hair and get knocked out all in one go*. At least I had a Dakar trophy.

As soon as we got to the Red Bull tent after the trophy presentation, out came a pair of clippers that someone had bought in Peru. Laia started at the front and shaved off most of my hair as she worked her way towards the mullet – only for the clippers to run out of juice before she got there. Nobody had bothered to charge them up. 'That's it,' I said. 'That's God's way of telling us the mullet has to stay.' Most of the mullet survived, but boy, was I left with a rude-looking haircut.

Next up was her end of the bet. I looked over my shoulder and there was the boyfriend. I was in enough pain with my wrist, I didn't need a broken nose too. I decided to be a gentleman and give her a kiss on the hand, like the Queen of the Dakar that she is. I let a few people down by not honouring the bet in full, but whatever. It was still a good laugh, which is all it was ever meant to be.

Reflecting on that 2019 event, it dawned on me that every time I went to Dakar not thinking about winning, just trying to survive, I got a result. When I competed there as the reigning champion in 2017 and tried too hard, I crashed out. I genuinely believe that you can't try and win the Dakar. It doesn't matter if you've done all the prep work and you've got a great bike underneath you. Your frame of mind has to be about survival, not victory. You've got to get through the 10,000 kilometres before you worry about whether you're first or last. There's so much you have no control over. It sounds corny, but the Dakar gods will have their say at some point.

Unlike my first Dakar win, there was no time for long celebrations or holidays. I knew my wrist was in a bad way, so within hours of crossing the finish line I booked an appointment to see Dr Steve Andrews, an upper limb specialist in Brisbane. The next morning I was on a plane home. I landed a day later, spent another day at home unpacking and getting my feet back on the ground, and then saw Dr Andrews. He did a couple of X-rays and scans, and as soon as they were up on the lightboard he shook his head and said, 'Yeah, this doesn't look good. You're falling apart. We need to do more surgery and we have to do it soon.'

It was no surprise to me. I knew there was terrible news coming. It would have been a full-on miracle if it had somehow held on through ten days of bashing through the Peruvian desert. He was only confirming what I already knew.

Basically the screw that Dr Mir had put in my wrist in Barcelona had turned into a windscreen wiper, wearing away bone as it moved back and forth. It had broken the bone apart, it was just floating there in pieces. The screw wasn't doing anything. 'This is going to be complicated,' Dr Andrews said. 'I don't know how you were able hold onto a bike; you shouldn't even be able to hold a coffee cup! Your wrist won't be quite the same, but we'll get you back on a motorcycle. It will just take a while.'

Before I knew it, I was on the operating table. The only way to fix it was to put in a new screw at a different angle, then take a bone graft from my hip and use that to build the scaphoid back to the shape it needed to be. After that, it was all about getting good blood flow to the bone so that the graft would take and the injury would heal.

The surgery meant I was a bit banged up for my traditional Australia Day party. I always try and get back home from Dakar by Australia Day so I can have a few friends and family over and blow off some steam, whether I've had a positive result or a negative one. Given I was fresh off from surgery, I had to behave a little. No jet skis in the swimming pool or anything like that. But we still gave it a good shake. We took the shoey to a whole new level by doing what we called booties – drinking beer out of a ten-day-old riding boot. The fungus inside of that thing can't have been good for us.

Chaz Mostert, Supercars driver extraordinaire and one of my close mates, made a mess of my kitchen tiles at that party. He decided he wanted to feel like a Dakar winner, so he began chucking some of my gear on. The next thing he'd fired up one of my bikes. He started the bike up easily enough, so I figured he knew a thing or two about dirt bikes. Suddenly he was wheeling the thing through my house with the engine bashing on the rev limiter. I didn't realise he'd clicked it into gear until he got onto the tiles, dropped the clutch and did a burnout. I only found out later that the guy has no idea about bikes. If he'd accidentally dropped the clutch while he was walking it through the house, it would've taken off and gone through a wall.

Chaz got in a bit of hot water for it the next day, and it had nothing to do with my tiles. Someone posted a pic of him on my bike, dressed in all my Red Bull riding gear, on social media. He was sponsored by a rival energy drink at the time and it did not go down well.

I'm always adamant that winning the 2019 Dakar was worth the damage I did to my wrist. But I paid a price for that trophy, no doubt about it. As Dr Andrews warned, my wrist isn't what it used to be. I've lost some movement, and you can see it when I'm on the bike these days. I have to drop my elbow on the throttle side to compensate. I can't imagine my wrist will age well, either. I guess I'll have some pretty gnarly arthritis to deal with in the not-too-distant future.

I often get asked if I'd ever take that same level of risk with an injury to win a Dakar again. The honest answer is yes.

16
Paulo

I basically spent the first half of 2019 recuperating from the post-Dakar surgery. I wasn't on a bike at all.

We made a decision pretty early on that, even if my recovery was tracking well, it would be too risky to tackle the Finke Desert Race on two wheels. I wanted the best chance of being fully fit for Dakar 2020 and that meant playing it safe.

It was a bummer not to be able to go for a seventh title on the bike, but I still had the trophy truck. You can drive one of those things one-handed, so I decided to get back out there and see if I could finally get that elusive win on four wheels.

Being able to focus solely on the truck made life a lot easier. We absolutely went for it, we were as prepared as you could possibly be. From the moment we got to Alice Springs we were ticking boxes. My navigator Jason Duncan and I topped the prologue, so we were first on the road for the Alice–Finke leg. And we had a dream run out there too.

I crossed the line in Finke in an hour and 44 minutes, which left us with nearly eight minutes clear of the rest of the field.

The crew went over the truck that night and it was perfect. No leaks, no issues, nothing. All evening people kept congratulating me, telling me we were definitely going to win. I kept saying things like, 'Nah, there's a long way to go,' but deep down, I had to admit it tasted like a win was coming. I really started to believe it was going to happen.

But it didn't. When we got near the 150-kilometre mark on the run back to Alice I began to hear something. We were cruising along, not pushing at all, so I thought maybe it was my mind playing tricks on me. The next thing I lost drive. The truck blew a third member and tore all of the gears out of its rear end. There was nothing we could do to fix it there in the desert. Jason and I sat on the side of the track for a while and watched everyone else race past.

That one really hurt. We'd gone close in the truck before, but not that close. Everything was brand new in the truck; the rear end had only done a limited number of kilometres in testing. The longer I sat next to the broken-down truck, the more I wanted to take a match to it and burn it to the ground. The helicopter couldn't come fast enough to take us back to Alice Springs.

When we returned to camp, there wasn't much else to do but drown our sorrows. We gave it a good shake as well. I remember sticking Jason to a palm tree with cling wrap at one point. But it was all just to mask the disappointment. It was a tough one to swallow, it haunts me to this day.

Once I was back from Finke it was time to start ramping up my training on the bike. It was important for me to get a feel for where the wrist was at. If we needed to do any clean-up surgery, I wanted there to be plenty of time before the Dakar. Luckily it all felt pretty all right and I could plot my return to competition.

I made my comeback at the Atacama Rally in Chile, South America, in September, which was the penultimate round of the FIM Cross-Country Rallies World Championship. I hadn't looked at a roadbook since January and my wrist was still a little tender so I just worked my way into the event. I started off somewhere near the back of the Top 10 on Stage 1 and then worked my way forward. I was fourth fastest on Stage 2 and fourth again on Stage 3, which was the first leg of a marathon.

My KTM teammate Sam Sunderland, who was fighting for both the round win and the world championship, hit a rock and bent a rear brake disc on that third stage. Because it was a marathon we had no access to spare parts between stages, so I gave him my straight rear disc and used his bent one the next day. It wasn't ideal but I was still able to take the stage win. Leading the way through the dunes on the final day wasn't easy, but my main job was to support Sam. He finished second for the rally and secured the world title. I was absolutely stoked for him.

Next up was the world championship season finale, the Rallye du Maroc, in Africa in the first week of October. I made good headway, but the new roadbook system we used for the rally wasn't great. If you were one of the first few bikes on the stage it was tough going. I really struggled with navigation on Stage 2 and then, starting back in the pack, won Stage 3. I was absolutely nowhere on Stage 4 and then won Stage 5. It was that kind of rally. I finished fourth overall, which was pretty all right.

A few weeks later I found myself in Mexico once again for another crack at the Baja 1000. After the disappointment of our first attempt, all I wanted was to get through the event and make the finish. I was meant to team up with Jesse Jones like last time, but before we got there he crashed off a scooter and busted up his leg. He couldn't drive, but he still wanted his truck to race. After a last-minute scramble we managed to get Nasser Al-Attiyah out from Dubai to replace Jesse. Nasser is one of the top rally racers in the world on four wheels, a four-time world champion and a three-time Dakar winner. But he arrived in Ensenada with zero trophy truck and Baja experience. That made me the 'seasoned' one in our team, and yeah, I'd done the Baja before but I was hardly a truck guru. With the Finke disaster fresh in my mind, I still felt unsure about how hard to push in one of these things. It's a fine line between being too slow and beating the shit out of the machine.

Jesse had built a brand new Mason all-wheel-drive truck for the race, it hadn't even hit the dirt until we got to Mexico. It was an absolute weapon with over 1000 horsepower. All-wheel-drive technology was the new thing to have in trophy trucks, but boy, it made the trucks expensive. About double the cost of a two-wheel-drive truck. It was a big investment from Jesse, but he really wanted a good Baja result.

We weren't considered contenders going into the race. We weren't there for qualifying, which meant we had to start right at the back of the field. I think we were the third-last truck over the line. We were going to have to deal with the dust and slower cars and all the other madness that you encounter when you're down the order.

But the weather was on our side. Three days before the race this huge storm rolled through Mexico and washed half the track away. There was a mad rush to repair sections of the track and plot new courses around the flooding. The start was delayed by a day and, for the most part, everyone's course notes were rendered useless. That was great for us; we'd done a lot less pre-running than most, so it levelled the playing field.

Suddenly, running from the back of the order was an advantage. The moisture would neutralise the dust factor and the rest of the trucks would clear the water out of the holes and ruts. We had the front-runners offering to buy our starting position, everyone wanted to go from the back. But we weren't giving it up for anything.

I was in the truck for the first stint. My job was to keep it clean and hand the truck over to Nasser in one piece. That's it. Without going nuts I got through almost 840 kilometres, picking off other trucks whenever I had a chance. I think I was close to the top four by the time we stopped for the driver change.

Once Nasser was in the truck he went ballistic, he was so quick. He crossed the line third on the road and we were classified second on corrected time. In the same year I'd stood on the Dakar podium I was now on the Baja podium. I was ecstatic, particularly after what had happened at Finke. It took plenty of people by surprise too – everyone was buzzing. There was a sense of redemption, I guess, given we'd failed to even make it to the finish three years earlier. But more than that, it was nice to pay Jesse back for his faith and investment in us.

When we got to Saudi Arabia in the lead-up to the Dakar a few weeks later, there were lots of riders asking about Baja. I mean, guys like Stéphane Peterhansel, Cyril Despres, Sebastien Loeb, Carlos Sainz . . . huge names in the rally and Dakar world. They all wanted to know what the event was like and how to go about getting a drive over there. They'd been wanting to do it for years but never had the opportunity. To think that the Baja 1000 was on the bucket list for all of these legends, and I'd been there and done it a couple of times, made me really appreciate how lucky I am.

After Baja I flew back to Australia for a few weeks to try to sort out some things on the home front. When I won my first Dakar in 2016 I bought a five-bedroom house on the Gold Coast, a beautiful place right on the water. It had a pool, its own jetty and pontoon so you can walk straight out and jump on a boat or jet ski, the lot. But because of all the travel I never really had a chance to enjoy it. I hadn't used the pool. I didn't own a boat. I did have a jet ski, but

I barely touched it in four years. The whole place was going to waste.

I also needed somewhere to keep all my tools and toys, so I bought a warehouse building. I decided I would fit the upstairs offices out as living quarters and move in there. I wanted to be able to work on my cars and bikes until ten at night, walk upstairs, jump in the shower and go straight to bed. I didn't need a big luxurious house. After 14 years of living in a caravan, an apartment above a workshop was enough luxury for me. The fit-out on the offices started just before Christmas and my plan was to move in once I got back from Dakar in January. I was already renting out a couple of the rooms in the house, I'd just rent out my room as well.

Meanwhile, my parents had spent the last few years managing a property in Singleton. That contract ran out at the end of 2019 and their plan was to be nomads, living in a caravan with no fixed address. That didn't sit well with me. After all the sacrifices they'd made for me when I was younger, I saw another opportunity to give something back to them. I'd been looking to hire a full-time mechanic to take care of my bikes and the trophy truck. And I always needed help with both my life and business admin. So I basically offered them both jobs and told them to move into the workshop with me. I'm not sure how many 30-plus-year-old two-time Dakar winners still live with their parents, but I do. To be honest it's the perfect arrangement for all of us.

Dad wears a lot of hats, from mechanic to truck driver. When I head off to go racing Dad says, 'Just leave me a list of what needs doing. When I get home he'll have gone through the entire thing, and there'll be a practice bike freshly prepped and ready to go. He'll normally come out with me on practice runs as well, just in case I come off the bike and need to be scooped into the car and taken to hospital. Mum runs the office for me. She handles all my administration and makes sure the bills are paid on time.

It's made my life so much easier and has opened the door for bigger and more ambitious projects. It's a bit of an insurance policy too; there's some pretty expensive gear in that factory and I like to know there are people I can trust keeping an eye on it all while I'm away.

Right after Christmas I was off to Saudi Arabia, the new home of the Dakar Rally.

After all those years in South America, heading to Saudi in the Middle East was a new experience for everyone. We didn't quite know what to expect. But I arrived in the port city Jeddah, feeling fit and in fine form, confident that I could have a solid crack at hanging on to that #1 plate.

The Dakar got off to a weird, but ultimately good, start. It was all smooth sailing for the first 140 kilometres of the rally before my roadbook started to get jammed. A small rubber piece which spins the roadbook snapped and then fed itself in between the paper and the rollers. Eventually it stretched the paper and tore the roadbook in half.

Fortunately for me my KTM teammate Matthias Walkner, who'd started in front, had a few dramas and I caught up to him. I latched onto the back of his bike and stayed there for the rest of the stage. If he'd got away from me at any point, I would have been lost and in big trouble. I thought we were just cruising – we'd all agreed before the stage that we didn't want to win and have to be first out the next day. But we didn't judge our pace right, went too quick and I headed to bed on the first night with a two-minute lead over Honda's Ricky Brabec.

The second stage was a strange one. Usually on the Dakar you get the roadbook for the next day as soon as you finish a stage. It means you can have a good look, mark some things out with highlighters and feel nice and prepared for the upcoming stage. But in 2020 the organisers decided that for six of the 12 stages we'd only get the roadbook in the morning, 25 minutes before the start. Not only did I have very limited time with the roadbook, I was first out on the stage too, so I had nothing to follow. And it was the first leg of a marathon.

It was a tricky combination of factors and it meant I had to be conservative. I just looked after the bike, tried to limit navigational mistakes and got to the end in one piece. I came in ninth, seven-and-a-half minutes behind new leader Sam Sunderland.

I had a better road position for Stage 3, but it turned out to be another shocker. An issue with the GPS meant some of us couldn't find a waypoint near the end of the stage. I got lost looking for it and dropped about 20 minutes. The organisers rightly decided to not count the last 38 kilometres, which moved me up to sixth in the overall standings and around 12 minutes off the lead.

I had a pretty quiet run through Stage 4, finishing about where I started in terms of the overall standings. We spent most of that stage on these tricky, rocky roads. I expected Saudi Arabia to be nothing but sand, so it was surprising to spend so much time riding over rocks. For Stage 5 we continued on fast, rocky tracks before heading back to the dunes about midway through. It was a bittersweet day for us: I had a great run, winning the stage and ending up second overall, nine minutes down on Ricky, but poor Sam came off the bike and had to be airlifted to hospital. He broke his shoulder and some vertebrae but was generally okay. It could have been a lot worse.

Stage 6, the last before the rest day, definitely belonged to Ricky and the Honda crew. To put it frankly, it was a kick in the guts for us. Opening the road was bad enough, but then, late in the stage, the bib mousse – which is a solid foam tube we run inside the tyre – let go on me. I tried to keep going on what was effectively a flat rear tyre but eventually it rolled off the rim and got tangled in the back end of the bike. I couldn't move, I was stranded.

I laid the bike on its side, grabbed some tools and pulled out the axle. My plan was to get the rim and tyre out, then put the rims, sans tyre, back on the bike and see if I could keep going. It was a long shot, but they're the risks you take on the Dakar.

While I was doing that, Andrew Short, who was riding for the Husqvarna factory team, pulled up to see if I needed a hand. While we weren't technically teammates, we were kind of connected through the common ownership of the two brands. And, mechanically, the KTM and the Husqvarna are identical bikes. Shorty had had a bad start to the rally and was already out of contention. Being the rad, down-to-earth guy he is, he said, 'My race is done anyway, I'm happy to help keep you in the race. You take my tyre and I'll ride back on your rim. If we get any strife, from the teams we'll deal with it later.'

Once we'd swapped wheels I pushed pretty hard through the last 40-odd kilometres to try to make back some time, but I still dropped 13 minutes and slipped to third, a full 25 minutes behind Ricky. In second was my old mate Pablo Quintanilla, but even he had a 20-minute gap to the leader. KTM's winning streak was starting to look vulnerable. This was fast becoming Honda's race to lose.

After the rest day in Riyadh, the second week kicked off with a long competitive stage, nearly 550 kilometres, down to Wadi ad-Dawasir. It was the longest stage there'd been on the Dakar in five years. Because of my Stage 6 dramas I started back in the pack, and all I remember is that the stage was fast. Crazy fast. We were basically pinned all day.

It was so fast that it tested the fuel range of the bike; when I got to the 200-kilometre refuelling zone I was running on fumes. It's always tough for a while after a fuel stop. When the motorcycle is close to empty it feels great, so light and agile. And then you stick 32 litres of fuel in the thing and its dynamics change entirely. You feel like you're riding a cruise ship.

By the time I reached the stop I was running behind Paulo Gonçalves. As I was just finishing refuelling he took off back into the stage and, about four minutes later, I went after him. The track quickly wound its way down to a long, flat piste between the dunes. It was mostly hard compacted ground but there were some soft spots too. It was wide open, full gas. As I started to come to a bit of a crest the ground changed from being quite moist to feeling more solid. Just before I hit the top of the crest my Iritrack went off.

I slowed right down and checked out the tower to see what was going on. When I looked back up I could see a bike that appeared as if it had exploded. There were parts and bits and pieces lying everywhere. As I came down the other side of the crest there was a square, hard-edged wall. I pulled up next to the crashed bike and Paulo wasn't too far away from it. I knew immediately that it wasn't a good situation. It was going to be a tough few minutes.

I hit the red button on my bike, then hit the red button on Paulo's bike. I needed to get the medical helicopter there as quickly as possible. I went over to Paulo and he was completely unresponsive. I checked for vital signs and couldn't find anything.

I had a tremendously bad feeling about what I was seeing and the panic quickly washed over me. I ran to my bike and frantically tried to call the control centre on the Iritrack. I was rattled, I felt like his life was in my hands. But there was no life there anymore.

I finally got through on the radio. 'You need to get someone here ASAP!' I shouted. 'We're in big trouble.' Or something like that. I'm not sure I made that much sense, to be honest, but surely the alarm in my voice told the story.

They had the location, so it was just a case of waiting for the helicopter. A minute or so later, privateer KTM rider Štefan Svitko pulled up and I screamed at him to call the control centre as well. I just wanted to keep things moving. Then I completely shut down for a minute or two. I didn't know what to do, I didn't know how to help. I just froze. There was too much happening and nothing I could do. I was desperate for the helicopter to arrive, but at the same time I knew what the doctors were going to say when they got there. I knew this was the last time I was ever going to see Paulo.

Stefan and I tried to do some chest compressions on Paolo, but it didn't help. We were too late. I mean, I was four minutes behind Paulo on the road. He'd spent four minutes lying there all on his own.

Eight minutes after I got to the scene the helicopter arrived. The paramedics burst into action and spent a good 45 minutes working on him. But there was nothing they could do, either. They called the time and that was it. I don't really know how to describe it except to say it was shit.

As they loaded Paulo into the helicopter, I had that familiar feeling: why do I put my family through this? Paulo wasn't going home to his family. And, like any of these crashes, it could so easily have been me. The race wasn't on my mind at all, I couldn't process anything like that. I was rocked to my core. I'd lost good friends before, but I'd never been there on the scene. I'd never had somebody's life slip through my hands like that.

I sat down in the sand, and as the adrenaline wore off it really hit me that Paulo was gone. He was such a lovely, easy-going guy. He was a bit older, from the generation of Dakar riders before mine, but he was one of the real heroes. I shared my first Dakar podium with him and Marc Coma in 2015. Even though he rode for a rival team, I spent a lot of time with him. Every time he saw me in the Bivouac, he'd come right over to say hello and have a joke and a laugh. We weren't best friends, we didn't chat on the phone weekly, but he was a mate, a competitor and someone I looked up to a lot.

It took me about an hour and a half to get back on the bike. I didn't care about the race, but I couldn't just sit out there in the desert all day. I had to return to the Bivouac. A lot of cars and bikes had gone past us by then, and we hadn't let anybody else stop at the crash scene. They didn't need to know what was going on and we didn't need a crowd. Anyway, it meant there was a visible line on the ground I could follow through to the end of the stage. I wasn't even rolling the roadbook or checking the GPS or hitting waypoints, I just rode to the finish. To be honest I don't really remember much about the ride back, I was completely numb. I vaguely remember thinking about how Paulo was gone and the world was still spinning, which made the

Dakar feel so unimportant. Was trying to win this thing really worth the risk? If you die trying, the world will go on without you.

By the time I reached the Bivouac the news had got around. I rode into the tent, handed the bike off to the crew and went straight to the camper. I sat in my gear for about an hour. Normally you try and get that dirty, sweaty stuff off as quickly as possible, but I didn't have the energy to get changed. Sam had already gone home because of the crash, so I was on my own in the camper. That first hour I just needed to sit there on my own, to try and process everything.

After a while I reluctantly ventured out of the camper. It was a sombre mood in the paddock. The media crews wanted to talk to me but I told them to piss off and leave me alone. I wasn't the only one hurting, Paulo's death had rocked the Bivouac. But I was one of the very few who had been there and seen it first-hand.

At that point I had no idea if I was going to finish the race or not. All I knew was that there was no way I'd be able to get up the next morning and hop back on the bike. Everyone was rallying to get Stage 8 cancelled as a sign of respect for Paulo. We all needed a day off to get our heads around things a bit more. Thankfully the organisers agreed.

The following day I started to open up a bit. I had to talk about it, maybe even try to understand it a little, if I was going to get to the end of the race. What really blew me away on the day off was the wave of support from Portugal, Paulo's homeland. It was a difficult time for the Portuguese fans, they'd lost one of their sporting heroes. But the support they gave me . . . it felt like I'd been adopted by another country.

I decided to put the heartache to the side and continue the Dakar. It sounds cheesy, but that's what Paulo would have wanted.

I got the time I'd spent at the crash scene on Stage 7 taken off, so I went into the last four stages sitting fourth overall, just under 29 minutes off the lead.

Stage 9 took us into Saudi's Empty Quarter (Rub'al Khali) desert. I had a pretty clean run and ended the day second behind Pablo, but Ricky was in cruise mode, protecting his huge lead. I had a plan to finish further down the order on Stage 10 so I could have a real crack at the leaders on the last two days, but that was ruined when the stage was shortened due to strong winds and I was credited with the fourth-best time.

Between my road position, and the fact that so much of the stages was wide open throttle, it was going to be impossible to chase down Ricky unless he had a problem. On Stage 11 I almost ran out of fuel, getting into the service park with less than a litre left in the tank. I pulled six minutes on Ricky, but it was a drop in the ocean – he was still 22 minutes down the road. I did, however, move back into third overall, after Honda's Joan Barreda was handed a penalty for changing his engine.

The final stage was a 447-kilometre run from Haradh to the ceremonial finish in Al-Qiddiya. I gave it everything, but Ricky was just too far ahead. I finished third on the stage and third for the rally. It wasn't a win, but considering everything that had happened I was proud to get to the finish. And I'd kept my own little streak alive – four Dakar finishes and four Dakar podiums. But KTM's amazing winning streak was over after 18 years.

We were all immensely proud of the winning streak, and there was a hint of disappointment it had reached its end. But after Paulo's death it wasn't something any of us were in the mood to dwell on. To be honest, the sport needed it. Big races like the Dakar thrive on rivalries and having the same team win over and over again is a bit of a buzzkill. Anyway, 18 in a row was a heck of a haul. I don't think I'll see a manufacturer go on a streak like that again in my lifetime. It was an honour to be part of it.

I'll never forget those eight minutes with Paolo. The longest eight minutes of my life. I'll never forget how I was trying to do everything I could but I felt so helpless. And I'll never know for sure if I did everything right. Maybe I did something wrong. Maybe I shouldn't have touched him. Maybe I should have turned him on his side. It's a train of thought that's hard to shake. There's no doubt that experience changed me as a person. It drove me even closer to the idea that you have to appreciate the small things and the good people you have around you at any point in time.

To this day, that third-place trophy stirs up mixed feelings when I look at. On one hand, it's a constant reminder of those eight terrifying minutes in the desert. On the other, it's a tribute to an amazing man and competitor. That's why I keep it in my office, right next to my other Dakar trophies.

Being able to reflect on the positive times is worth the pain that comes with it. And it gives momentum to my own resilience in a way too. I made it to the finish of that race in the toughest circumstances I can imagine.

It means a lot to have that trophy in the cabinet.

17
Last Flight

During the first week of the Dakar, right before Paulo was killed, I was offered a drive in a trophy truck at the Parker 425 desert race in Arizona, USA, in late January 2020. I jumped at the chance and booked some flights to the States straight away.

My initial reaction after Paulo's crash was to call it off. All I really wanted to do when that Dakar was over was to go back to the Gold Coast and hide myself away from the world. But everything was already booked and my mate Reggie had organised to come with me. He'd never been to a trophy truck race in the States and he was really keen to go. I didn't want to let everyone down, so I decided to just press on. I flew from Saudi Arabia to Australia, had one day at home, and then Reggie and I jumped on a plane to the US.

It proved to be a good decision. I needed the distraction; sitting around overthinking about what had happened wouldn't have been healthy for me. It was a great trip. We finished fifth in the class in the race, and Reggie and I spent another week cruising around. A couple of mates just hanging out. It was exactly what I needed.

During that week news started to kick off about this coronavirus. Like most people, at that stage we weren't too worried. We had no idea the damage it would do or how it would change the whole world.

After our holiday we flew back to Australia and I went straight to Adelaide to race in the Stadium Super Trucks at the end of February. A week or so later I was on a plane again to Europe and then Morocco, to get a head start on testing for the 2020 world championship. My stomach churns at the idea of going to Morocco at the best of times; I don't know why, but I always manage to get sick while I'm there. I'll eat a bread roll at the hotel and, bang, I'll be crook. I often end up travelling with no spare clothes, because I can only take two bags and one is full of food and the other with riding gear. With these rumours about the virus, I was even more apprehensive than usual, but what could I do? I flew to Spain, spent a few days there and then carried on to Morocco.

I hadn't been in Morocco long when things began to ramp up with COVID-19. We still didn't think it would shut the world down, nobody did, but there was a sense that something serious was going on. There was talk that borders would start closing and we wouldn't be able to get back into Spain, let alone Australia.

We tried to carry on with testing, but each day more flights were cancelled and more countries were heading into lockdown. When France closed its borders to the rest of Europe, the team decided to call it. It was time to get out of there. The idea was that we'd all go home, let this thing blow over and then return to Morocco to finish the test. We thought it would only take weeks. A month, tops. The team decided to leave the equipment – two big trucks, two vans, eight practice bikes – in Morocco for when we got back. I think I was on the very last flight out of the country. If we'd waited even another day, we would've been stranded.

By the time I reached Dubai, Australia was starting to really crack down on its borders. And while I was in the air between Dubai and Brisbane, the Australian Government announced that all new arrivals had to do 14 days of quarantine. Nobody on that plane knew about it until we landed. I turned on my phone when we hit the tarmac and there were messages from friends and family saying, 'Hey, you won't be allowed to leave the house for two weeks'. At first, I had no idea what they were talking about. It seemed a little far-fetched. But when I got to border control I was told, 'Sorry, sir, there's been a change to the rules since your flight left Dubai. You'll have to go into quarantine.'

Cue mass confusion at the airport as everyone on the flight tried to process what was going on. There were Australian Border Force agents everywhere and we had to go through all this paperwork. At the time it was home quarantine, not in a hotel, so I had to nominate where I was going to spend the next two weeks.

It was all a bit complicated, because I had nowhere I could isolate on my own. I was still technically living at my place by the water, but I had housemates there. My new apartment at the factory was almost finished, but my parents had already moved in. At that stage we knew so little about the virus and tests weren't widely available, so I had no idea how much of a risk I might pose to other people. I didn't really want to spend four grand on a hotel room for two weeks, but I didn't want to put my housemates or parents in danger, either. I sat at the airport for an hour and a half trying to work out what to do. I rang Mum and Dad, and we agreed I'd go to the workshop and lock myself away the best I could. I spent the first week wearing a mask around any common areas in the factory, just in case I developed any symptoms. Thankfully, I hadn't caught anything on my way home.

In the weeks that followed the world was turned upside down. The restrictions on international travel got tighter and tighter, and professional sport basically ground to a halt around the globe. I didn't think the world would shut down, but it did. I assumed it would all blow over pretty quickly, but it didn't. It became clear we were dealing with a once-in-a-generation thing that was bigger than any of us could have predicted. It was a nerve-wracking time and I was uncertain about the impact it would have on my life and my career. Given my earning capacity depends so heavily on both international travel and sporting events, two things that were smashed by COVID, I was worried about the future. Would there be a Dakar in 2021? And if there was, would I be able to even get out of Australia for it?

I spent the next five months hanging out on the Gold Coast. As the initial anxiety of the pandemic started to subside, I actually began to enjoy being home. My feet had barely touched the ground in six years; I'd travel somewhere for a race or for testing, then come home for a week or so just to wash some clothes and repack my bags before boarding the next plane and leaving the country for the next three or four weeks. I felt like I'd spent most of those years sitting on a plane, so to be able to stay in one place for that long, it was a breath of fresh air. It was a chance for me to get my life back together. I could finish building the apartment at the workshop and properly move in with Mum and Dad.

It also did wonders for my enthusiasm for the sport. Injuries, Paulo's death and the general fatigue of constantly travelling had taken its toll. During the time off I really missed competing, and when it came to get going again I was extremely excited. I bet I wasn't the only sportsperson out there who felt that way about the pandemic. We all reach points in our lives where we desperately need a break, but you very rarely get the opportunity to take one without it tanking your career.

What was good for the soul wasn't necessarily good for the bank balance, though. A lot of my income is from sponsorship deals, where I deliver exposure to a brand at an event. No events meant no exposure and no exposure meant no income. It wasn't ideal, but I was under contract with the team so there was still some money coming in. And compared to the millions of people affected by the virus around the world, my problems were very, very insignificant.

I spent plenty of time on the bike during the break, but maintaining my fitness routine was tricky. The world championship rounds were basically cancelled one by one. I'd start training and getting organised for the next event, and all of a sudden it would be called off. Eventually the entire world championship season was cancelled, but Dakar was apparently going ahead in January 2021. There were rumours it wouldn't happen, but that wasn't a chance KTM could take. Until the event was officially called off, it was happening. And if it was happening, we had to get back to testing. In August I got the call from the team. It was time to hop on a plane and head back to Europe.

I wasn't overly impressed about having to leave but there wasn't much I could do about it. The next challenge was actually getting permission to leave Australia. There were so many rules and restrictions, and so few flights leaving Aussie shores. Exemptions to go overseas were only being given to essential travellers, so I had to fill in a mountain of paperwork begging the government to let me out so I could do my job. There were heaps of emails and plenty of visits to the doctor. It took me the best part of a month to go through the process. Given it was such a pain in the arse to get out, I knew there was no way I would be coming back to Australia before the Dakar. I called the team and said, 'Are you guys prepared to pay for me to spend the next four, five, even six months away? Because realistically, that's what we're looking at.'

According to my contract, once I leave the front door of my house I'm on KTM's dime. All of my expenses are covered, hotels, meals, transport, everything. To pay for me to live in Europe for five months was a big commitment, even for a factory team. The price of flights had absolutely skyrocketed as well. And at that point we were still running on hopes and dreams in terms of the 2021 Dakar actually going ahead. There was a risk that KTM would pay for me to spend months in Europe only for the event to be cancelled. But it was a chance they felt they had to take. I ended up making a deal that, in between official team duties, I'd cover the cost of food just to lighten the financial load for the team.

Once the paperwork was done and I had permission to leave, I flew over to Austria. When I landed, I made a throw-away comment on social media about being in Europe and it stirred up a bit of an unexpected reaction back home. It wasn't crazy hate mail, but there was a wave of comments that went along the lines of, 'How come you get to travel while we're all stuck in Australia? This is bullshit! What makes you so special?' and so on. I didn't blame anyone for thinking that way, everyone was getting frustrated by the pandemic. It was the height of the Melbourne lockdown and there was anger and conspiracy theories flying everywhere. I tried to calmly point out that I was just trying to do my job.

I spent a week in Austria doing some filming for KTM and then it was off to Spain and Portugal to get stuck into

Dakar preparation. We'd taken the end of the KTM streak on the chin, but that didn't mean there was no impact. The team used it as a shot in the arm. When you're winning it's hard to make too many changes to your approach. You don't want to mess with a recipe that already works. But we were in a new era of the Dakar Rally, the Saudi Arabia era. The structure and processes we had in place for the original Paris–Dakar and then the South American Dakar weren't quite as effective in the Middle East. We took it as a good opportunity to look for ways to improve.

None of us had competed since the 2020 Dakar, and for a while it looked like we'd be going into the next edition cold, particularly when the Rallye du Maroc was cancelled three weeks before it was meant to start. But after a late scramble by the organisers, the event was shifted from Morocco to Spain and renamed the Andalucia Rally.

The whole rally was a bit of a yo-yo for me. Because it was so last-minute the structure wasn't all that solid and there were constant changes to the rules and the roadbook.

I topped the prologue, but then had to lead the way for 240 kilometres on the first stage. The roadbook was hard to follow, and all I could really do was stay upright and hope I didn't bleed too much time. I ended up 17th overall and 17 minutes off the lead. Starting back in the pack made the navigation slightly easier on Stage 2, but the dust was horrendous. Again, staying upright was all I could worry about, particularly as my teammates Sam, Matthias, and Daniel Sanders all crashed on that stage. Finishing fifth for the day and only dropping another minute to leader Kevin Benavides from Honda was a decent result, all things considered. Ahead of the third stage I was awarded some of my time from the first day back due to some issues with the roadbook. I still finished the day 15 minutes off the lead, but at least it put me in the top five overall.

For the fourth and final day, we were mostly covering old ground. There were plenty of tracks to follow so, for the first time, I felt comfortable pushing a little. I finished second on the stage to Daniel, to make it an Aussie one-two, and ended up fourth in the overall standings. A podium would have been nice, obviously, but really the results didn't matter. The race didn't mean anything, it didn't count for the world championship. The main objective was to get through the event fit, healthy and at least somewhat prepared for the Dakar.

We stayed in Spain to do a bit more testing before heading to Austria for fitness training at the Red Bull Athlete Performance Centre. While there, I went to see a new physio I hadn't seen before. He cracked my back and all that stuff, and for the first couple of days I was fine. But on the third day my lower back started to hurt. It clearly didn't agree with something the physio did. I spent the next few days playing catch-up, trying to sort out what was going on. We managed to get on top of the problem by the end of the week at the Athlete Performance Centre, but I missed out on a lot of the training I was meant to be doing. It was disappointing.

At the end of October I moved to Igualada, in the province of Barcelona in Spain, where I was planning on living for a couple of months. But all of a sudden another wave of COVID-19 infections swept across the country and everything started to lock down again. There were no cooking facilities in my hotel room, so I was relying on being able to eat out to get some fresh food. But once Igualada went into lockdown, all of the restaurants closed and there was an 8 pm curfew. It seemed like it was only going to get messier, and I was worried about getting trapped in Spain. So I called KTM and said, 'Look, I've committed to being here, but I can't live like this. I've got to get somewhere else that's a bit more open.' Our plan was to fly to Dubai to do some testing in a month or so anyway, so I asked if they could change my flights to get me out of Spain ASAP. They agreed it was a good idea and, within a couple of days, I was back in the Emirates.

Life was a lot easier there. I had to wear a mask whenever I was outside of my hotel room, but I could go and buy groceries, and I could eat at restaurants. It was great for training and riding, as well; the city is surrounded by plenty of lonely desert I could ride through. It was as close to a normal life I'd been able to live since I'd left Australia.

A few weeks later the team joined me in Dubai, and we carried on with our proper testing program. We spent a week-and-a-half out on the bikes. Because there'd been so little racing, we had to do a lot of testing to catch up. Our schedule felt never ending. When we weren't testing, we were catching up on filming and promotional stuff for Red Bull. It was a very concentrated, intense build-up to the race.

Being busy was a good thing, really, because it helped keep the homesickness at bay. At least until my brother, Matthew, and his wife had their first baby while I was in Dubai. That was hard. I became an uncle and I felt like I was a million miles from my family. Matthew and I have grown a lot closer in our adult years. It's not that we weren't close as kids, but there's six years between us. He finished school not long after I started, so we didn't have the opportunity to hang out all that much back then. But as we got older the age gap has less impact, and we've become great mates and close family. So when Marley was born, and I was stuck in Dubai, the full gravity of not being able to jump on a plane and duck home for a few days hit me at once. It made me think about all those people who thought I was selfish for leaving the country. Trust me, that wasn't how I wanted to be living. I spent Christmas on my own in a hotel room. I've been travelling most of my life, but until then I'd never been away from my family during Christmas. I was completely on my own. It was really hard. All I could do was focus on January 2021 and the reason I was making these sacrifices.

COVID-19 was an unusual wildcard for the final preparations, particularly in the immediate build-up to the event. If I tested positive at any point in those last three weeks, that would have been the end of my Dakar campaign before it had even started. The closer we got, the more I locked myself in a hotel room as much as possible. The only exception was when I was out in the middle of the desert, on my own, on the bike. It was pretty lonely, but I felt so prepared. There was nothing else to think about except Dakar and I was pumped to get into it. I was fit, I was happy and I was ready to go and win the thing to make all the sacrifice worth it.

Between Christmas and New Year, the COVID-19 situation started to get a little dicey in the Middle East. We had flights booked from Dubai to Saudi Arabia, but a few days out there were news reports that Saudi Arabia was shutting its borders. There was no international flights and no road or sea transport. They just shut the country down. I checked the status of my flight and it was cancelled. I couldn't believe it; I'd gone through all this, missed out on time with my family and friends, and now the event was going to be called off. Five months of my life gone, all for nothing.

Thankfully the ASO, which runs the Dakar, has a good relationship with the Saudi government. They struck a deal for the race to go ahead, but it meant we had to fly in on private charter flights. Those flights weren't free, either. KTM got a refund for commercial flights it had booked for us, then had to buy seats on the ASO charter planes.

The final hurdle was a nervous wait for test results. We had to get tested for COVID-19 before the flight and again once we landed. A positive test and it was over, you'd be kicked straight out of the race. I'd been very careful the last few weeks in Dubai, but it was still a scary prospect.

We had to quarantine for two days when we landed in Jeddah before going to a full-on laboratory for more health checks. The Saudi government wanted to make triple-sure none of us were carrying the virus. It was like when you get stopped for a random breath test when you're out in your car – you get nervous, even when you know you haven't had a drop of alcohol. It was a very stressful time, it felt as if we were in a race just to get to the race. There was so much riding on every little twist and turn. It was mentally and physically draining, and undid a lot of the good preparation work I'd done in Dubai.

The whole saga also cast a question mark over tactics for the race. Usually you start out slow, focus on getting the best road position for the first week and then think about attacking after the rest day. But what if there was a huge COVID-19 outbreak a couple of days into the race and it was called off? Would they declare whoever was leading at the time as the winner? It made me wonder if the best approach would be to push like mad from the word go, just in case. But then, what if the event ran its full course and I'd gone too hard, too early?

Nobody really knew what the right answer was, but my gut feeling was that the ASO would fight tooth and nail to keep going, whatever happened. There'd been so little professional sport happening since the pandemic had started, so this was Dakar's time to shine on the world stage. Even people that may not normally be Dakar fans would tune in because it was something to watch, something to follow, something to cheer for. Some small piece of normality during the weirdest thing that has ever happened to us. So, I opted for my usual slow and steady approach.

Of course, that meant I won the first stage without even trying. Typical. I had a decent road position and I planned to just cruise along, but I had no idea the guys at the front were getting lost and having all sorts of issues. I caught a few guys on the stage and thought I'd settled into a nice rhythm, until I got close to the halfway point and saw everyone else who had started in front of me together in a big group. That wasn't a good sign, some of those guys had gone 20 minutes before me. Then I figured that maybe some of the guys who'd started behind me would use my tracks and catch up and pass me. But that didn't happen, either. At the fuel stop I thought, *Shit, I'm probably leading this stage.* But the damage was done. I couldn't switch off too much and risk going too far the other way. All I could do was keep cruising along. I finished the day 30 seconds ahead of Honda's Kevin Benavides and dobbed myself in to be first on the road for Stage 2. There was a rule change for 2021 that meant we were only allowed six new rear tyres for the entire 12-stage event. Winning the stage wasn't ideal, but at least I was happy with how the bike looked after its rubber.

Boy, was I in for a shock on Stage 2. I knew there would be some pretty wild swings in results day to day based on road position, but I couldn't have predicted what happened on that second day. It was a strange old stage. I got lost three or four times at the start, which put the guys who started second and third on my tail. They settled in behind me until I made another mistake, and suddenly the guys who started fourth, fifth and sixth were behind me. Before I knew it, I was in a group of ten or 11 riders, doing all the navigational heavy lifting for them as they made up time on me.

Then there was the fuel issue. When we refuel out on the stage, we don't exactly drop into the local service station. The organisers sub-contract to a wholesaler that dumps a fuel tanker in the middle of the desert. There's a lot of trust involved that the contractor will provide nice, clean fuel but, on Stage 2, that wasn't the case for a few of us. I ended up with about a litre of water spread across the two tanks and as I bounced across the desert it mixed with the fuel and got into the injection system. My bike was constantly mis-firing and carrying on, and I had to keep switching between the front and rear tanks to keep going. As if the navigational issues weren't bad enough, I lost more time dealing with that.

The fuel thing could have been worse; Shorty's Yamaha shit itself after drinking too much water and he was out of the race on the spot. But I still went from leading to being 32 minutes off the pace. It was only the second day but I felt like I had this mountain to climb.

When you fall that far behind, it's easy to end up down in the dumps. That night I sat in the camper and thought, *What's the point? I should just pack my bags and go home.* But a very important part of tackling the Dakar is knowing how to hit the reset button. Even when you win the damn thing you're going to have bad days; it's impossible to avoid them on an event that goes for so long. The Dakar is so unpredictable that, as crazy as it may seem, you can nearly always recover from a bad day. But convincing yourself to put it behind you can be difficult. It takes discipline to say, 'Right, I lost half an hour today but it doesn't matter. Tomorrow is a new day.' Letting your frustrations compound from day to day is a waste of energy. Anything can happen on any given day. And you need to have your best foot forward at all times, in case your luck turns. If you're sulking about something that happened a day earlier, you can miss your opportunity to get back in the game. Things change instantly. Get one note wrong and you can see the most comfortable lead disappear. And exactly the same thing can happen to somebody else.

And that's how it played out on Stage 3. Suddenly the leaders were doing the hard yards out front, and I was the one charging through the pack. I pushed through the soft dunes like a madman. I won the stage and wound up third overall, less than a minute off the lead. I made up that half hour lost from the day before in a single stage.

It was up and down for the next few days. I led the way again on Stage 4 and dropped to eighth in the standings, seven minutes off the lead. On Stage 5 I was back in the pack again; I finished third on the stage and moved to fourth overall, three minutes off the lead. I was only seventh fastest on Stage 6, but still went into the rest day in Ha'il with a two-minute lead. It was a crazy rollercoaster of a rally, but I felt good. It wasn't so much that I was leading, because there was plenty to play out, but I thought, big-picture-wise, I was right in contention. The swings and roundabouts were eventually falling my way. I started to feel like I was working out how to attack the event. And it seemed as if a third title was definitely within reach.

The course for the second week took us out of the dunes and into the mountains, back towards the coast. The challenge shifted a bit from trying to navigate through endless kilometres of soft sand dunes to having to deal with stones and rocky riverbeds. It was the sort of terrain that was really going to test the six-tyre rule.

We started out with the first leg of a marathon from Ha'il to Sakaka. I made a decent start to the stage, but when I got to the fuel stop and took a look over the bike my heart sank. I'd clipped a stone somewhere and it had sliced the rear tyre. As part of the new rules for 2021 I wasn't able to work on the bike during the fuel stop, so I had to nurse it through the second part of the stage – which was something like 180 kilometres of competition and another 60 kilometres of liaison. Somehow I made it and my pace was all right; I was seventh for the day and held onto second overall, one second behind Honda's Nacho Cornejo.

But at the same time my race was pretty much fucked. There was no way that tyre was going to last another 709 kilometres to get through the second leg of the marathon. And because of the new rules I couldn't swap tyres with another rider, like I'd done with Shorty the previous year. If I put a different tyre on the bike, I'd be facing a 30-minute penalty. It just wasn't an option. I'd be better off doing the next day on the rim.

Being a marathon, there was no crew in the Bivouac to help think of another solution. It was up to me to figure out some sort of bush-mechanics fix to try and keep my race alive.

Losing air isn't the issue on our bikes, as we run the solid rubber bib mousse under the tyre. But what was going to happen was that both the tyre and the bib mousse were eventually going to disintegrate. My only hope was to try and get the tyre to hold its form, using either what was in my toolkit or in the limited spares truck we get to share on marathon stages. I got some race tape and wrapped it around the tyre and the rim to cover the hole. Then I got a heap of zip ties and put them around the race tape. They were big zip ties, you need a tensioner gun to tighten them. And I went through about 50.

It was a crude fix and, to be honest, I didn't think it was going to work. Because of the COVID-19 regulations, it was one of the more comfortable marathon Bivouacs, because we were able to use our campervans rather than spend the night on the ground. But while everyone else got a good night's sleep, I was wide awake, tossing, turning and stressing about that tyre. There was no way my fix was going to work. I was going to be riding on the rim by the time I was 20 kilometres into the stage.

As I was lying there, staring at the roof of the camper, different ideas were running through my head. Maybe I should go outside and look for a wire fence that I could hack into. Then I could wrap some wire around the tyre and the rim. But then I got scared that the wire might get loose and get wrapped in the brake or the chain or the sprocket and break the engine. Or even whip me in the back and slice me open. That would end in disaster.

In the end I couldn't come up with a better solution than my original tape-and-zip ties idea. That's what I was going to have to pin my Dakar hopes on.

I took off on Stage 8 with absolutely no idea what was going to happen. I lost a couple of the zip ties on the liaison to the start of the competitive stage, but at least I was still running. Once I got into the competitive stage I took it pretty easy, trying to stress the rear tyre as little as possible. I tried to rail the left-hand corners as hard as I could, get really aggressive on the gas. Then on the right-handers I'd coast and roll. I would try and carry speed into the corner but then avoid the throttle, so I wasn't tearing the side of the tyre at all. The bike was ugly to ride, I could feel the rear shock fluctuating and moving due to this one heavy spot on the rim. I should've thought about the wheel balance and spread zip ties around the whole rim. That made me start stressing about something else breaking, like a wheel bearing.

When I got to the fuel stop, about 200 kilometres into the stage, there was one zip tie left. And it was hanging on by a thread. I reached down and touched it, and it just snapped off. Well, that was the zip-tie trick done. It was time to see if the tape would get me to the finish. I got about 10 kilometres from the end of the stage, and I couldn't believe my luck. The tyre was holding on. By that point I felt that, even if the tyre fell off, the bib mousse would probably hold on just long enough to get me to the finish.

Somehow I got there. I don't know how. I was still second in the overall standings too, just a minute behind Nacho.

It was the ultimate great escape. But boy, it took its toll on me. Between getting very little sleep, and the stress of lasting through the stage, I was exhausted when I got back to the Bivouac. The team were blown away when they took a look at the tyre. I chatted with the guys for a few minutes to explain what had happened and then decided I needed to get off my feet. As they went about fitting a brand-new tyre for the next day, I laid down on the tarpaulin flooring in the tent and immediately fell asleep. I was out to the world for an hour and a half. After a bit of shut-eye and some hydration and food, I started to feel human again.

I think that was the turning point in the race. If I could get through that, I could get through anything. I reckon the Honda crew were a bit worried too. If I could stay within a minute of Nacho, with my rear tyre held together using zip ties, I clearly had some pace up my sleeve.

Stage 9 got off to pretty much a perfect start. After all the stress of the last two days it was nice to be able to just focus on the bike and the navigation. I hit my rhythm straight away and it wasn't long before I began to see a bit of Nacho's dust ahead, which meant I'd already made up a couple of minutes on him. It was all going well . . . until I came off the motor-cycle at the 155-kilometre mark.

As usual, to this day, I don't know what happened. All I know is that I was in a rocky riverbed with a piste at the bottom, but I'm not aware of what I hit and I don't remember hitting the ground. I must have hit my head hard because, while I wasn't fully unconscious, I had a good concussion.

I don't remember Sam or Ricky Brabec stopping to help me, but from what they've told me I was in La La Land, asking the same questions over and over again. Apparently I was complaining that I couldn't breathe because my air vest had inflated on impact and hadn't gone back down. They didn't know how to manually deactivate it, so Sam grabbed his Leatherman and stabbed a hole through to deflate it.

I guess it's helpful to black out when you have a big crash like that because it means you don't cop the brunt of the pain. But it's frustrating to have no idea what went wrong. Was there an issue with the bike? Did we get the set-up wrong? Did I just make a stupid mistake? It'd be nice to know so we can try to avoid it next time. But racing is an isolated sport, and so often there's nobody around to see what happened.

The medical chopper came to collect me and according to those who were there I was complaining about soreness in my wrists, a shoulder and a leg. The first word to reach the Bivouac was that I'd broken the lot of them. That rumour spread like wildfire and sent the team into a spin. It must've been a huge crash to do that much damage. But at the hospital in Tabuk, there was better news. The scans showed that I'd damaged my AC joint and broken my collarbone, and there was a fracture in my right wrist. But my left wrist was fine and my leg was okay, apart from a big gaping hole. That was an easy fix with some stitches.

The hospital took great care of me, but I didn't really understand how they were going to go about the surgery on my AC joint and collarbone. They didn't seem too confident about it. So I decided I would try and go under the knife in Australia instead.

I checked out, returned to the Bivouac and started working on getting home. Usually you'd just book a flight, go to the airport and get on the plane. But COVID-19 added a whole new layer of complexity. First, I needed government approval to get back into Australia. And then a quarantine plan. And then I had to get a seat on one of the very few international flights heading to the country. It was a hell of a fight to get the paperwork in order and for Queensland Health to sign off on it. We managed to get on a flight to Brisbane that left in three days. If that fell through, Plan B was to head to Europe and have the surgery there.

For the next three days all I could really do was hang around in the camper, travelling with the Bivouac. It wasn't that much fun, bouncing along the highway with a fractured wrist and broken collarbone. The Saudi roads aren't exactly silky smooth, either. And not only was I in pain, but I was bitterly disappointed that my race was over. That was one that really slipped through my fingers. To add some salt to the wound, Nacho crashed out the next day as well. The bloke I was racing for the win. If I'd just got through that stage, I would've been in control of the rally.

One evening in the camper I tried to get some answers from Sam about what had happened to me in the riverbed. 'I don't really understand it myself,' he told me. 'It was like you rode the bike to a stop, laid it on its side and sat down next to it. I could see you were in pain but none of it made sense. There was no broken plastic, no broken bits of bike. It was weird.'

We later got more details from ASO. According to them I crashed, then got back on the bike and rode for another 500 metres before stopping at the spot where Ricky and Sam found me. I don't remember that at all. It's a scary thought, really. I could've ridden anywhere when I was in that daze. I could've ended up in the middle of nowhere. They would've been able to track me with GPS if needed, so I couldn't have got too lost, but I could've ridden off a cliff or into a bank or something.

It wasn't until 8 pm on the final day of the rally that I finally got on a plane back to Australia. That meant I got to see Sam, Daniel and Matthias cross the finish line, which was cool. Particularly as Sam finished third and Daniel was fourth. But I also felt like I'd let everyone down. I completely blew KTM's chance to get the Dakar crown back.

Because of the COVID rules, I had to serve two weeks' quarantine when I returned to Brisbane. But because I was all busted up, I couldn't do it in a hotel facility. So I was loaded straight into an ambulance and taken to Princess Alexandra Hospital. That meant I could have proper pain management, and the doctors and nurses could keep an eye on me. It was pretty confronting, though; every time someone came in the room, even just to deliver my dinner, they had to be dressed in head-to-toe protective equipment.

Because I'd been tested for COVID so many times, I was hoping they might be able to do the surgery during the quarantine period. Then I wouldn't be wasting two whole weeks of recovery just lying in a hospital bed. No such luck. I served my two weeks, went home for a day and then went straight back to hospital to finally have my shoulder operated on – three weeks after the crash. The surgery was a bit more complicated than Dr Andrews, the specialist who'd treated me before, was expecting. My shoulder was in a pretty bad way. There was some floating bone that had to be cleaned up, my collarbone had to be screwed down with fake ligaments and the AC joint had to be reconstructed.

The shoulder is well on the mend now, but the crash still hurts. It will for a long time. My third Dakar win was within reach; I was exactly where I needed to make it happen. It's a missed opportunity that, unfortunately, I'll never get back.

***

In May I found myself about as far as possible out of my comfort zone – at Government House in Brisbane hanging out with Queensland Governor Paul de Jersey – as I officially became Toby Price, OAM.

It all started back in December when I was hiding out in my hotel room in Dubai. Ainslie McCormick, who's part of my management team, broke some big news in our management group chat. 'Tobes,' she wrote. 'You've been awarded an Order of Australia medal. It's top secret until it's announced in January.'

I looked at the text for a minute or two. I had no idea what she was going on about. 'Ummm, what's that? I've never heard of it . . .'

That gave the crew a good laugh.

'It's a very important medal that is awarded to a few select people each year who have done Australia proud,' Ainslie responded. 'Someone put you on the shortlist, we gave the government some more information about you – and you got picked!'

'It's like getting the key to the city, but better. It's the key to the country,' added Dave Ellis.

I started to realise that this was a pretty big deal.

'Shit, that's badass,' I wrote. 'Never thought riding a dirt bike would get the Aussie government's attention . . . That's insane. Does this mean we get to fly private now?'

There is normally a big ceremony each year for new recipients of an OAM, but due to the COVID-19 restrictions it was split into small private ceremonies. And that's how I found myself at Government House with my parents, Ainslie, Matty Macalpine and the Governor of Queensland. Out of my comfort zone, but genuinely very proud to be there.

***

The Finke Desert Race was cancelled in 2020 due to the pandemic, so I didn't get my shot at four-wheel redemption in Alice Springs until June 2021. After all those disappointments and near misses, I decided it was time to go all out. I ordered a brand-new trophy truck from TSCO Racing in the US and struck a deal with Mitsubishi to create my own one-of-a-kind custom Triton body.

From the outside looking in, it seemed that we were better prepared than ever for Finke, but to be honest that wasn't the case. Apart from having a new truck and a new transporter, our preparation wasn't different to previous campaigns. If anything we were a little underdone in terms of pre-running – thanks to shipping delays we didn't get hold of the truck until quite late, and I didn't get a lot of seat time before we went to Alice Springs. I headed into the prologue with about 60 kilometres under my belt, that was it.

Despite the lack of testing I was fastest in the prologue. I was surprised at how comfortable I felt from the get-go. The next day we set a new record from Alice Springs to Finke, getting down there in an hour and 39 minutes. That gave me a two-minute lead for the run back to Alice Springs. It was a perfect day, but I've had those on the Finke before. You can never count your chickens, and when I went to bed that night I knew the job was far from done.

Sure enough, we had a problem on the way back to Alice Springs. Things started out okay, but with about 100 kilometres to go a warning light flashed up on the dash. The water temperature was too high. I couldn't believe it. I wanted to pull the thing over and give the sport away on the spot. The Day 2 curse strikes again. My co-driver Joe Weining and I tried to diagnose the problem on the fly. We couldn't fix whatever was wrong with the motor, but we could try and manage the issue.

As soon as I backed off a bit the temperature came down to a safe range, but when I tried to push again the temperature would take off. The only option was to try and manage the pace and the gap between us and the guys behind.

I slowed down and kept an eye on the mirrors. The plan was that the second I saw Josh Howells, who was running second, coming, we'd go flat out. I wasn't going to finish second or third – we were going to win or blow the thing up.

Meanwhile, there was another complication I wasn't aware of. There was a mix-up back at the start line and Josh left a minute after I did, not two minutes. So my lead had effectively been halved. I'm sure it was an honest mistake, but it put unnecessary pressure on us when we were trying to manage the engine problem.

We were about 70 kilometres from home when I first saw lights in the mirrors. It threw me a bit; I wasn't expecting Josh to catch me that quickly. It was go time. I put my foot to the floor and prayed to the Finke gods that the motor would hang on.

The big V8 didn't like it. Anything over 150 degrees is pretty bloody hot, and I saw it get as high as 153. If the oil temperature had started to climb as well we would have been in big trouble, but as long as the oil temperature and pressure held steady we were still in the running. We just kept on trucking and, somehow, made it.

There was a huge sense of relief when we crossed the finish line. *Five years* I'd been trying to win Finke in a truck. I thought it would be so easy after finishing second on that first attempt, but it took five years of heartbreak to get the job done. It was an amazing feeling to stand on top of the truck and celebrate.

Not that the celebrations would last long. We'd just got through the podium and sprayed some champagne when someone told us there had been an incident back down the track. Initially we didn't think much of it, until word started to filter back that it was serious. The unofficial reports were that a car had left the track and hit a group of spectators.

That's one of the real dangers at Finke. The spectators line the track and there's no crash barriers like at a racing circuit. There's been a lot of close calls in the past, with cars collecting quick shade tents and things like that. Sadly, I guess it was inevitable that something like this would eventually happen.

And this was the year.

It was a horrible feeling as we sat and waited for some official news to come through. Eventually we were told what we really didn't want to hear: two guys had been hit by a car and one of them had died.

We quickly changed our post-race celebration plans. We held our own little presentation back at the Desert Palms so I could thank the crew that had helped me finally get that win, and then we went to bed. Normally the town is buzzing after Finke, and we'd be at the casino until the wee hours of the morning. But it just didn't feel right. None of us wanted to party all night when there was a family out there grieving the loss of a loved one.

The tragic end to Finke took the edge off the celebrations, but I still woke up the next morning immensely proud of what we'd achieved. I know there are people out there who look at our Finke set-up, with the new truck covered in sponsor stickers and the big transporter, and think, *Yeah, of course this guy is going to win.* I see it all the time in comments on social media posts. Some people honestly think I'm paid millions of dollars to race that truck. But that's a long way from the truth. Yes, I'm lucky to have some great sponsors that make it possible to race at Finke, but the backing only subsidises the costs – it doesn't cover them (or turn a profit). Winning that Finke title in the truck still cost me $60,000 out of my own pocket.

As awesome as it was to finally get that win on four wheels, I still feel like I have unfinished business at Finke. I want to win the ironman. I want to have my name on both trophies on the same weekend. That never leaves the back of my mind. I want at least one more crack at it. I just need to convince KTM to give me permission to have another go on the bike.

I guess that's the competitive mindset, always wanting more. It's the same with Dakar. I've won it twice, but I want more.

At the same time, I don't take what I've already achieved for granted. To think that I'm a two-time Dakar winner and a rally world champion still feels completely surreal. I often think about how I ended up here and wonder if it's the most random thing in the world, or something that was perfectly orchestrated through my life of highs and lows.

I never even set out to be a Dakar rider, I only ended up there through trial, error, failure and pain. I was too big to be a MotoGP rider, so I tried to become a supercross champion. My body failed me when I attempted that, so I was left with no choice but to become an enduro rider. My plans to conquer the US enduro scene dissipated with my crash and Kurt's death, but that opened the door for me to do the Dakar for the first time. For so long it felt like every time things started going well, there was something terrible right around the corner. One step forward, three steps back. Everything I tried led to failure. It didn't matter how I approached it, what I did, it would either implode or explode and I'd be left on my arse.

It always led to a dead end.

But in hindsight I wasn't really failing, I was just finding my way to Dakar. It was a journey I was blind to, I was too naive to know I was even on it. Once I made that switch to rally everything felt right. Sure, there've been some lows since then, but I feel like I'm on the right path. I'm doing what I, as a rider, was built to do.

Sometimes I wonder why I didn't see it earlier, but in all honesty I don't think I was meant to. I had to go through all the hardships, all the injuries, all of those moments when I wanted to give up on the sport, or even give up on life, to get here. Those experiences combined taught me how to be a stronger person. It taught me how to grit my teeth and take every opportunity in front of me no matter how much physical pain it will take. It taught me how to take the bad times with the good, because in a sport as volatile and dangerous as this, breaking even is actually about as good as it gets.

That's where I'm at. I feel like my scales are about balanced at this point.

ACKNOWLEDGEMENTS

I'm grateful for the support of Mum, Dad, my brother Matthew, Jeff Leisk, Alex Doringer, Arnaud Duhamel at Red Bull Motorsport, Ben Brabham, Matty Macalpine, David Ellis, Ainslie McCormick, Ben 'Reggie' Richards, Jesse Jones, Joe Weining – and anyone who has ever supported me on my journey.